Beyond
Curriculum, Pedagogy and Teachers' Training for

Environmental Education

Beyond
Curriculum, Pedagogy and Teachers' Training for

Environmental Education

Edited by
Rajarshi Roy

SHIPRA

Rs. 1250; US$ 42

ISBN: 978-81-7541-401-3

First Published in India in 2008

Beyond
Curriculum, Pedagogy and Teachers' Training for Environmental Education

Published by:
SHIPRA PUBLICATIONS
LG 18-19, Pankaj Central Market,
I.P. Ext., Patparganj, Delhi 110092, India
Ph.: +91 11 22235152/6152
Email: info@shiprapublication.com
Website: www.shiprapublication.com

Preface

Most discussed and less practiced issues among the contemporary conscious humanity centers round environmental protection and concerns thereof. It is agreed upon that development of science and technology is essential to ensure economic and social advancement of the humankind. Leadership in science and technology is an indispensable facet of knowledge-creation and application. Progress in science and technology can significantly open new avenues for industry and could be an engine for providing crucial knowledge services in developed and developing countries across globe. It is also simultaneously understood that same 'science and technology' could be well utilized for protection of 'environment', may be it 'natural' or 'artificial'. Here comes the question of sustainability of protecting environment. Experience across globe reveals that nature is sustainable. Hence special attention needs to be focused over 'natural environment'. It aught to be call of the age to make the future generations aware about the need to protect the nature and environment.

It is often quoted that 'nature can meet the human need, but not the human greed'. In present juncture of time, we are rapidly observing a paradigm shift from natural to the artificial way of life, which is putting tremendous adverse impact over our body, mind, and finally over the lifestyle of the social atoms.

In the age of knowledge-explosion, where in one hand, we are supposed to take an account of upcoming knowledge, on the other hand, we need to integrate the existing pertinent knowledge components with that of the newly generated knowledge. A synthesis of this two is prerequisite to utilize the pertinent knowledge and to turnoff from obsolete knowledge.

History reveals that almost each and every society possess their 'own' indigenous knowledge, some of which are drowsed in the waive of time due to lack of appropriate infrastructure of recording and retrieving the same. From the oriental countries, we may re-explore such indigenous knowledge, which are felt, essential for protection of the environment. Scientific bases of indigenous knowledge help to protect environment in a much easier and sustainable way. Most of the cases, the only prerequisite for thee is an affirmative feeling and attitude of the masses.

Emergence of consciousnesses about 'environment', within which we leave and grew up, doesn't appear from vacuum. It is the resultant of the societal effort for betterment of, and also for a sustainable future. In view, the task of generating awareness appears as a responsibility of the formal system of education to make the human components informed about the environment and thereby to enable our future citizens conscious about the environment. The task remains with the teachers involved in varied levels of formal educational institutions. To create the awareness, environmental education emerges as an approach to integrate various subjects of studies in tune with environment, its protection and ensuring its sustenance. In the present volume, an attempt is being made in the very line. It is fact that theoretical knowledge hardly possesses any space in creation of specific practice among the society at large, until the inner-self is desirous for so. However, teachers of the day, who act as an important pivot of knowledge-dissemination system, aught to be equipped with the strategies and tactics of developing concerns for environmental education among the students. This is possible following integration between 'ongoing subject of studies' and 'developing concerns about the environment'. The present volume makes a humble attempt in this direction. Contributions in the volume includes issues like evolving disciplinary approach for environmental education, integration of environmental knowledge of the past and present, implications of teachers' training in environmental education, prospective educational profile for environment and safety, approaches of teaching environmental education, exploration of trend of doctoral level research in environmental education and related curricular and pedagogical issues. The volume also includes a few empirical study-reports, linked with environmental education.

—Rajarshi Roy

Contents

Environmental Concerns in the Vedas

A Lesson in Ancient Indian History

R.P. Singh

> "The men of firm intention bind that, the men who are well-versed in the knowledge of *Atharva-Veda* bind that, which the men of anatomy and medicine being strong break through the fort of disease-creating things."
>
> —*Atharva-Veda; Book X. VI.20*

What has Man done to the only planet where he must live? In the infinite, ever-changing Cosmos the space where alone life could be sustained is Mother Earth. But in the name of competitive nationhood, scientific advancement and material progress, we have come to a stage where holy or otherwise rivers are reduced to becoming sewer lines, where potable water is scarce, lush green fresh fruits are heavy with pesticides and the air that we inhale carries unsustainable anti-life germs and killing particles.

Having destroyed the Nature all around and making even the glaciers melt, we are very soon going to clutter up the outer space too because of our unlimited greed for both lucre and power; and a strong desire for killing instantly our potential enemies. When not engaged in killing each other or plotting to conquer the weak, humankind is frightfully busy discovering other solar systems that could be populated by the power-hungry. We refuse to accept the reality that the only enemy Man has is Man himself.

There are a few questions that one needs to answer. Do we ever think that the only reality is change and the only certainty is death? Time was when there was no earth and there will again be time when our solar system itself will have disappeared along with the earth. But so long as we live, it is our bounden duty to protect it so that life could be sustained. Still we, the *asharful maqhluqat* (the best of the Beings), have not learnt enough to live in peace and remain in harmony with the world around us.

Long before the civilizations grew and man learnt to conquer nature. There were men and women who taught us to live in harmony with the nature around us and treat all (both animate and inanimate) with respect and learn to be humble before the unknown. Long before others came to realize the value of environment. The ancient Indians had perhaps intuitively learnt that trouble comes from unknown sources and therefore it is better to take care of the immediate neighborhood first. This neighborhood is environment. By definition 'environment' means 'the aggregate of circumstances surrounding organisms or group of organisms including the social and cultural conditions affecting the nature of individuals or community.' Hence, the following prayer:

> 'May the five types of men, born to offer (the butter of) affection, and eager to perform the sacrifice, be pleased with my discharge of the function as an invoker; may the earth preserve us from the troubles that come from heaven'.
>
> 'May you, spinning the thread of divine knowledge, follow the splendid light of the illuminator, and protect the pathways well..'.
>
> 'The great river of life-conflicts flows alone, be alert; rise up, cross over, my friends; here let us leave those who are wretched and hence unhappy; may we cross over (this river) to secure auspicious boons.'
> —*Rig-Veda* X.54.5-7

In whatever form *the Vedas* have survived, they tell us enough about the nature, life and the concerns of the ancient Indian. Since author selected *the Vedas* therefore it is not portraying an analysis of the archaeological findings of Indus Valley civilization to show how the urban populace of those times had evolved amazingly the most sophisticated and scientific urban water supply system and also the sewage system. But the *Vedic* society is no less careful and knowledgeable about the world around them. The *Vedic* seers appear to have foreseen the catastrophe. Man was likely to invite for his own destruction, therefore they had forewarned against indulging in such acts.

Experience informs us that mere knowledge is rarely enough to prevent trouble, and it is also true that we rarely listen to reason until the catastrophe takes over and we are left with nothing else but regret. In the modern high-tech world, people have little time and even less patience to go deeper into any text even when it might have enormous value for one's guidance. Indeed, it is no longer considered necessary to read scriptures or may be it is even considered un-intellectual, if not infra dig, to try discovering any particular sense in reading them. Perhaps it is the job of a priest who is put paid for his services to read the same out in bits and pieces on ceremonial occasions.

Indian historians took considerable time to discover the meaning and the message that *the Vedas* carry and that too only when the western scholars had started using *the Vedas* and their text for purposes other than those of mere scholarship. One must admit that it is the occident that initially led the path back to our glorious past and furnished insight to find for us gems that had been lying hidden in the obscure homes of the neglected but venerable scholars.

The Vedas are correctly regarded as repositories of all knowledge and the acme of ancient Indian wisdom. In them lie the seeds (at times the finished products) of our modern knowledge. One should accept *the Vedas* as ancient historical documents (and not mere liturgies), wherein the ancients have left for us nuggets of their foresight to take guidance from. But it would be foolish to try finding principles of steam engine or airplanes in them. The present author does not have any quarrel with a scholar who interprets *the Vedas* differently. Actually they are the foundation of knowledge and are not necessarily the finished products, true for all times to come. Yet there is hardly any branch of knowledge viz. music, astronomy, physics, modern mathematics, yoga, alternate medicine, philosophical systems, literature, grammar and prosody etc. whose foundations cannot be traced back to them. Few know that the binary system, which gave birth to computer sciences, has its origins in *the Vedas*. The yoga and the alternate medicine, which is the current rage in the West, and therefore in the East too, have also been the gifts of *the Vedas*. True, we have outgrown many of the discoveries and findings. But there are numerous areas of knowledge where we are still groping in the dark alongside the ancients. In some ways the contemporary astrophysics has brought us back to the *Nasdiya sukta* to compare notes. Be that as it may, we share with them the desire to learn and discover.

The author proposes to cite here relevant hymns on each of the manifested contemporary environmental concerns from the text of *the Vedas* and show that the ancient Indians had the knowledge of the environmental problems but their future progenies alas did not have the 'Will' to act. The message is clear. If we failed once there is still time to mend our ways. This is the sole purpose of learning history. Historians as interpreters of facts are capable of delivering subtle messages to the posterity.

Although all the four *Vedas* were supposed to have appeared simultaneously the common belief is that the *Rig-Veda* came first. It is in this *Veda* that we see *vayu* or air being regarded as the soul of human beings. They realized the value of the air and talked of its curative powers. 'Lord *vayu* is the soul and spirit of *Indra* and all other gods and living beings and is the seed of the world. Such a divine lord flows according to its own Will. We can only hear it but cannot see it. We bow before this lord *Vayu.*'—[*Rig-Veda X.168.4.*]. Additionally they came to realize that air had its own curative powers. Therefore, they prayed, '*O Vayu!* Bring your medicines and do away with all the ailments here because you are the only one who is full of curative powers.' In the history of Indian philosophy there is discussion about the evolution of the concept of *Atma* or the source of life, which was at different point in time was variously identified with air, water, food etc. Even now we call soul as *prana vayu*. Since they rated all these elements as divine and identified with soul or life itself, it was unimaginable for them to have even thought of polluting any one of these.

In terms of Western history this concern dates back to 1962 when *Rachel Carson* wrote *Silent Spring*. This book focused on the enormity of ecological damage brought about by industrial waste being dumped into the rivers. Then came the papers by *Barbara Ward* and *Rene Dubois* in 1972 'Only One Earth.' Their project had been funded by UNDP. It brought to the fore the conflict between biosphere of Man's inheritance and the techno-sphere of His creation. Since then the voices of concern for the safe upkeep of this creation have not been silenced. The concern clearly is about keeping the environment livable. The express desire is for striking a balance between material prosperity and human sustenance. The 'Club of Rome' —funded by independent scientists, too has shown similar concerns and proposed almost identical schemes to sustain life on this planet

The 'Limits to Growth,' brought out in1972, reported research findings based on a data collected at global scale on a mathematical model. The model predicted Doom and stated that continued resource shortages, crowding, pollution, famines etc will soon control current trends in population growth, natural resource exploitation and capital investment in agriculture. As expected the model heavily criticized. Since then the problem remains where it was seen for the first time. As of today the problem is whether or not based on non-renewable resources is it possible to maintain a certain rate of sustained growth forever? We should remember that when academic concerns cross over the bounds of polite drawing room discussions, it is no longer possible to remain ideologically neutral. Today's dialogue about global warming has entered precisely the same stage as I mentioned above. We are no longer ideologically neutral.

The Indian concern for the environment is as old as our civilization's origins. But did the ancients understand the meaning of the term 'environment'? Perhaps they did. But then what exactly do we mean by this term. 'The environment (after all) is sum total of water, air and land, inter-relationships among themselves and also with the human beings, other living organisms and property.' This definition appears in the Environment (Protection) Act, 1986.

In modern terminology if one wanted to have a comprehensive knowledge of the subject the minimum requirement is to go through several stages of a variety of subject areas, - such as Botany, Zoology, Microbiology, Genetics, Geology, Biochemistry, Biotechnology, Oceanography, Atmospheric science, Statistics etc. It would appear as though we hold the view that if the ancients spoke on all these subjects with equal command like us then alone they would be considered knowledgeable enough for our good failing which, let us keep them under covers for a few recluses and the lonely.

Let us examine *the Vedas* on all these counts all the same.

For instance, see in this quote a desire that we have in common with the ancients, i.e. work so that one could meet one's physical needs and an airy house to live in.

> 'I resort to agriculture and craft for removing poverty and ministering happiness to all. May I feel joy in domestic life! May our houses be sufficiently commodious, airy, fully comfortable, and built in the middle of an open space'. — *Yajurveda, chapter 1.11.*

For an obvious reason an individual engaged in agriculture knows the value of timely and plentiful rain. In this sense we have not outgrown this basic requirement.

> 'Let us see with respect that earth, which loves the rains and is looked after by the clouds, in which is grown food grains like rice and barley, and where live all the four castes, and the other five types of people.'
>
> —*Atharvaveda, chapter /12/1/42.*

> As one reads the Vedas one is made to realize that the ancients suffered from the same weaknesses as we do, but they prayed to get rid of them through sustained efforts called the *yagnas*. For them, 'the *yagna* keeps away the thieves, refines and sweetens the speech, is productive of foodstuffs and is the bestowed of knowledge and vigor.'
>
> —*Yajurveda, chapter1.16.*

We see in the following few pages the type of knowledge they had of the Nature and its capacities. They desired that we do not transgress boundaries and remain within acceptable limits to avoid catastrophe. See here their knowledge about fire or heat.

'I describe the special features of Fire. It takes every type of matter forward. It softens iron ore etc. it burns everything. It emits light. It beautifies. It is set up before everything else. It performs many functions and is used during many activities. It is an instrument for attracting attention, give and take and for food preparation. Fire creates inside earth all varieties of gems and ores like gold, silver, iron, and diamonds.' — *Rig-veda chapter 1/1.*

In the following quote the reader could see that they had knowledge of *Vaastu* and were fully acquainted with the powers of the Nature's Elements.

> 'O husband and wife! We want to construct a house for you; that is fully lighted by the strong rays of the Sun. For Sun is strong and capable of giving happiness yielding light'.
>
> —*Rig-Veda chapter /1/155/6.*

About the Solar energy they say:

> 'Learn carefully about the presence of *Vaishwanar* Fire in us all. The same *Agni*/ Fire is located in all worlds and the same is working through *Vaishwanar* Sun doing all kinds of work such as producing light, growth of plants etc.' —*Rig-Veda chapter / 1/98/1.*

Here is a hymn from *Yajurveda (XXXIII.92)*, which talks of the functions of Sun: 'Just as the Sun, set in Heaven, the benefactor of humanity, increasing in power on earth, ripens medicines and grows food, removes darkness of night with his lusture, shines forth, so should ye dispel ignorance...".

> 'Just as lightning destroys insects that disturb sleep and spread disease, let us enjoy all the fruits and favors granted to us by the Sun and the wind and thereby let us feel safe against Nature gods.'
>
> —*Rig-Veda chapter / 10/36/4.*

Or read their knowledge about the relationship of Sun with the formation of clouds and feeding rivers with plentiful water:

> '*O Gurudev*! Just as strong, light -emitting Sun attracts the waters of these rivers toward itself and having done so distributes them through clouds all over again on the land, so do you attract students and instruct them with éclat.' —*Rig-Veda chapter 7/34/10.*

> The Seers therefore enjoin us to learn to 'Respect that special Guru who is powered by education, who is familiar with the work of *Agni, Vaayu*, Sun and other deities and knows all about the names, places and the births. You should respect those Gurus too who understand the speed of air and the lightening and who can tell you the exceptional ways to Salvation.' —*Rig-Veda chapter /7/ 58/ 1.*

They offer a lesson or two in human psychology for compassion toward one and all.

> 'May that intellect which is inside me let that be full of feelings of welfare for others! It is because of that the industrious, reflective and patient men work to gain both knowledge and the riches, and undertake to give charity, worship gods and work for mutual benefit, and that which is located in all living beings.' —*Yajurveda/ 34/2.*
>
> 'Even as all spokes in a wheel are joined together in the center may my intellect also carry feelings of welfare for others because of the coming in of knowledge from the *Rig Veda*, the proper methods of actions from the *Yajurveda* and of worship from the *Sam Veda*'.
>
> —*Yajurveda* 34 / 5.

We could see their concern for the education of all, more particularly of girls. At least in this sense they were far ahead of us. While discussing methods of instruction, the Seers also talk of how to practice writing. Incidentally, the following lines throw light on a historically disputed domain. Few historians dispute the fact that *the Vedic* people had no script and therefore writing was unknown to them. Probably it is possible to resolve that contentious issue whether or not the ancients knew how to write, what to write and the lack or otherwise of a script. The fact that they knew about the written word can be established even otherwise. For instance, on the demerits of gambling the *Rig-Veda (10/ 34 / 2)* says that the faces of the dice carried written symbols. At another place, viz. *Rig-Veda—10/62/7* there is a mention that the ears of the cows have the number 8 written on them.

Additionally, these lines also show that education of girls was common and prevalent. In their opinion female teachers are better teachers than their male counterparts.

> 'O girl students! Just as intelligent teachers introduce writing and reading of letters with the help of fingers, you should know lady teachers who know innumerable subjects and possess immeasurable learning. For your balanced development such an intelligent teacher will herself make all arrangements'. —*Rig-Veda/7/15/9.*

In case this is not enough to establish their knowledge about language or linguistics, then see elsewhere they mention that mere reading is never enough because people learn at a pace, which differs from individual to individual:

> 'A few do not understand the secret of the language even after reading it, a few others do not realize the reality even after listening to it, but there are others for whom the language presents her true form as does a beautiful bedecked bride reveals herself before her husband.'
>
> —*Rig-Veda 10/ 71/4.*

> 'Language through its own symbols explains the wide expanse of knowledge and is able to illumine all intelligence fully. Therefore, one should put language to good use.' —*Rig-Veda1/3/13/*

We see here the functions of language per se and its symbolic nature. It perhaps holds a lesson or two for the modern day linguists.

What did the *Rigveda* say about the nature of the universe (cosmology) / astrophysics that we live in? We may have advanced in varied ways but about the origin of the galaxies, stars and planets we are still nowhere being close to certainty. Even today we have not gone beyond the realm of conjectures in numerous academic areas such as astrophysics for instance; then how could we expect the ancients to be definitive about their knowledge, who definitely had no access to the present day scientific instruments, which make a Hawking so knowledgeable and relatively certain? According to the ancients, the universe consisted of three regions—the earth

(Prithvi), heaven *(Dyauh)*, and the intermediate world or the *Antariksha*. We are familiar with the term earth, but not with *Dyauh* because this is one term which was employed to denote the vault of the sky, which is the place where the sun and the stars shine. They had an idea that there was an invisible world too where these stars and the sun retired after their daily ritual or duty was over.

The *Rigvedic* hymns sporadically mention the abodes of *Padam* of *Agni, (1.72.2), Indra Pusan (1.162,2), Vishnu (1, 154,6)* etc. In reality they appear to think that the universe consisted of four regions. The name of the fourth region is *Satya Lok*. Read *Rg. (1.35.2)*, which says 'Causing immortal and mortal to rest, God *Savitr* returned (to his abode) by way of the *Satya Lok* (i.e. invisible) world; he comes on the golden chariot observing the worlds.' The *Satya Lok* was considered the abode of *Brahma*, the Creator. The later day developments have only added certain more *Loks* to the list. Only as a passing reference, it is mentioned here that seven *loks* that *the Puranas* talk about. From *Bhu-lok* upwards are *Bhuvar-Lok, Svar-Lok, Mahar-Lok, Jan-Lok, Tapo-Lok* and the *Satya-Lok*. Similarly, by that time the idea of seven 'nether' worlds had also grown and developed. They were called *Atal, Sutal, Vital,* and *Patal* etc. according to the depths at which different unwanted creatures supposedly lived.

Numerous references are made daily to the unusually wonderful understanding these *Rishis* had of the origin of the Creation, especially to the scientificity of their observations. For instance, the subject of Creation interested these *Rishis* immensely. The *Rigveda* talks of it in the *Hymn 10/ 129/7* and *Yajurveda* in *10/ 129/ 3* etc. It does amaze one to imagine that even without the benefit of any of the modern equipments and gadgets they could be, at times, so precise in their observations. For instance, *the Vedas* hold the view that in the beginning there was nothing but darkness. It was the state of Nature, which could drown all without a trace. That extensive Nature, which is hidden in the Cause form, the same with the shinning glory of the divine God appears in the physical form as its effect. Compare this piece with the findings of modern astrophysics and take your own decision.

Read the *Nasdiya-Sukta* and feel surprised at the latent modernity of reasoning and logic:

'What was the state during the *Pralaya* or total annihilation? Who is the Creator? What was the principal cause of Creation and what its principal instrument? During *Pralaya* there was no evil or good nor did the atoms fill the horizons? What was shrouded and by what? Who was the Protector? Did only the deep seas exist?

There was no death nor was there any life. Even the day and night had not taken birth. The lone Creator breathed without any life breath by his own will. Nothing superior existed beyond him.

'In that dark existed, the un-manifested Nature like seamless water. Everything looked small before Him. Nature gradually manifested itself because of the austerities of the Supreme Being.' *—Rig-Veda 10/129 [I-V].*

A Desire was superimposed on what existed in the form of inner-self during *Pralaya.* The seers could thus realize that the Good was latent in the Evil even as the light is in the dark. The creation could arise out of the un-manifested Nature. Slanted bright rays spread out of these three – God, Soul and the Nature. What was below was as amazing as the one who could serve as receptacles for that amazing semen above. If one went deep into the description of the origins of the Creation itself, we start dealing with the eternal questions of Philosophy whose definitive answers continue to elude us. Our understanding of the Reality is as remote today as it was when the ancients were trying to grapple with it.

In a hymn the seer says, 'One thing that is beyond this world is matter, the material cause of this world, another thing even beyond this is the soul which is remote in rareness and not within reach of ordinary man.' *—Atharvaveda, Book V, XI. VI.*

Interestingly, the *Atharvaveda* carries a section on the *Vaastusastra*—the art and science of architecture. Here a number of hymns talk of God being present in a three-room school or the eight-room school. One cannot imagine of a three rooms or eight rooms building without proper measurements and even building materials.

'Like the animal heat in the body and foetus in the womb, I, the master of the house live in the houses, which are built with two wings, four wings, six wings, eight wings, and are constructed in appropriate measurement'. *—Atharvaveda / 9/3/21.*

In fact, so great is the insistence on the proper measurement of the size of the rooms and the accurate mixture of mortar that one could seriously start thinking about the presence of the ubiquitous modern day contractor in that society too. One would be amazed to read about their express desire to make lighting arrangements that are necessary for a large room. The mention is of electricity and also of teaching-aids. It is agreed upon that, we have failed to be specific because we do not know whether this light is not lightning and teaching-aids something very elementary and highly primitive in character. These hymns in question are: *Atharvaveda 9/ 3/1* and *9/3/11* and many more. The fact that God is present in all these classes of the school does suggest that schooling was carried on in built enclosures and not under the shade of the trees or in the hermitages only.

It is not quite correct that all *gurus* had equal competence. But in terms of their insistence on respect, there is near unanimity. The impression that we have is that the *Guru* did not charge fees. May be, he did not do so in the beginning. But no student could leave the residence of the teacher without paying the appropriate amount in terms of tuition fees/ *guru-dakshina*.

On pupil's return home the following hymn specifically desires that the teacher should make some relaxation in the strict rules that one followed.

'O the best Guru! The restrictions that you had imposed on us regarding food, sensuality and travel, please relax them now. O luminous with knowledge, *Gurudev!* We shall continue to observe all the pure *vratas*, and shall continue studying with unbroken regimen, *the Vedas.' —Yajurveda. / 12/12.*

In fact, there is a mention that at the time of leaving the *Ashram* the student does say that he would like to know about the time one could leave the school and when does he invite the teacher home. *Atharvaveda (11/5/26)* describes how glorious the student looks on the completion of his education.

But here is one *mantra* wherein the teacher refuses to be admired by a student whom he regards to be a fool.

'O you, my pupil! Who shuns practice in learning, even if you are ready for employment immediately, I do not like your praise because you cannot repeat properly even those lessons that have already been taught. You, who are famous amongst fools, I do not like any praise from you. I would much prefer you becoming properly educated and earn reputation than what you are Right now. That would enhance my reputation.' *—Rig-Veda/ 7/22/5.*

'The teachers who teach at the lower levels and offer expertise, may they improve and grow. Those that teach at the middle and higher stages let them too progress and develop. The teachers of Som-knowledge let them too progress. Let all these teachers teach us the techniques and methods of prayer and the *yagnas*. Besides these teachers, those who know the techniques of the *yagnas* and are aware of *the way the Universe was created and are free from crookedness and have long lives may they too impart us instruction.'* —*Rig-Veda/ 10/15/1.*

Let us now take up an example of their concern for keeping rivers free from pollution:

'O God! Cast aside the vile man who pollutes rivers...' says the *Yajurveda* XXX, *8* and the hymn goes on to command,' *Nishad's* son, hankering after libidinous women; a degraded arrogant, friend of person harmful like a tiger; an uneducated person attached to low dancing and singing women; the demented, given to the application of magical rites; an untrustworthy person who befriends the serpents and fools, a non-gambler, who creates unnecessary excitement; a woman who creates split among the *Pishachas*, the thorny woman who favors the freebooters.'

Look at the way they desire the trees to be protected, 'He, who rears the trees by erecting barriers round them..conduces to our happiness.' —*Yajurveda XX.45.*

Read *Yajurveda* and see how in chapter XXII, hymns after hymns are talking of protecting oneself against the physical ailments and blesses those that help preserve environment. Hymn 5 in the chapter admires one who 'protects beautiful objects like the Earth.' The next hymn is even more explicit — 'Make the best use of fire. Take medicines. Derive joy for drinking water. Enjoy well the warmth and light of the Sun. Have knowledge of air and vital breaths. Perform *yagna* in fire.'

They knew that 'The Sun moves singly and alone. The moon is brought to life again. Fire is the remedy of cold. Earth is the vast field for production.' —*Yajurveda Ch.XXIII. 46.*

To the questions: 'what luster is like the Sun's light? What lake is equal to the sea? What is more specious than the Earth? What thing s beyond measure?' —The reply is given in the next hymn. *Yajurveda Ch.XXIII. 48 /* — 'God is luster like the sun. Heaven is a flood to match the sea. Sun is vaster than the Earth. Beyond all measure is speech.' It is difficult to find an answer better than this one from a Seer.

Let us now cite from *Yajurveda [ChapterXXIV],* wherein the Seers talk of birds and animals and their attributes and characteristics and where to locate them. The loving manner in which they talk of these birds and animals merely underlines the fact that they knew their beans about environment and wished to protect it. These hymns begin from number 11 and continue up to 40. There is not a single animal known to a veterinarian practitioner that is not described along with its typical characteristics. Read for instance, hymn 18 —'the animals of peace-loving parents are smoke–colored and of brownish hue. The animals of parents who sit in assembly for propitiating *yagnas* are brown and smoky-looking.' The next hymn commands — 'O men, bring into use the pre-mentioned agricultural animals' then comes the knowledge of the experts. — 'An expert in the knowledge of animals finds *Kapinjalas* in spring, sparrows in summer; partridges in the Rains; quails in autumn, *kakras* in winter and *Vikaras* in the dewy season.' —The *rishis* describe also the uses of each animal according to the class of people for whom they are intended. It is not possible to reproduce all the hymns to show the knowledge of the Seers or their desire to preserve all these species but it is perhaps enough if we appreciate their knowledge and perception from the following hymn (40): — 'Rhinoceros serves all warriors in preparing their shield; the black-dog, the long-eared ass. The hyenas are used for protection against the demons; the boar is for the king who wants to tear asunder his enemies; the lion is swift like air; the chameleon, the *Pippaka,* the vultures are used are used for making arrows; the spotted antelope is used for preparing *mrigshalas* for the learned people.'

The next chapter (XXV) opens with a hymn for protecting all objects worthy of desire. Read this hymn in totality, —'Learn for the teeth the act of biting; from the gums the method of protection; from tooth-sockets the way of pounding; sharpness from the fangs. Use the tongue tip for a learned utterance; learn the act of uprooting from the tongue; the use of palate by crying slowly; chew with both the jaws; drink water with the mouth. Acquire the knowledge of oozing semen from testicles. Recognize the *Aadityas* from the beard; know the path from the eyebrows; know the sun and earth from their motion; lightening from the pupils of the eyes. Observe celibacy for the protection of the semen; acquire knowledge through high character. *Objects worth acceptance are worthy of preservation.*

Objects after one's desire should not be resisted. Don't show disrespect to your own men. Friends and relation should be fostered.'

Whatever else may have been the motive of these seers in commanding mankind to worship God and perform *yagnas*, one thing is certain. They knew well their environment and wished to protect it.

What better could one offer in terms their understanding of the Nature's cycle around them than the following quote?

'When the clouds cultivate the earth with its waters; then winds are blown (for the rain to fall), lightening is struck, vegetation comes to life and grows, sky pours the raindrops and the earth then gets ready for the welfare of the world.' —*Rig-Veda 5/83/4.*

We should remember that they wrote an entire *Veda* on the science of medicine called the *Atharva-Veda*. They went into details how an herb has to be identified and then they describe its properties for different ailments. They achieved and left behind knowledge of an almost fully developed medical science, which is currently proving to be helpful to the entire Mankind. Therefore they had prayed, 'O God, create a man of iron determination for the implementation of a vow..a forest guard for the protection of a forest...and drive away a forest burner contemplating the destruction of jungles.' — *Yajurveda, Chapter XXX. 19.* One might as well put a question: — 'What else does a forest officer do other than protecting a forest and preserving wild animals and their habitat under his/her charge?' In the same chapter of the *Yajur-Veda* in hymn 10, the seer prays— 'O God create a physician for purifying our body with the eradication of disease; an astronomer for the advancement of knowledge; an inquisitive man full of cravings for knowledge; an extra-inquisitive man for desire of extra-knowledge; and a question-solver for establishing moral law.' If read closely, one can see the hymn telling us that all knowledge is located in curiosity and for extra knowledge one has to put in extra effort.

'O Spiritual juice (of wisdom and devotion) thou hast been prepared carefully for the soul. Let diseases stay afar together with the fiends of lust, anger, greed, pride and jealousy.' *Samaveda Hymn. 561.* This hymn clearly states, 'Those who are double-tongued or crooked, cannot take delight of drinking thee.' It would be clear to the reader that disease or physical ailment is as good as being crooked or a doublespeak. It is much better to avoid them both. It is only then that 'those who are of calm nature like the rays of the moon, (will) be full of strength and wealth of wisdom.'

A hymn *(Sam-Veda, 1837)* is cited here that has been interpreted differently by two scholars of eminence viz. *Satvalekar* and *Griffiths*, whose two versions are given below. Meanwhile the reader should also realize that it is quite common for the hymns being interpreted differently by different scholars. This is precisely what has been written in the beginning about the difficulty of agreeing on the common meaning of a hymn or even of a single word. *The Vedas* can be read for different purposes, as they are capable of giving more messages than one can imagine. In fact, it is impossible to understand everything they say and why do they say what they actually say. Majority of the Indians regard them as revealed books because no human being could have been so wise as to cover all themes and subjects, besides all aspects of human life as they do. Probably for this reason alone that F. Max Muller wrote the following:

> 'What can be more tedious than the Veda, and yet, what can be more interesting, if once we know that it is the first word spoken by the Aryan man?'

The Vedas has a two-fold interest; it belongs to the history of world and to the history of India. As long as man continues to take interest in the history of his race, and as long as we collect in libraries and museums, the relics of the former ages, the first place in that long row of books, which contain the records of the Aryan branch of mankind, will belong forever to the *Rigveda.*

So much for the glory of the *Vedas!* This praise comes from a man who learned Sanskrit and translated *the Vedas* only to make Hindus Christians.

Be that as it may, the first interpretation is of *Satvalekar:*

1. 'O Omnipresent Divine Mother! Thou art source of happiness. So endow us with strength and pleasure of great vision (realization) of truth.'
2. Griffith's translation: - 'Yea waters, ye bring health and bliss; so help ye bring health and bliss ye us to energy that we may look on great delight.'

It is interesting to note that this hymn has something to do with water. In the next hymn the reason why water is mentioned here is made clear. Because water is known to be the source of life as it is one of the five elements or *tatva* that constitute life and at the same time water is also a cure for numerous diseases even if used singly.

The hymn number 1638 from *Samaveda* has two meanings. — One is an external meaning and the other internal. The external meaning is as follows: 'O water! Let your most prosperous juice be ministered to us in this world with the readiness that affectionate mothers apply to their infants.'

The other interpretation is spiritual in character. — 'O Divine Mother! May thy most auspicious juice of bliss be ministered to us in this world with the readiness that affectionate mothers supply to their infants.'

The next hymn talks of water being used for removing diseases. It is significant that the use of water as a medicine was known to them and therefore it becomes even more meaningful that this water has to be clean or pollution free. Look at it from an ordinary person's point of view by the time the Seers came to writing the *Atharvaveda* they had learnt through experimentations as well as through empirical evidence the curative value of the usages of both herbs and lotions including water. This *Veda* is a living testimony to the fact that science grows only empirically. And the seeds of modern laboratories were first grown in the *Vedas*. This is one History lesson that one should learn from reading *the Vedas*.

To end the write-up let us cite *the Rig-Veda X.1/ 46*

'Lady of the Forest! Lady of the Forest!
Who seems to vanish from sight in the distance?
Why do you never come to the Village?
Surely you are not afraid of us.
When the grasshopper replies
To the lowing of the cattle,
As though to the sound of tinkling bells,
The lady of the Forest makes merry.
Sometime you catch a glimpse of her,
and think it is cattle grazing
Or a house, far away
And at the evening you hear the Lady of the Forest
Like the distant sound of moving wagons.

Her voice is as the sound of man calling his cattle.
Or as the crash of a felled tree,
If you stay in the forest in the evening
You will hear her like a far voice of crying.
But the Lady of the Forest will not slay
Unless an enemy draws near
She eats the sweet wild fruits
And then she rests wherever she will
Now I have praised the Lady of the Forest
Who is perfumed with balm and fragrant
Who is well-fed although she tills not
The mother of all things of the wild.'

And what greater respect could Man show towards all the elements of Mother Nature than the prayer from *Yajurveda, 36/17* for peace or recite the *Shanti mantra*, which desires that 'let there be peace in the heaven, horizons—where the Earth and sky meet, peace in the vegetation, peace on earth, peace in everything' etc., and this prayer is always sung at the end of any holy anushthan or ceremony and this Shanti mantra may be accepted as the ultimate for any environmentalist.

Environmental Education and Beyond

Implications for Teachers' Training

DZINTRA ILIŠKO

The present world situation is unsustainable. Therefore, professionals in all levels of education are engaged in finding ways to meet the needs of current generation by not reducing the capacity of future generations' needs. The complexities of the problems that have led to unsustainable development are broadly acknowledged by international scholars.

The ecological crises require a new approach based on different ways of thinking and acting. In the light of the current situation in the world, including the obvious degradation of the global ecosystem, population crisis, there is a need for education that puts forth a clear vision of holistic ecological approach. Constructing a sustainable future is an essential response to the current state of the world's ecological crises. Education for sustainable development has the capacity to teach students systematic ways of perceiving and addressing ecological problems.

The challenges for reorienting teacher education towards sustainability in Daugavpils University, Institute of Sustainable Education are illustrated here. It offers theoretical and methodological framework, as well as cases of efficient practice in changing students and teachers' values and behaviors towards sustainability. The challenges of reorienting teacher education towards sustainability are enriched by the insights from works of ecofeminist thinkers. The author also traces the development of few sustainability initiatives at the Institute of Sustainable Development and identified obstacles to education for sustainable development.

The Concept of Sustainability

The importance of ecological concerns is linked to an awareness of ecological crises. The Soviet centralized education did not leave much space in school curriculum for the environmental concerns. During the 1970's, an emerging body of literature in science, philosophy and cultural theory highlighted the new emerging perspective called 'holism' *(Miller, 1996, Fogarty, 1991, Schreiner, Baney & Oxley, 2006).*

Holism emphasizes the challenge of creating a sustainable, just, and peaceful society in harmony with the Earth and its life. It involves ecological sensitivity. A holistic approach inspired many educators in public and private schools in Latvia. Holistic education refers to the worldview that opposes reductionism, positivism, and the Cartesian dualisms of self, other and the world. The emphasis of holistic education is on the ultimate unity, relatedness and inherent meaningfulness. Holistic education can be described best by the following underlying assumptions: education brings dynamic human relationship; learning is a life-long process; learning is active, self-motivated and supportive *(Schreiner, Baney & Oxley, 2006, 90-91).*

In the early 90's in Latvia first attempts were made to define environmental education by introducing the concept of sustainability. Since then a much stronger emphasis in teacher training programs has been placed on integrating thinking and action around ecological, social, political and economic systems. On a university level, it was a shift from a narrow definition of programs that focused on ecological aspects to the acknowledgement that environmental problems need to be addressed through economic, social and political change. The group of thinkers from the Institute of Sustainable Education in Latvia *(I. Salite, A. Pipere)* with the support of UNESCO Chair *C. Hopkins* and in cooperation with the partner institutions from the international network of Western and Eastern Europe, Canada, Scandinavia, the United States, and Asia has initiated country-wide reforms on reorienting teacher-education towards sustainability.

Defining Sustainable Education

Sustainability is a concept, which still remains ambiguous. Sustainability comes from the Latin word *'subtenir'* that means *'to hold or to sustain'* from the bottom, and also implies the meaning of stability, balance, unity, and harmony (Allaby, 1994).

The ambiguity of the concept lies in the *Brundtland Report* (1987), definition of sustainability that later was elaborated in the United Nations Conference on Environment and Development report held in Rio de Janeiro in 1992.

Sustainable development was defined as development that 'meets the needs of the present without compromising the ability of future generations to meet their own needs' (*Our Common Future, 1987, WCED, p. 8).* This definition was enriched in a United Nations Environmental Program report *'Caring for the Earth'* as *'improving the quality of life while living within the carrying capacity of supporting ecosystems.'* This definition recognizes environmental limits. The carrying capacity, ethically speaking, is a narrow definition of sustainability that allows humans to make rational choices about controlling life processes.

Lele (1991) points to a literal, ecological and social aspects of the term. The literal meaning refers to the continuation of anything. The ecological meaning relates to maintaining the 'ecological basis of human life' within a time-based structure, indicating concern for the future and the present. Social meaning focuses on maintaining desired social values, cultures, and other social aspects.

Orr (1992) elucidates that education for sustainability means '..uncompromising commitment to life and its preservation', as well as the interrelatedness of all disciplines and the practical know-how to use knowledge and emotion to promote sustainability (p. 133). At the Institute of Sustainable Education the term of 'sustainability' is used to describe a positive movement towards environmental accountability and social and environmental responsibility. The author believe that as citizens of the 'global village' universities should be totally committed to searching sustainability issues and in advancing knowledge which is able to meaningfully add to the long-term goal of a fully sustainable environment.

Sustainable development is a constant process of transformation of a society to maintain and nurture life. The concept includes all aspects of human and non-human existence; it involves deep questions about human responsibility and destination, and can be seen at different levels from micro to global and through different perspectives. Therefore, sustainability is essentially a holistic and interdisciplinary issue. The concept of a sustainable education encompasses a vision of education that empowers every individual to assume responsibility to create a sustainable future.

The Examples of Sustainable Practice at the Institute

The scholars at Daugavpils University from the Institute of Sustainable Development believe that modern educational system in Latvia reflect a deep crisis of our culture: the inability of the predominant worldview to address the social and planetary challenges. The researchers who are engaged in a deeper study of sustainability issues *(Salite, 2006; Ilisko, 2005; Pipere, 2006)* believe that our dominant cultural values and practices have been destructive to the health of the ecosystem and human development.

The concept of sustainable education is a topic of discussion among the academicians across Latvia *(Salite, 2006; Ilisko, 2005; Pipere, 2006)*. The group of scholars from the Institute of Sustainable Education at Daugavpils University in Latvia is trying to define a workable definition of sustainability, by capturing the essence of key concepts, such as ecocentrism, biotism, and clarifying the components necessary to embrace all aspects of sustainability. By working towards formulation of a definition of sustainable education, the scholars propose practical strategies and steps in reorienting educational curriculum and teacher training programs towards sustainability *(Salite, Ilisko, Pipere, Grabovska)*. Several members of faculty took time to restructure their own thinking by learning the basic facts about new topics, finding appropriate texts with the purpose to integrate sustainability issues in their curriculum.

An example of integrating sustainability issues in the University curricula is the course on "The Environmental Education' offered by professor Ilga Salîte. During the classes, the students from the Faculty of Education and Management of Daugavpils University were engaged in constructive discussion formulating the definition of a sustainable education. One of the tasks of the course was to encourage participants to explore the complexity of sustainability. At the end of the course they were asked to write an essay on their understanding of sustainability.

Relevant scholarly literatures provided the course-participants with the opportunity to explore, to examine, to discuss and to critique societal unsustainable reality. Students acquired knowledge about the notions of eco-centric attitude, anthropocentrism, egocentrism, ecophilia, and ecophobia as well as the connectedness of these notions with the concept of sustainable education.

While formulating the notion of sustainable education, the students discovered the aspects of sustainability as, 'rational use of the resources,' 'purposeful action towards the interdependence of a person and the environment,' 'the respect towards the future generations,' as 'one's moral obligation to improve the quality of the environment,' as well as 'action for ensuring a sustainable development' ('*Students for Sustainability*').

As the main obstacles for hindering sustainable development, students mentioned insensitivity, anthropocentrism, alienation from nature, and cruelty. The characteristics that are needed to adapt a sustainable way of life, as mentioned by students in their essays, are ecocentric attitude, tolerance, and biotism. After completing the course it was evident that the students were able to identify all aspects of sustainability: ecological, economic, environmental and social.

Other members of faculty undertook similar initiatives by integrating sustainability issues in their study-courses. Within the framework of the course on *Multicultural Education* and *Christian Faith* delivered by Dr. Dzintra Ilisko, sustainability issue was integrated by discussing the issues of diversity (biological, cultural, religious) and inclusion. The increased interest of students in Eastern traditions, such as Hinduism and Buddhism that stress the interdependence of all things provided them with the space for discussion about building a sustainable future. Religion has played a key role in the global and historical human dialogue about morality, human rights, and social justice. Many religious traditions have stories of creation and concerns for human suffering, morality, human rights, and social justice. Religion course is one of examples how the sustainability issues can help students to think about necessary behaviors and actions for a sustainable future.

The course participants where also acquainted with the ideas from the scholarly works of ecofeminist thinkers *(McFague, 1993, 1997; Soelle, 1984)* that emphasize a responsibility of humans to participate actively in God's continuing creation by mending 'one's broken relations to the earth, to each other and to God. So, as Soelle (1984) concludes, 'the more a person develops creativity, delves into the project of liberation and transcends his or her limitations, the more God is God' (p.24).

International Framework

Sustainability issue was broadly discussed on a worldwide scale at the number of international events. One of such worldwide events was the UN *Conference on Environment and Development in Rio de Janeiro in 1992* where the policy makers signed a global contract that binds governments around the world to strengthen a Global Biodiversity by implementing a strategy of a sustainable development. Another world wide event to be mentioned is *The United Nations World Summit on Sustainable Development in Johannesburg that* took place in South Africa in *2002* where the participants defined four interdependent and mutually reinforcing pillars of sustainability, such as economic, social, environmental, and political.

UNESCO (2002) proposed pillars of sustainability which are grounded in four interdependent systems:

- Biophysical systems that provide the life support systems for all life, human and non-human;
- Economic systems that provide continuing means of livelihood for people;
- Social and cultural systems that provide ways for people to live together peacefully and with respect to human rights and dignity;
- Political systems through which power is exercised fairly and democratically (p. 8).

This definition points to the capacity of educational establishments to construct culture that reflects the policy of sustainability-oriented teacher-education.

Alongside with reaffirming the educational objectives of the Millennium Development Goals and the *Education for All* frameworks for action, the Summit announced *the Decade of Education for Sustainable Development*. *The Earth Summit* had a clear focus on reorienting education in order to foster values and attitudes of respect towards the environment.

Paradigm Change: Towards an Eco-Centered Worldview

There is a growing consensus among the scholars that current philosophy and strategies are unsustainable. This requires a paradigm shift in the relationships between humans and the environment in a way that is mutually beneficial and sustainable.

The meaning of any reform does not mean rearranging old things in a new way. For the reform to be sufficient that requires a radical change in thinking, this requires a major shift in the worldview. Feminist thinkers *(Durka, 1990, Finson, 1987)* believe **that when educators arrive at critical awareness, they have a capacity to recreate and transform the world, and therefore, build new models of relationships between humans and the Universe.** Freire (1970) describes this as a process of conscientization when people move from lower (naïve) levels of conscience towards critical conscience when a person makes a commitment to face the injustices.

As Sterling (2001) wrote, dominant paradigm 'sustains unsustainability'- through uncritically responding norms, by fragmenting understanding, by relocating a narrow spectrum of human ability and servicing the consumerist machine. The dominant mechanistic and anthropocentric worldview demarcates the reality in dichotomies: humans/nature, present/ future, local/ global, while ecological view emphasizes relatedness. Such thinking is not systemic but linear, not integrative but rather fragmentary.

The traditional subject - centered classrooms nurture dichotomous thinking and inhibits empowerment and convergent thinking. A school and university setting where the student is submerging to subject matter are contrary to a democratic and sustainable classroom community. Such a classroom promotes dichotomous thinking and conveys a message that democracy, diversity and sustainability are something very theoretical. Until one acknowledges that sustainability can be strengthened by integrating the diverse perspectives, there will be little commitment to a sustainable future. According to Dewey (1963), every experience changes the person who had the experience and, therefore, the quality of subsequent experiences. If experiences are provided in which sustainability is seen to have a positive influence, the effect that experience has on the student is more likely to influence future experiences positively. However, all knowledge – constructed, experienced or received – has little value unless it is reflected upon and internalized in same meaningful way. As Breault (2003) argues, sustainable future implies a certain trust that most students can come to that same belief on their own, if provided with the right balance of new experiences and reflection.

For any reform whether it takes place in the society or in the realm of education to be sufficient, it needs to begin with the transformation of self. Transformation of self means transforming individual's entire way of thinking and being in the world. This means moving beyond the boundaries of one's individualistic self towards an expanded sense of self. The assumption that humans are the crowns of creation, the measure of all things is deeply imbedded in Western philosophical, social and political traditions. Anthropocentrism and homocentrism is an exaggerated sense of the human in relation to the rest of the world. Expanded sense of self moves one beyond 'the limits of one's egoistic self to 'something which is more inclusive than individual self' *(Fox, 1995, 1999).* Conceptualization of self as an ecosystem existing within a larger ecosystem can facilitate the shift from thinking of self as a separate, independent entity to recognizing its complete interdependence in the totality *(Ilisko, 2006).* Similarly, eco-feminist thinkers *(McFague, 1995; Gebara, 1999; Durka, 2003)* define relatedness as the most essential condition of a human being. In the cosmology proposed by eco-feminist writers, there is no such thing as an isolated human being. Individual is always a part of interconnected events. As O'Sullivan (2001) states, expanded ecological self integrates dimensions of differentiation, subjectivity and communion. Fox (1995) points to three identifications of ecological self, such as personal, ontological and cosmological. Personal identification refers to experiences of communion with other entities, while ontological dimension refers to transpersonal and a radical openness to all the existence and a cosmological dimension of self refers to experiences of communion and point to a single unfolding reality.

Teachers Facing Paradigm Change

Latvia Human Development Report (2001) indicates to a number of causes for the fall of teachers' active involvement in processes of initiating changes in the society.

First, with the fall of communism and the processes of liberalization teachers regained their voice in pursuing changes in education, but they had neither skills nor experience for initiating changes. Huge workload and bureaucratic requirements diminished teachers' time and motivation for societal action to a great extent.

Secondly, the critical deficiency of liable policy-making impedes the development of the country, and does not permit the formulation of a sequential and goal oriented public policy. Irresponsible policy-making is an example and a justification for a cynical public attitude against the regulations of state institutions.

Thirdly, many teachers do not participate actively in educational processes, because they do not believe that they can make significant impact upon the educational policy processes. They view school as a political corporation geared to no higher ideals than its own maximized self-perpetuation according to optimal input/output rates. Teachers firmly place all the effective forms of public influence in last place among a broad scope of alternatives available.

Fourthly, the majority of teachers live under conditions of economic hardships. There is also a lack of teachers' consciousness with regard to an environmentally friendly institution and moving away from 'comfort zone'.

Problems, which undermine teachers' initiative and meaningful work, as mentioned by the teachers, can be classified in the following categories *(Ilisko, 2007)*:

The 1st category: the policies and procedures:

- Discrepancy between educational standards and a real situation;
- A gap between what Ministry requires and a real life situation;
- Frequent changes in requirements initiated by the Ministries;
- Never ending reforms in the country;
- No time been given for self-reflection about the necessities of changes.

Irresponsible and closed policy-making leads towards passive society and teachers' low self-esteem. Teachers firmly place all the effective forms of public influence in last place, among a broad scope of alternatives available.

The 2nd category: inadequate resources:

- Shortage of resources,
- Low financing of schools,
- Low technical supplies for schools and classrooms;
- Economic hardships (primarily teachers energy has been directed in making ends meet);

The 3rd category: bureaucracy:

- High, unrealistic testing requirements set by the state;
- Conflicting expectations;
- The bureaucratic structures of their work;
- Models of teaching imposed from above;
- Bureaucratic inflexibility to change.

The 4th category: job related responsibilities:

- Loads of paperwork;
- The overload among teachers;
- Imposed changes and the timeliness for their implementation;
- Innovation overload;
- Lack of confidence in one's power and doubts about the significance of one's actions;
- Unrealistic demands for teachers;
- Discomfort with ever changing educational policy.

The 5th category: teachers' motivation to make changes in education:

- Low motivation;
- Teachers do not believe that they can make significant impact upon the educational policy processes;
- Teachers perceive school as a political corporation geared to no higher ideals than its own maximized rates among other institutions;
- Teaching job prestige is very low, social guarantees are minimal;
- Low financing of teachers' further education

Educational Change: Problems and Gains

Hargreaves (2005) point to several difficulties for teachers while facing educational change: the change is poorly conceptualized, the change is too broad and ambitious, the change is too fast for people to cope with, it is poorly resourced, and there is no long-term commitment, and the change is pursued in isolation. Some of implications of understanding educational change are a complex, paradoxical and chaotic phenomenon. Attempts to coerce teachers into change results in the intensification of teacher's work and 'burnout' *(Byrne, 1994)*. Therefore, greater attention needs to be paid to the personal influences on what teachers do. Change strategies that ignore the meanings, emotions and cultures of schools, are doomed to failure *(Fink & Stoll, 2005)*.

To overcome some of the difficulties for teachers dealing with change, the professors from the institute of Sustainable education have a good practice by gradual reorienting of education towards sustainability by integrating elements of sustainability as it was described above.

Prior to encouraging teachers' active engagement in making changes in education processes, the primary step is engaging teachers in critical evaluation of their views, assumptions, believes, conditions, meanings, and values and empowering them as to make changes in education.

As Mezirow (1991) suggests, a teacher needs to be engaged in critical reflection of his/her experiences, which in turn leads to a perspective transformation. "Perspective transformation is the process of becoming critically aware of how and why our assumptions have come to constrain the way we perceive, understand, and feel about our world; changing these structures of habitual expectations to make possible a more inclusive and integrated perspectives; and, finally, making choices or otherwise acting upon these new understandings". Perspective transformation is quite helpful in explaining, how the meaning structures that adults have acquired over a lifetime become transformed. These meaning structures are frames of reference that are based on teachers' cultural and contextual experiences that influence how they behave and interpret events. As Taylor (1998) suggests, meaning schemes can be deconstructed and acted upon in a rational way. This happens through such stages as self-examination, critical assessment of assumptions, recognition that others have shared similar transformations, development of competence and self-confidence in new roles, and reintegration into life on the basis of new perspectives.

Education for sustainability needs to move away from an agenda focused on awareness raising and behavioral change towards process which Paulo Freire calls *'conscientization'* that leads to transformative action. Education, which focuses only on 'awareness-raising', is disempowering and insufficient. 'Conscientization' involves challenging teachers to explore sustainability issues through a deeper power perspective.

Methodological Recommendations for University Academicians

The recommendations concern policy makers, curriculum developers, teacher trainers and teachers who have an agency in reorienting education towards sustainability.

University is a microcosm of the larger community. Therefore, it can teach students the ways how to foster environmentally responsible living and to reinforce values and behaviors of ecological livelihood by teaching students ecological footprint of their activities.

Universities and teachers' training institutions have a capacity in organizing seminars and workshops for policy and decision makers. Decision makers need to ensure that awareness, knowledge, and understanding of sustainability become a part of the mainstream consciousness, both nationally and internationally, since concern about the environment, economic, and equity must become rooted in public consciousness. Individuals involved in decision making have an agency to foster action for sustainable practices and produce commitment of all individuals to work towards a sustainable future.

University's research centers have a capacity to strengthening networking and participation among international partner institutions, conducting research into the emerging trends of a sustainable education. An example of such cooperation can be mentioned BBC (Black and Baltic Sea Consortium) network of researchers engaged in the research around the sustainability issues.

The environmental crisis challenges university faculty members to re-educate themselves and then to teach students new patterns of thinking and acting. They have an imagination and power to envision a community that stretches from its comfort zone to increased cross cultural understanding, - a community that avoids oppressive hierarchies but advocates for inclusion, respect and cooperation of all members.

Particular attention should be paid creating research agenda to address issues of sustainable education by increasing research on quality teaching and transformative learning approaches.

This is essential to integrate sustainability issue in the educational courses that focuses around understanding diverse aspects of sustainability. Several scholars have made attempts to integrate the issues of sustainability within the framework of the following study courses on all educational levels, mainly, Bachelors, Masters and Doctoral level: 'Multicultural education,' 'Environmental education', 'Theoretical and Practical Aspects of Adult Education.'

The following shifts need to be considered for redesigning educational approach of teaching:

- From individual learning to collaborative learning;
- From theory dominated learning to praxis – oriented learning;
- From content–oriented learning to self-regulative learning;
- From emphasizing only cognitive to higher-level cognitive objectives to also emphasizing affective and skill related objectives.

Hutchison (1998) names this education as 'education for ecological renewal' or 'the pedagogy of possibility'. The 'pedagogy of possibility' focuses on meaningful learning and finding a sense of purpose within a natural world while paying critical attention to cultural context in which everyone is embedded.

The initiatives for the administration of faculties and research centers in universities are the following:

- To develop a spirit of interdisciplinary cooperation;
- Helping faculty to explore a shift in pedagogy from a paradigm of a teacher as an expert to teacher as a facilitator of learning, becoming a co learner with the student;
- Engaging faculty members in doing research on sustainability issues.

Universities have a task to educate students as the future custodians of the planet, to act ethically and responsibly and to demand less consumer goods. In this regards curriculum must be revised.

Methodological Suggestions to Reorient Education for Sustainability

Teachers need to become facilitators of the paradigm shift and supporters of the value of diversity. Feminist educators can enrich educational practice by valuable suggestions. They believe that people have a capacity to recreate and transform the world, and to build new models of relationships between humans themselves and the universe. Moore (1998) suggests several strategies for the transformative action:

1) Suspicion towards the dominant norms, symbols and assumptions underlying institutional and societal rules.
2) Grace and care are powerful strategies to build one's relationships with God and Earth;
3) Hope for the better and a more sustainable future that implies one's power to envision a transformed world-ecological, personal, social and global, and finally;
4) Solidarity will help befriending the stranger, offering hospitality to the outsider, rejected and silenced.

Teachers need to be aware that 'all education is environmental education' *(Orr, 1992)*. By this students learn that they are a part of the natural world. This helps students to adopt an attitude of careful stewardship towards the Earth.

By transcending the frames of traditional education, teachers can encourage students encounter with the nature. Natural diversity can be the source of human creativity.

Teachers should be encouraged to use an inquiry based methodology in their classrooms, by implementing experimental approaches for conducting students' research; by introducing hands-on-activities and field trips with their students. Learning should be viewed as eco-centric, empowering and participatory. Student participation in designing their curricula should be welcomed. Learning process should be connected with students' lived experience. By studying local issues in connection with their lived experience, students will learn to investigate larger systems and their interconnectedness with local problems, and how these systems affect humanity economically, environmentally, and socially. In this way students will become invited to participate in the community.

Teachers need to use strategies to motivate environmentally sound and socially just behaviors of students. Enhancing students' 'ecological literacy' *(Orr, 1992)*, means developing students' broader understanding of how people and societies relate to each other and to natural systems, by comprehending the dynamics of the modern world. The ecologically literate person will have a positive view of life and a sense of connectedness with the universe. Such view will enable a student to look upon the human experience positively and at all things compassionately. As Orr (1992) comments, the ecologically literate person "will appreciate something of how social structures, religion, science, technology, patriarchy, agriculture and human cussedness combine as causes of our predicament". The ecologically literate person is a responsible lifelong –learner who strives to improve the human condition and the environment within the context of self, human groups, the biosphere and the ecosphere. The person will find meaning for life by aspiring to higher levels of balanced growth, in his/her cognitive, affective, reflective, intuitive, creative and spiritual capabilities. Dyer (1996) provided us with a pedagogical model to achieve environmental literacy. His model promotes the idea of including environmental issues in existing university and school courses as well as having direct courses in which content is uniquely the environment and sustainability.

As the experience indicates, that through the process of discussion and rigorous intellectual explorations, students can develop an ability to think critically and deeply about issues of sustainability and their assumptions about the world and their vocation in the world *(Students about Sustainability*, 2007).

Another challenge for the schools is creation of research-culture. Teachers' research helps teachers to become problem-solvers in their classrooms, leading to a greater capacity to find, develop, and implement strategies that meet the learning needs of their students. Further, teachers' research improves students' learning when school-contexts foster problem-solving research done by teachers. This is most likely to occur where school administrators promote continuous learning for teachers through in-service professional development, making schools as centers of inquiry.

The other challenge is how to join school administration in common efforts with the staff of the university staff encouraging and supporting teachers' research by engaging teachers in exciting research projects where teachers are capable to share their finding with other colleagues though publications. Enhancing visibility for research findings to other teachers provides scaffolding for the development of research-based practice for teachers not currently involved.

Methodological Suggestions to Curriculum Transformation

In majority of schools in Latvia, teachers are not committed to designing holistic curricula; they prefer to work within the given curriculum-framework where disciplines are separated and distinct *(Ilisko, 2005)*. However, they make efforts to relate topics within the discipline. As the obstacles they mention lack of time and availability of resources, doubts about academic test scores, and difficulty in planning and scheduling. Teachers who had a longer teaching practice admit that they have no prior experience in implementing integrated curricula in a basic and secondary school level *(Ilisko, 2005)*. The majority of teachers prefer to teach in the same way as they have taught before by changing nothing in their work. As teachers report themselves, standards define much of a schools curriculum and what teachers need to do in their classrooms, so that teachers 'adapt' and conform to their reality. The context of top-down, unquestionable standards, and anti-intellectual culture of schools are hindering teachers' desire to be challenging and inspirational teachers. Instead the role of the teachers is reduced to a low-skill activity, where teachers are treated mainly as craftspeople. State standards specify what is to be taught, how it to be taught is, and what constitutes student-teacher competence.

Training teachers as implementers of state standards turn teachers into a role of a technicians rather than designers of their own reality. As Wilson, Wineburg & Samuel (1988) comment, a set of absolutes that label what is right and wrong, effective and ineffective only contributes to the comfort level of those who assess teachers' effectiveness but does not do well to teaching process in the classroom.

Though there are many successful cases of curriculum integration at the pre-school level. The group of scholars from the faculty of Education and Management in the cooperation with ISEC representatives has designed suggestions for the curriculum integration for the preschool level, which has been successfully integrated in practice. Therefore, the suggestions for the curriculum designers and implementers at schools should include the following:

Sustainable education should not be seen as series of projects or initiatives, but as an integral component of school-curricula. The challenge is the integration of a core curriculum at all levels, which emphasizes unity, and interdependence of humanity, as well as all species.

Environmental issues should be integrated across disciplines and even at the core of all education. Students have to become confident in a holistic education if they are to become the future custodians of the Earth.

Curricula should be organized in such a way that it teaches that the responsibilities of humans extend further than their neighbors to all life on a planet *(Ilisko, 2004)*. This involves family, school, and a wider community, assisting students in their encounter with different others and with creation, taking seriously the role of education towards responsibility. By learning responsibilities for themselves, students will gradually learn that the moral vocation in life is also to be responsible to all beings and all people.

Environmental issues are complex and cannot be understood through a single discipline. Therefore, holistic curriculum can encourage interdisciplinary education.

Sustainability oriented curriculum need to emphasize: system thinking, the interdependence of humans and the environment, including the relationships among population, culture, economy and the environment.

Curriculum should reflect four interdisciplinary themes, such as ecological literacy, ecological responsibility, a sense of community, experiential learning and developing ecological self.

Curriculum should be built on specific basic understandings, such as intergenerational thinking, systems thinking, dialogic, and inquiry based processes, embededness in a natural world.

While designing curricula, particular attention needs to be paid to accord scope in providing students with the opportunities to explore their own values and attitudes towards sustainability issues, as well as challenging them to participate in decision making.

An integrated curriculum reflects educators' concern with connecting and integrating ideas, which Bonds, Cox, & Gantt; – Bonds (1993) describe it as a synergetic teaching which goes beyond the blurring of subject lines to a process of teaching where all subjects are taught in a synergetic way.

To develop a transformative agenda for redesigning educational curricula that integrate the economic, ecologic, and social well-being issues of sustainability the insights of eco-feminist thinkers are particularly valuable here.

Eco-feminist thinkers prompt guidelines for building a holistic curriculum based on the following principles:

- Everything has intrinsic value. Any curriculum transformation must respect that all nature has intrinsic value.
- Human beings should not attempt 'to manage' or control nonhuman nature, but should have a special vocation to safeguard the Earth.
- Redistribution of power relationships is not an answer to the environmental and educational crises. In order to deal with the environmental, social and educational problems, educators need to move beyond power over towards an ethic of mutual respect.
- The personal is political. Every individual has a power to make changes in the society.

Eco-feminist thinkers *(Moore, 1989, Harris, 1989)* suggest that curriculum should be organized in such a way that teaches students responsibilities, which extend towards all life on the planet. This means expanding boundaries of community beyond immediate family and friends, and embracing all peoples. Such extension is a respect for the rights and needs of future generations that help students to live with a sense of kinship with nature and an ethics of ecological responsibility.

Concluding Remarks

Sustainability-education has evolved as a decentralized movement without a professional organization, national standards. At the international level, United Nation has declared 2005-2015 as the Decade of Education for Sustainability. Sustainability education infuses a sense of purpose and relevance across disciplines while providing a rigorous response to academic debate.

Designing a sustainable future requires a paradigm-shift towards an ecocentric worldview, which encompasses the complex interdependence of individual, social, cultural and economic and political activities.

The Earth Chapter outlines the challenges to bring forth a sustainable global society, focused on respect towards the other. As an imperative there is a call for everyone to undertake a responsibility to recognize that in the midst of a magnificent diversity of cultures and life forms, 'we are one human family and one Earth community with a common destiny (2000).

A major paradigm shift is required in the thinking, value education and actions for a long-term effort to make sustainability concerns a central theme in the education. Institutions of higher education bear a profound moral responsibility to increase public awareness, knowledge, skills and values, necessary to create a sustainable future.

Sustainable education should embrace the following features:

- It should be interdisciplinary and holistic: learning for sustainable education should be embedded in the whole curriculum;
- It should embrace critical thinking and problem solving;
- Participatory decision-making; involving all the participants;
- Locally relevant: addressing local as well as global issues.

Formal education plays a crucial role in raising awareness of young people about the issues of a sustainable development, developing their skills they need to implement the idea of sustainable development in practice. Focusing on sustainability provides an opportunity for assessing epistemic development and the new ways of thinking (the paradigmic challenge). Integrating sustainability into higher education brings academics into new experiential, epistemic, and systemic world. Education is a key to creating necessary behavioral and policy changes. Sustainable living can be learned. Sustainable development principles must lie at the core of the education system. By linking teaching to issues of direct concern to students, their personal quality of life, and the wellbeing of the communities and the environment around them- their learning becomes more relevant.

Industrial Safety, Public Health and Environment

A Prospective Educational Profile

S.C. Santra, S. Kar and A.C. Samal

Since UN Conference on Human Environment at Stockholm, Sweden in 1972, global concern on environmental education was focused. In response to the above UNESCO in cooperation with United Nation Environmental Programme (UNEP) launched the International Environmental Education Programme (IEEP) in 1975 at Paris. The major objectives are to make people aware of the nature of the relationship between humanity and the environment on which mankind depends, to impart knowledge and skills to understand and solve environmental problems, and to enable people to acquire the attitudes and motivations leading to sound decisions and civic actions for the protection and improvement of the environment and its quality.

In India, there are three major ways of initiation of environmental education, viz, non formal education through NGOs, Institutes & Govt. bodies; formal education and training at school, college and University level; specialized technical education for skill-development and application in solving environmental problems. In every education there is need for a goal, target groups, and modalities of teaching with specified contents. The approach will be highly variable with these issues. Thus environmental education is something is very complex to design and needs to reoriented every-time with new experiences and expertise.

Industrial safety and health hazards are common in many economic sectors and affect large number of peoples in our country. Approximately 30-50 per cent of workers report hazards physical, chemicals or biological exposures or overloads of unreasonably heavy physical works that may be hazards to health and working capacity; an equal number of working people report psychological overload at work resulting in stress symptoms *(Rao and Lundgren, 1955)*. With the rapid growth of technology and globalization of economic review, transfer of technological knowledge has taken place throughout the world at an increasing rate. This technological application have often led to benefits such as improved productivity and reduced physical exertion. Conversely the misapplication of such technology has given rise to hazards threatening safety and public health. Rapid changes in modern working life associated with increasing demand of developing new skills, need to adopt new type of work, time, pressure and with growing psychological workload and stress among the work force.

With the increasing awareness about the environment world over, most of the countries have enacted legislations for protecting environment and establish machinery for their implementation. With a view to promote good standards on environmental practices, International Organization for Standards has developed ISO 14000 series which specifies requirements on environmental management systems.

Hence there is urgent need for strengthening human-skills, developing newer competencies and broadening our knowledge in the area of Industrial Safety, Occupational and Environmental Health. Environmental Education, Awareness and Training [EEAT] play significant role in encouraging and enhancing people's participation in activities aimed at management of the industrial safety and protection of health, essential for achieving sustainable development. The government therefore, accords priority for the promotion of non-formal environment education and creation of awareness among all sections of the society through diverse activities using traditional and modern media of communication.

Industrial Safety

Industrial safety is now the prime concern in developing world including India and everyone hoped that industrial world would take appropriate measures to ensure safety in industries. But even after so many years, nothing has been done after Bhopal massacre to improve the safety in Indian industries. Whatever has been done is insignificant in comparison to what needs to be done. Although the Ministry of Environment and Forest (MoEF), which is the nodal ministry for handling safety of chemical industries claims to have initiated great measures to ensure safety. Bhopal tragedy is with which not only India but also the whole world learnt lessons on need for industrial safety. Though industrial safety has not reached a comfortable level, there has been a substantial improvement in industrial safety in India after Bhopal incident.

However, what makes above claims immensely interesting is the statistics on chemical accidents in India. In 1985, release of hexacyclopentadiene killed 200 people in Cochin. In 1988, fire and explosion in a factory in erstwhile Bombay killed 35 and injured 26 people. Same year, a fire in an oil refinery in the same place took lives of 35 and injured 16. Similarly, 93 were killed and 53 injured when explosion and fire happened in Medhvan Khind in 1991. Same year, 100 more people were exterminated by LNG caused explosion and fire in Bombay Ahmedabad highway. Two years later, Sulphuric Acid release from a factory in Kalyan, Maharashtra killed 49 and injured 1123 *(ICR, 1996)*. MoEF has come out recently with a comprehensive list of chemical accidents that have occurred in India after Bhopal. According to the report, there have been as many as 119 industrial accidents in between 1984 to 1995 involving hazardous chemicals *(ICR, 1996)*.

Public Health

As the trend in India is towards industrialization, the industrial development both in size and complexity, industrial safety and public health will pose new and more difficult problems. Government has recognized the need for protecting the health of the workers. To assess the health conditions of the industrial employees, number of inquiries have been conducted and were submitted to the Government of India by many experts *(Rajgopal, 2002)*. The important reports in this connection are: Adarkar's Report of the Health Insurance for Industrial Workers (1945); Report of the Health Survey and Development Committee (1946); Report of the Health of Industrial Workers *(Thomas Bedford, 1946)* and Report on the Health of Workers in Plantation *(Jones, 1947)*. The Government of India have given practical shape to some of the recommendations contained in these reports and have introduced certain legislative measures pertaining to both the curative and preventive aspects of occupational health. Most important among these measures are the Indian Factories Act, 1948, The Coal Mines Labour Act, 1948.

At present, there is no comprehensive occupational health service in India. However, there are various organizations active in the field of occupational health. The organization of the chief advisor of factories now Director General, Factory Inspection and Advisory Service was set up in 1945, to functions an integrated service to advice the government, Industries, and other interests concerned in matters relating to health, welfare and safety of industrial workers. The organization deals with questions relating to the administration of the Factories Act and other Acts and the rule framed there under and the training of Factory Inspectors.

For scientific study of the various aspects of industrial safety, occupational and public health, particularly the 'human factor' in industry, the Central Labour Institute was set up in Bombay in 1960. Three regional labour institutes at Kanpur, Calcutta and Madras have also been set up. These institutes are dealing with a variety of activities important in the field of safety and health. They have a museum of Industrial Health, Safety and Welfare, Industrial Hygiene laboratory, Training section and Library Occupational Physiology sections. At the state level the Department of Health and Labour, through the Chief Inspector of factories and Industrial Health Inspection Services are: rendering assistance by making studies and undertaking surveys at the plant level and enforcing the legal standards laid down in the various acts.

In addition to the above, the following Research Institutes are active in the field of occupational health. The Central Mining and Research Station, Dhanbad under the Council of Scientific and Industrial Research (CSIR), Industrial Toxicological Research Center, Lucknow under the CSIR. Occupational Health Research Institute, Ahmedabad under the Indian Council of Medical Research, National Environmental Engineering Research Institute at Nagpur, The All India Institute of Hygiene and Public Health, Kolkata, Indian Institute of Technology, Kanpur. Beside these the Indian Council of Medical Research has an occupational health division. The Indian Association of Occupational Health is playing an important role in the promotion of occupational health.

Environmental Education for Prevention and Control of Pollution

Though formal education is the mandate of the Ministry of Human Resource Development (MHRD), the Ministry of Environment & Forests has been interacting with the MHRD, NCERT, State Departments of Education etc. to ensure that environmental components are adequately covered at the school levels by infusion into the school curricula at various levels introducing industrial safety and occupational health. Govt. of India and various international agencies support NGO's and institutions to promote non-formal environmental awareness education. For last 30 years such a practice is going on as a recurrent activity. But adequate follow-up for action-oriented activities in the field of environment protection/conservation is lacking so far. Commitment or motivation towards environmental issues is grossly inadequate in every education programme in our Country.

Regarding industrial safety and occupational health, the workers need to be aware of the industrial processes and technologies adopted. Besides they should be given adequate protection against direct contact by protective clothing, gloves and boots and other precautionary measures. There should be available a plentiful supply of warm water, soap and towels. The workers should be encouraged and educated to make frequent use of these facilities. Adequate washing facilities in industries are a statutory obligation under the factories act. There should be periodical medical check-up for all workers for early detection and treatment of any kind of occupational disease. In other way, the prevention and reduction of industrial health hazards should be needed for better utilization of resources and maximizing the production in terms of good factory management and practices, adequate pre-placement examination, good human relations and application of ergonomics *(Parikh and Kashyap, 1995).*

Periodic inspection of working environment provides information of primary importance in the prevention of occupational disabilities. Various aspects of working environment such as temperature, lighting, ventilation, humidity, noise, cubic space air pollution and sanitation, which have an important bearing in the health, and welfare of the workers should be monitored. Employees should be acquainted with raw materials, processes and products manufactured. Workers should have knowledge about the various aspects of occupational physiology such as occurrence of fatigue, night-work, shift-work, weight carried by the workers and render advice to the factory management on all matters connected with the health and welfare of the workers. Also cooperation would be needed among safety engineers, industrial hygienists and psychologists.

Environmental Monitoring

An important aspect of industrial safety and health programme is environmental monitoring. It is concerned with periodical environmental surveys especially sampling the factory atmosphere to determine whether the dusts and gases escaping into the atmosphere are within the limits of permissible concentration. The use of 'permissible limits' has played important role in reducing occupational exposure to toxic substances. Thermal environment, ventilation, light would also have to be monitored. Such monitoring should be done by joint collaboration of doctors, engineers and skilled persons.

Despite the enormous progress that has been made in developed countries, continuing vigilance is required not only to maintain the effective control of established hazards but also to rapidly detect the emergence of new or unsuspected disorders that might appear as a consequence of changing technology or work practices. In developing countries, where lack of awareness, malnutrition, communicable disease are seen, it is prudent that health promotion programme at work site should be comprehensive and complete and should encompass all aspects of workers health including occupational health *(Dorman, 2000).*

Health Education and Counseling

Ideally, health education in industry should start before the worker enters the factory. All the risks involved in the industry in which s/he is employed and the measures to be taken for personal protection should be explained to the worker. The correct use of protective devices like masks and gloves should also be explained. Simple rule of hygiene- hand washing, paring the nails, bodily cleanliness and cleanliness of clothes should be impressed upon him. They should be frequently reminded about the dangers in industry through the media of health education such charts, posters and handouts. The purpose of health education is to assist the worker in his process of adjustment to the working, home and community environment.

Education and Training in Occupational Hygiene in India

Occupational hygiene has been defined as the practice of science and art devoted to the identification, evaluation and control of occupational stress. The objective of occupational hygiene programme involves reorganization, evaluation and control of work environment in industry. It is broadly concerned with the chemical, biological and physical stress that may impair the health and well-being of the workers. For the last few years, in occupational hygiene programme, the effect of outside environment, i.e., community environment of the people at large is also considered as an important factor.

The global strategy on 'Occupational Health for All' will yield an immense aspect on the health and safety of workers in the long run. The leading principle of this strategy is that 'Every citizen in the world has the right to a healthy and safe work environment and to one that enable socially and environmentally productive lives' *(WHO, 1995)*. It means that for healthy life of every citizen, safe, comfortable and clean work environment is a necessity. Practice of occupational hygiene and Industrial Safety can bring safe and comfortable work-environment in Industry.

There exists a general shortage of various categories of Occupational Health manpower at all levels in most of the developing countries. Regular courses at graduation or post-graduation levels for personals, such as occupational hygienists, safety officers, occupational health nurses and ergonomists etc. are rare and generally lacking in details. India is no exception to it. However short orientation and specialized training courses, symposia, seminars, conferences and educational campaigns are conducted regularly on occupational hygiene in India by the National Institute of Occupational Health (NIOH), Ahmedabad and Mumbai, All India Institute of Health and Hygiene and Public Health, Kolkata, Industrial Toxicology Research Centre, Lucknow. The Master of Industrial Hygiene course being conducted by the Sardar Patel University, Anand, Gujrat since last five years in collaboration with Cincinnatti University, USA is an exceptional effort.

Existing Facilities for Education and Training in Occupational Hygiene

Physicians, chemists, physicists, safety officers often perform some of the functions of occupational hygienists in the developing countries. Similar trend is prevailing in India. After getting practical experience in this field and basic training as well as orientation in occupational hygiene, they perform the duties of occupational hygienists in the country. More often they are scientists or engineers drawn from different disciplines with on-job training in the field.

Full time courses leading to a degree (may be, graduate or post graduate level) in industrial safety and hygiene are currently available in many developing countries. The industrial hygienist is supposed to be trained in a variety of disciplines in these courses. As a rule, chemistry, microbiology, physics, Environmental Science, medical practioners or engineers are admitted in such courses, which have exposure or brief experience or willingness to study this course.

The principles of occupational hygiene forms a part of the curriculum in public health diploma courses to doctors and is covered in about 20 to 25 hours of lectures, demonstrations and field visits. The graduates in engineering who are qualifying for a master degree in public health are also given a similar orientation in the subject. Almost 30 per cent of the nine months of diploma in Industrial Hygiene (DIH) course and 25 per cent of the one-year diploma in Industrial and Occupational Health (DIOH), courses are devoted to Industrial Hygiene. Master of Environmental Science and postgraduate diploma in Industrial safety also cover about 60 hours of lectures, demonstration and field visits. Even then it is considered that these trained persons do not acquire adequate confidence or quality for independent practice of industrial hygiene, despite the sufficient theoretical knowledge they have acquired during the course.

Future Development of Education and Training on Occupational Hygiene

There is a growing demand for Industrial safety and hygienic services in large industries, especially those, which obtained ISO certificates or manufacturing eco-friendly products or have foreign collaborations. It is essential that such specialized training in occupational hygiene should be given in this country.

The training could be at two levels, namely training at lower level for occupational hygiene technicians, and at higher level for occupational hygienists. In addition a few training programmes in occupational hygiene is necessary at the undergraduate level for both medical and engineering students, who are expected to be involved in public and occupational programme in future.

Functions of Occupational Hygienist

The following are the major functions of the occupational hygienist—

(*i*) Planning of occupational hygiene programmes,
(*ii*) Recognition and evaluation of work-environment,
(*iii*) Interpretation of the results of examination of the work-environment and environs, in terms of nature of health impairment, work efficiency and community nuisance and/or damage, and presenting specific conclusions to authorities/parties such as health officials and management,
(*iv*) Determine the need for control measures, when necessary, recommended suitable and effective procedure for the environment and environs,
(*v*) Present expert testimony before court of law, hearing boards, and workman's compensation commissions, regulatory agencies and legally appointed investigative bodies covering all matters pertaining to occupational hygiene,
(*vi*) Conduct programme for education of workers and the public in general for prevention of occupational disease and community nuisance,
(*vii*) Establish or improve threshold limit values or standards as guidelines for maintenance of health and efficiency,
(*viii*) Conduct research for advancement of knowledge on the effects of occupation on health and means for the prevention of occupational health hazards and problems related, community air pollution, noise nuisance etc.

The teaching curricula in occupational hygiene will have to be made in such a way that it addresses the demand of the country. These curricula should be practicable and problem oriented with extensive academic and field training. Occupational hygiene education may be taught as under graduate, post graduate and specialized course.

Occupational Hygiene Education: The Scenario in Developed Countries

The World Health Organization (WHO), the Commission of the European Communities (CEC), the International Commission of Occupational Health, and the American Conference of Industrial Hygienists have organized International Workshop on 'Training and Education in Occupational Hygiene' in Luxembourg (1986) and they recommended the need of such type of specialized courses in Industrial hygiene in developed and developing countries. They also felt that there is an urgent need of Industrial Hygienists in developing countries *(Phoon, 1985).*

First academic programme in 'Industrial Hygiene' in the US was organized in 1918 at Harvard University and provided training to industrial physicians. The Social Security Act passed in the 1930 provided funds for industrial hygiene training in several universities like, California, Columbia, Harvard, Michigan and Yale. The University of Cincinnati began its M.S. and Ph.D. programmes in industrial hygiene way back in 1952. The National Institute of Occupational Safety and Health (NIOSH) currently supports industrial hygiene programmes in different Education and Research Centers and Training Programme Grants having M.S. and Ph.D. programme.

The Singapore National University offers graduate programmes in industrial hygiene. Australia and Taiwan also have such graduate course. In countries like USA, UK, Sweden, Germany, Yugoslavia also supported graduate and master programmes in Industrial Hygiene making this field as a well established and defined one.

Suggested Programme/Activities

Indian Council of Medical Research (ICMR) has recently prepared a report of the Working group on 'Environmental and Occupational Health' for the 10th five year plan on behalf of the Ministry of Health & Family Welfare, Government of India *(ICMR, 2001).* Their recommendation indicates the importance of education and training in occupational health and hygiene. They also suggest that such specialized education in occupational hygiene should be initiated at graduate and postgraduate levels through Universities/Institutions.

It is also necessary to have diploma courses for trained graduates in science in the field of occupational hygiene technology. The institutes like NIOH, ITRC should develop more refresher courses on occupational hygiene. The facilities for training developed at NIOH should be made available to other developing countries for training of candidates in occupational hygiene according to their individual national requirements. For organizing latest training in occupational hygiene, suitable fellowship programme of experts and equipment should be made available from international sources.

Occupational Health and Industrial Safety Management System

The Indian Factories Act, 1948 with its numerous amendments, and the Factory Rules in the states, encompasses almost all the requirements of recording and notifying occupational accidents and diseases in the factories. Indian statutes on this subject are in line with requirements of the International Labour Organization (ILO). Health and safety are important aspects of an organization's smooth and effective functioning. Good health and safety performance ensures an accident-free industrial environment.

Awareness of Occupational health and safety (OHS) has improved in India considerably. Organizations have started attaching the same importance to achieve high OHS performance as they do to other key aspects of their business activities. This demands adoption of a structured approach for the identification of hazards, their evaluation and control of risks *(Chakraborty, 1967)*. Bureau of Indian Standard (BIS) decided to formulate an Indian Standard on OHS management systems considering this fact and a great demand from the industry for a comprehensive framework of OHS.

National Priority on Occupational Health and Safety Management System

Recognizing that the workplace safety and health is a decisive factor in an organizational effectiveness, several management frameworks have been proposed to implement cost-effective occupational health and safety (OHS) in preventing workplace ailments and promoting health and welfare of workers revolving around the International Standards organization families of management standards (ISO 9000 and ISO 14000). Broadly an ideal OHS management system should provide a structured process to minimize potentials of work related injuries and illness, increase productivity by reducing the direct and indirect costs associated with accidents, and increase the quality of manufactured products and/ or rendered services. It must provide a direction to OHS activities in accordance with the organizational policies, regulatory requirements, industry practices, and standards, including negotiated labour agreements. This approach has drawn significant attention among the standards organization, the accreditation and certification bodies and the national agencies in formalizing, implementing and evaluating OHSMS.

Occupational Health and Safety Policy

The OHS policy is the basis for developing, implementing and improving and organizations OHS management system. A documented policy statement that gives an overall sense of direction and sets the principles of action for an organization should be produced and authorized by the organizations top management. It sets OHS objectives for OHS responsibility, performance and continual improvement throughout the organization. The policy reflects the formal commitment of the top management towards good OHS practices and management. The organization needs to be aware of how its' activities are affected by applicable legal and other requirements, and to communicate this information to relevant personal. The organization must have procedures for identifying and accessing information and identifying which requirements apply and where and monitoring the implementation of controls consequent to changes in OHS legislation *(Redinger, 1997).*

Organization should have effective procedures for ensuring the competence of personal to carry out their designated functions. Competency is required for individual roles. Analyses of training needs, training programme for individual employees, including the range of training courses/products available for use within the organization and training records and records and evaluation of the effectiveness of training would be needed.

Conclusion

Industrial safety and healthy working environment are among the most vulnerable assets of individuals, communities and countries. Occupational health is an important strategy not only to ensure the health of the workers, but also to contribute positively to the productivity, quality of products etc., work motivation, job satisfaction and thereby to overall quality of life of individuals and society.

To improve and strengthen the activities and programmes of Occupational Hygiene and conducting Occupational Health and Hygiene services in Indian Industries, It is necessary to introduce training and education in occupational hygiene for Engineers, Chemists, Physicists, Medical practitioners, Microbiologists etc. at both under graduate and post graduate levels. Refresher training courses for the Factory Inspectors, Safety Officers, Industrial Physicians and Industrial Chemists, apart from teachers should also be organized.

An effective industrial programme can identify potential exposures and provide programme of action to protect health of workers. This increases work productivity by keeping employees on job during the work year. An effective programme decreases sick-time and reduces retraining costs, reduces turn over among employees and increase work place morale. One needs to look at competency model from legislative requirements. Industry needs, employee demands, geographical demands and from occupational physician's perspective [i.e. Technical and behavioral competencies].

The awareness of politicians, the authorities, employees and the general public of occupational health and safety issues should be increased by various ways to indiscriminate information. This creates a basis of strengthening political will to create the prerequisites for improvement of working conditions and thereby worker's health. A system of participation and positive incentives would further ensure the development of health at work in all societies.

How Shall I Explore My Environment?

A Physicist's View

M.N. Bapat

This module aims at involving the learner in activities intended to enable her/him to restructure and refine her/his concepts through hands on experiences regarding environment and consolidate the learning happened. In order to make pupil explore her/his own environment we will place her/him in the robe of an investigator, we impart responsibility and show concern in her/his doing as a researcher. For this we give certain instructions as how to proceed and how serious the inventor has to be to start with. The pupils will then be exposed to certain situation.

But for sure, exploring environment entails keep it as healthy as nature has meticulously done over centuries, seeing it in right spirits, ensuring that it is not over exploited and so on. But this is not a job only of certain class of people or the government. It is an activity for the benefit of all living beings where participation of maximum number of individuals is desirous accessed as invaluable. The cooperative work extracting and making use of right ability of each is not only imperative but also useful in educating people when they start expressing concern for its degradation/deterioration. The participatory approach gives confidence, learning and satisfaction to each member of the team. Further it makes a difference in the quality of the output.

When such an approach is adapted for class/school activity learning is concretized. The underlying assumptions are:

(*i*) Each individual is capable of doing some thing in better manner than the others.

(*ii*) Everybody cannot do every job with equal proficiency.
(*iii*) Each work needs some skill to do it neatly and in minimum time.
(*iv*) Doing task in groups is joyful, competitive and encouraging.

With this background when the teacher involves the students in exploration s/he also prefers groups of mixed ability.

Exploration starts with planning, imparting instructions, doing field work, consolidating the data, presenting findings, extracting group inferences, asking questions for validity of the results and ultimately culminating in reporting.

The Process

When placed in certain challenging situation (this word need not be taken literally, when we say children doing research s/he discovers some thing unknown to her/him. Similarly challenging situation is a situation that is exciting at that age group or level of understanding) inventor looks around and finds what interests him /her most.

The instructions to the students can be like –

You are given 100 minutes time for exploration in the field after which all members of each group will report back.

Each and every member of the group under the control of the group leader has liberty to explore what ever fascinates them. On reassembling the groups will interact with the other groups.

The group will submit their observation under following heads

(*i*) What was observed?
(*ii*) What among it was most conspicuous?
(*iii*) What significant transpired in inter group deliberations?
(*iv*) What is outcome of excursion in terms of its usefulness and learning happened?
(*v*) Experiences narration that would serve a guide to next excursion group?
(*vi*) Feedback to teacher in respect of organization.

We discuss here a few exemplary projects and modules at different levels of learning, which might serve a guide for teacher who is directly involved in handling and nurturing students' curiosity instinct.

PROJECT 1

Cooling of water in earthen pots.
(Level VIII in age group of 11 to 13 years)

After going through this module, pupils will be able to discriminate the pots (for better cooling), to understand the process of cooling, to recall that water contains invisible but suspended impurities that can block the pores in the earthen pot.

Fact: Earthen pots are prevalent for cooling water (mostly in summer).

Process: Water sneaks out from the pores and evaporates at the outer surface.

Principle: Evaporation of water needs energy. Which in this case is taken from the water - earthen pot system.

Corollary: More surface exposed (to the air / draught of air) for evaporation, more cooling results.

Hypothesis: Longer is the duration of evaporation more is the cooling of water.

Exploration question

⇒ Why is the heat of evaporation taken from the water-earthen pot system and not from the surrounding air?
⇒ Is evaporation-taking place at boiling point of water?
⇒ What is the role of the temperature of the surrounding?
⇒ Is there any limit to cooling?
⇒ What parameters would make cooling faster?
⇒ What is the ideal shape for the earthen pot to make it more effective for cooling?

Methodology and Discussion on answers correlating with daily life experiences

Teacher takes students to an exploratory cum activity class (It is proposed that each school be advised to make a provision in their time table for such a class / hour at least once per week) and poses a question of the sort.

In summer we prefer cool water to hot one. What are the possible reasons?

Responses include answers to suggest: for soothing action, for relief, to quench thirst, to keep oneself cool, it tastes good etc.

Teachers' comments- Water has large specific heat. So it can absorb large quantity of heat without getting itself much hotter.

In summer we need to cool our body. Cold water helps in this aspect. In winter we do not want to further cool our body hence we do not bother about cool water in winter.

Open question for the class:

Why do we not take cold tea in summer and hot (ice) cream in winter?

Student teacher- demonstration

Teacher takes a little spirit on cotton and lightly applies on the back of hands of a few students. The students recall that spirit quickly evaporates and produce sensation of cold at the spot where it was applied. Teacher names a few more liquids that show this effect (telling precautions of their use).

Teacher next suggests students to wet their handkerchiefs, remove its excess water and put it on the bare part of their body e.g. forehead, hand etc. (Teacher asks whether they have seen such an action by their mother in their homes any time?).

Teacher's comments- Evaporation of water takes place from handkerchief and heat necessary for it is taken away from the part of body it makes contact with. S/he makes students to recall the actions they had witnessed earlier.

Teacher generalizes the observations that evaporation of liquid is accompanied by cooling of the system from which evaporation takes place and the environment.

Teacher asks about different water-cooling gadgets available in students' daily life. S/he adds that getting cold water from earthen pots is the only environment friendly device easily available and accessible to a large population of our country.

Intermittent question to keep curiosity alive

- *Why brass / steel / glass pots do not produce such cooling?*
- *Bring pots' opening near your ears and try to listen. Is the sound same for all kinds of pots? If the pot is faulty or has crack is the sound produced the same?*

The teacher summarizes the responses: Earthen pots have pores through which water can sneak out. These miniscule water droplets when reach the surface of the pot quickly vaporizes to produce cooling.

How big the pores should be?

With this background the teacher makes inhomogeneous grouping of the class. S/he assigns a question each (except Q.6) to each group, gives instructions to under take an activity or do the experiments they wish. They may seek help from the parents and community for the search of the answer. She further suggests that in the next class they would analyze the findings and conclusions.

The possible findings are summarized below:

1. Water inside the pot was cooler than the surroundings. Why? they did not know. Wild guesses were untenable.
2. Cooling does not increase linearly with increase in the temperature of the surrounding.
3. Fresh pots cool more effectively. Rate of drop in temperature (cooling) gradually reduces and ultimately further cooling stops.

Teacher adds the fresh pots have pores. These are blocked by dust and other suspended impurities present in water etc with the repetitive use. In short the contamination in water settle in the pores with use.

4. Draught of air makes cooling faster.

Teacher provides further information: A few decades ago when access to ice and cooler were not in wide use, the travelers used to carry canvass bags. Auto vehicles used to fix such canvas bags in the front panel so that air draught would be more to cause rapid cooling.

Probing questions

⇒ *How to avoid blocking of pores of the earthen pots purposed for cooling water?*

⇒ *Can reheating the pot in fire unblock pores?*

⇒ *What kind of earthen pot should be used as container and for cooking food?*

Evaluation

Hot water would cool faster in earthen pots because...

1. Will ice cool water be further cooled in earthen pot?
2. Some people cook food in earthen pots. Why should it be possible?
3. What is the structural difference between new and old earthen pot?

4. For drying clothes we wave the clothes. What are the reasons?

Assignment

Visit places in your city where such pots are made. See the process and if possible interview the pot-maker and gather more information to share with others. Try to investigate what shape is ideal for making an efficient earthen pot. Should you make use of mathematical analysis?

Module 1

Transients (Level graduation: age group 17 +)

After going through this module, pupils will be able to recognize the significance of the impulsive forces, and identify situations when and where they happen.

What we know?

Impulse. it is a violent change of motion brought about by a very strong force that begins to act suddenly on bodies that come under its influence for only a short duration.

The average force is determined by

$$m\hat{a} = (mv' - mv)/\Delta t$$

Where m is the mass of the body, v is its initial velocity and v' is final velocity after it has made an impact with some other body.

The value of it obviously is more if v and v' are almost equal in magnitude but opposite in direction. We can appreciate it through life experiences such as cricketer hitting a fast approaching ball or a ball bouncing back. Though the magnitude of the force cannot be uniform during the impact yet we can for all practical purposes take an average to calculate the effect, as suggested in the figure.

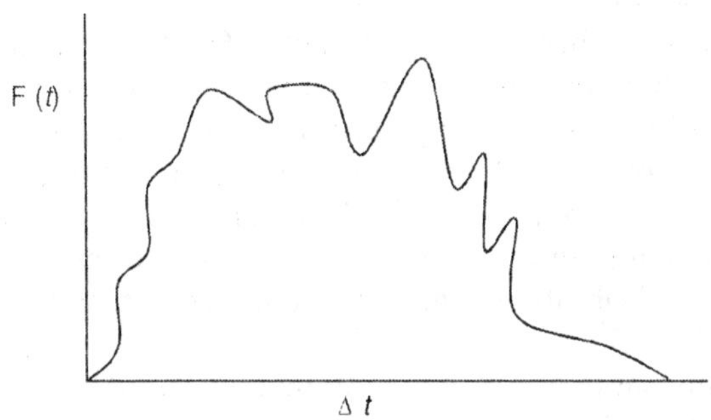

Development of the concept of transient through deduction

Let us discuss the equation

$$md^2x/dt^2 = -kx + F(t)$$

Suppose that the force F(*t*) can be represented by simple relation as

$$F(t) = F_0 \cos \omega t$$

Assuming in general that $\omega \neq \omega_0$, ω_0 being the natural frequency of the system.

Let the solution of this differential equation be

$$x = C \cos \omega t$$

We find that C has to be

$$C = F_0/m(\omega_0^2 - \omega^2)$$

The instantaneous amplitude *x* depends both on C as well as ω. However the amplitude depends on *w* for a given. When the frequency of the driving force is very low, it is the natural force that determines behaviour of the system. But if the frequency of the driving force is large only the driving force decides amplitude. In extreme cases when w is too large the amplitude becomes almost zero.

INTERMITTENT QUESTIONS

Hold a cricket ball and experience its force on your hands. Does a falling ball or the ball thrown at you impart same force? Is the impulse felt till too long?

Visit blacksmith and notice its impact on target. On what factors the impulsive force depends? Have you noticed spark coming at the site of impact? What is it due to?

Can you notice vibrations on a thick but short steel bar? What are the parameters that enable you to observe the vibrations in rods?

Let us examine these cases with daily life situation. Take a stick and hold it horizontally. Now push the other end and release. The free end of the stick starts vibrating. The vibration frequency depends among other factors on the length. For a given length exert external force periodically. This can be done by waving the fixed end or applying a periodic force at the free end. Observe the magnitude of vibration in each case and correlate with the theory suggested.

All this happens only when thing are started just at the right moment (we call it so when applied force is in phase). Otherwise there is a part whose effect is tremendous but dies down with in a short period. It is called the transient response to F(t). Let us see how? If $\omega \cong \omega_0$ the amplitude can become anything we like (save for dissipative effects).

Where do we notice the transients?

When we discuss LCR circuits we talk about steady state condition of a circuit. We assume that sufficient time has elapsed before we start our analysis of the circuit. Otherwise when the source is connected (or disconnected) there may be an additional surge of current or voltage, which can damage the delicate electronic system. The nature of these transients depends on the time in the cycle when the circuit is connected (or disconnected).

Probe questions

⇒ *Have you ever witnessed the lightening event?*
⇒ *What do the earth tremors do?*
⇒ *Are the after effects and immediate effects of an explosion similar?*

Evaluation

1. Should effect of impulse always be disastrous?
2. The impact of impulse stays longer. Write pros and cons.
3. Fluorescent lamps need large initial input power. How does it get?

Assignment

Survey situations where transients work. Delicate instruments are to be protected against transients. How it is done? Get information.

Project 2

Twinkling of stars
(Level X: age group 15 +)

After going through this module, pupils will be able to reason out as to why stars twinkle?

Background information: Looking at the sky in the night is an interesting activity. Stars of a variety are seen. Some stars are bright. Some are very weak. Some shine with almost same intensity while other appears to twinkle. Scientists have noted that the planets do not twinkle whereas stars do. The reason may not be always convincing. Let us try to find for ourselves what can be the reason.

Recalling our experiences: Many of us have seen fire. Around the flame there is a colourless flair / aura generally called plasma. Careful observation of it allows us to notice that the density of this plasma appears to change continuously. If we happen to see any object laying the other side through this aura, the object appears blurring. More furious the fire is more apparent is the experience.

Let us recall our visit to lakeside in the night. If on the other side of the lâke there were a lamppost or lighthouse our observation would be more asserting. In winter, the lamp appears to be quite bright and clearly shining. See this lamppost while it rains (for this we need not go to lakeside, a simple street lighting would do). We may notice that lamp appears blurring. We know it is due to inhomogeneous refraction of light coming to us. But if we visit the lakeside in the summer night we can see two distinct phenomena:

1. The lamp, that is not so high above the water level do not twinkle.
2. The lamps standing at height twinkle.

The observation however fails if the lamp appears too big. To observe this we need to be quite far from the lamp or size of the lamp is small and less bright. The other requirement is that the night should be quite hot so that lot of evaporation of lake water takes place.

Hypothesis: Water vapour of fluctuating density is responsible for twinkle.

Arguments in favour of our hypothesis: If we see through the glass over which water is spread non-uniformly it obstructs clear vision. When the passage of light is through different thickness of a medium the clarity of object is affected.

Experimentation

Place a tub like vessel filled with on the stove so that evaporation takes place. Have a torch bulb lighted at about two meters high on one side of the tub. Make room dark and sit on the floor on the other side of the tub so that a long path to see light bulb is achieved. Identify the conditions under which the twinkling effect is noticed.

INTERMITTENT QUESTIONS

We believe there is no material medium in space. How then to account for variation in refractive index?
Why planets should not twinkle when both stars as well as planet lie beyond earth's atmosphere?

Exploration questions: Water vapour may not be available beyond a few tens of kilometers above earths' surface. Then which thick ness or refractive index varies?

Distance between star and us remains almost same. Then why should we talk about thickness of the material medium?

Student -Teacher interaction: Discuss modification wherein different coloured lamps can be seen for twinkling effect. One can on the basis of observation and existing theories predict what colour is most suited for experimentation. Why red should be a poor candidate?

Evaluation: Ether and spirit is quickly evaporated can we venture to do such an experiment with these?

When we get petrol from the petrol sumps colourless fumes appear to come out. Is it plasma?

Assignment: Identify the star, which blinks best. Find its details such as its size, its brightness, and its distance from us and calculate its angular size. Try to reproduce our experiment for that angular size.

Project 3

Vegetable preservation system: (Level VI: age group 10 – 12 years)

After going through this module, pupils will be able to recall factors that cause vegetable to spoil, and to learn technique of vegetable preservation.

General information: To feed our large population we need lots of grains/edibles and vegetables. Grains and vegetable need to be preserved for long duration use. Various techniques are in vogue for different food species. When we buy them they can be fresh but in our houses in no time they get degraded. A fridge is most common household item that serves the purpose of preservation of cooked food and other vegetable items. Much of our population may not have access to it. And on top of it, it is not environment friendly.

Facts: Humidity, high temperature or dry air and jamming of items spoil vegetables.

Methodology: To ensure the above factors are done away with.

Student teacher interaction

⇒ *How does our body maintain its temperature?*
⇒ *What do we do in summer to cool the environment?*
⇒ *How would we avoid hot dry wind hitting us?*

Suggestive set up: Take metallic container. Pack loosely the vegetables brought. Close the container. Wrap a wet cloth over the container. If it is too hot we can wet the cloth intermittently.

Probing questions

⇒ *Why should we take a metallic container?*
⇒ (More it is heat conductive more effective it is. Thus copper vessel would be the best.)
⇒ *Why should we close the container?*
⇒ *How should we try to prove or disapprove the hypothesis that jam packing spoils things?*
⇒ *What is the role of wetting the wrapped cloth?*

Confirmation: Open the preservation system and record your observations.

Evaluation

⇒ *What is the reason you notice a little water deposited at the base of the container?*
⇒ *Why do we need to avoid use of non-conducting vessel?*

Assignment: Make your own vegetable preservation system. Use different materials of different conductivity and verify the assumptions. See what happens when we use earthen pot for this purpose. Provide appropriate comments.

Module 2

Spinning for stability—(Level +1: age group 15 +)

After going through this module, pupils will be able to recognize how rotation brings in stability, recall that mechanical system take time for action, appreciate the role of conservation of angular momentum

What do we know?

The bodies can be in one of the three kinds of equilibrium: Static, neutral and dynamic.

Stability is decided by the factor whether the line joining the center of gravity of the body passes through base of the body that supports it. This is the reason why we make base wider for stability.

It is rather impossible to support a body on a pointed pivot, because several external factors affect the disposition of the body if one has meticulously adjusted the system for stability.

Let us recall the exhilarating experiences

Many jugglers show how they can hold bodies supported at a point for quite some time. A circus fellow rides on a single wheel cycle or one seen doing walking action on a thin rope. Do all these experiences falsify our established facts? The answer is for certain "NO".

If we pay rapt attention we find that the magic is done by continuously manipulating the spatial location of supporting point. Effectively s/he manages to gain more base for the body. The skilled or expert showman tries to minimize the base. We will appreciate the analysis for two dimensions first and will then generalize for three dimensions. In the following figure the effective base is (d + d) and not mere a point.

Hypothesis

The juggler moves the support in such a way that effective base area is increased. (In how many ways can it be achieved?)

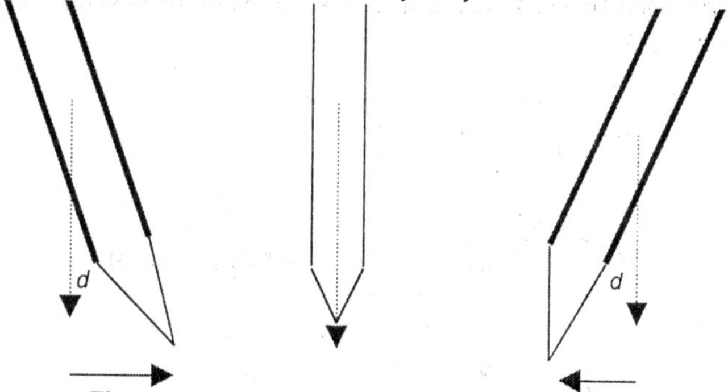

Fig. a Fig. b Fig. c

Let us define it by the above figure

Vertical arrows show the line joining center of gravity of the body to the center of the earth. Figure a shows the line goes far away from the base so does figure c. Figure b is just right but difficult to get.

Verification of the hypothesis

Support a body on a pivot as shown in the figure. The body begins to tumble. To avoid tumbling push the body so that it may tilt on the other side. Before it tumbles the other side push from that side. Keep on pushing appropriately making the body to be on the pivot always.

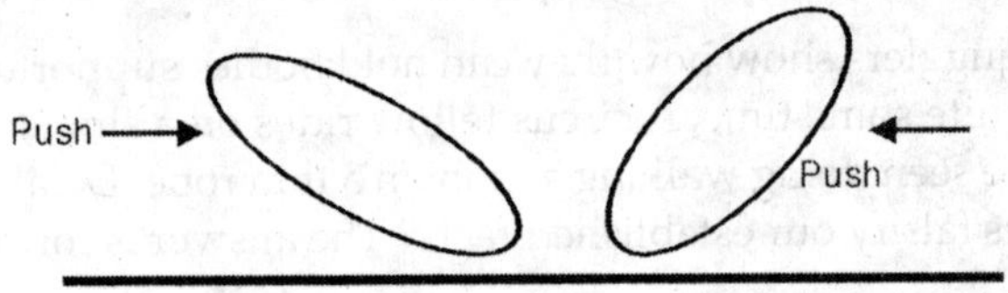

But this is two-dimensional aspect. Can we ignore our three dimensional world? To maintain balance we cannot go on pushing only from the two sides. We have to push from the side it tends to tumble. Here inertia comes to our rescue. Due to inertia body takes time to shift to a new position. So we can safely apply force intermittently.

What is the useful technique to apply force from all sides successively?

No one will advocate to apply a force only when need is felt in order to maintain stability. The clever way is to apply force from all directions successively. Let us see how shrewdly we can make system work.

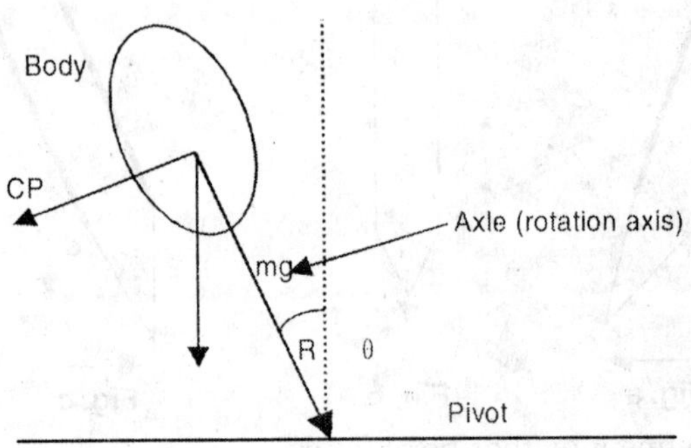

The force acting on a body not in stable equilibrium is m**g.** This can be represented by two components: **CP** that makes body tumble and **R** (that has no significance as for as rotatory motion is concerned). To restrain the object from tumbling a force need to be applied in opposite direction. Or the object be made to tilt in opposite direction quickly. The second option is relatively convenient. If the object precesses and goes to opposite quadrant before it falls appreciably our objective is achieved. Further we can notice that if q (the angle that rotation axis makes with vertical) is made less **CP** is small. For q equal to zero, there is no question of tumbling (but as we have seen earlier it is next to possible).

Let us now discuss spinning of a top. It precesses only if its rotation axis is not vertical.

What does spinning do?

When imbalance about rotation axis is minimal, precession is not conspicuous. To cause precession we need to apply a couple. Hence spinning object continues to spin till no external torque is applied. Once it is established we can immediately infer that like linear momentum, the angular momentum also should be conserved. Conservation of angular momentum entails that he orientation of axis of rotating body cannot undergo a change until an external torque acts on it.

Pupils' task: Find minimum rotational speed so that a top needs to be imparted to avoid its tumbling.

Can all bodies spin? Try out. Calculate energy associated with earth's spin and that associated with its rotation.

Evaluation

1. *Large bodies need larger spinning velocity than small bodies. Criticize.*
2. *What is the difference between spin and precession?*

Assignment: Moving bicycle does not fall whereas still does (if not on the stand or with other support). It is difficult to change orientation of a rotating object. Verify both the statements. Find energy associated with spinning object and rotating object. Which is more?

Project 4
Dry cloth is not as warm as wet one
(Level VII: age group 12+)

After going through this module, pupils will be able to recall that transfer of thermal energy gives sensation of heat, to recognize that water is good conductor of heat in comparison to cloth.

You have read in the book

On a hotter day in the summer the conducting objects sense hot while no-conducting objects do not. On a cooler day in winter the conducting objects sense cold while non-conducting objects do not.

The answer lies in the fact that conducting object quickly transfers thermal energy (heat). It is the quantity of thermal energy that decides our perception and not the temperature.

Other examples given are steam and boiling water though the temperature is same do not harm us equally.

Find it out yourself

- Note the room temperature. Is it safe to claim that temperature of our cloth we clad is same as room temperature?
- If room temperature happens to be different from our body temperature the chances of success of the experiment are more.
- Wrap a cotton cloth on some part of your body. Now pour some water on to wet.
- Do this now in reverse order. Wet your body and wrap cloth over drenched portion of the body.

Answer these questions

- *Did the cloth wrapped on your body give hot (or cold) sensation?*
- *Was water temperature same as cloth's? (A simple thermometer would find this).*
- *What was sensation in terms of hotness or coldness when water was poured over it?*
- *Does this sensation repeat for other than cotton cloth?*
- *What happens if in place of using normal water we user warm or cold water?*

Evaluation

1. *Water has large specific heat than why water does not absorb heat in place of transferring it to us?*
2. *Water temperature is usually low than that of surroundings then why water shows hotness?*

Assignment: Test for conductivity of easily available other liquids. Many stars are hotter than sun. But we do not feel their hotness. Identify the reasons. Establish with available literature that heat is misnomer we should talk only in terms of transferred thermal energy.

Module 3

Things found in Hills
(Level V: age group 8-10)

After going through this module, pupils will be able to appreciate the nature, classify things found around them and learn techniques of collecting samples.

Methodology: Undertake a field trip of pupils to nearby hill. Give useful and proper instructions as what to observe? How to observe? What they should not do? Etc.

Probe questions

1. *What are the things available around you?*
2. *How do you propose to classify them?*
3. *What is the criterion of you classification?*

Evaluation

1. *How many samples have you collected?*
2. *What were the difficulties in collection?*
3. *Is your collection as per instructions given?*
4. *Did you discuss your friend about your collections?*

Assignment: Collect materials around you that are unique. List special items that you have collected. Is any item useful in making article of daily use? Meet old people and find out what other interesting thing were available on the hill.

Teachers' task: The tender age pupils need to be guided at every stage. If need be some curiosity can be aroused before undertaking the trip. The parents need to be consulted and if they offer let them accompany. This brings variety and novelty in your job. This is suggestive module. Field trips for hands on experiences can be organized for various places depending on your vision and accessibility to those places like: lakeside, agriculture field, foundry, industry, zoo etc.

Module 4

Importance of free body diagram
(Level +1: age group 15 +)

After going through this module, pupils will be able to notice significance of concentrating on isolated bodies for analysis, solve numerical related to equation of motion, draw free body diagrams for a body in equilibrium.

Introduction: Free Body Diagram is a diagram showing the body and all the forces acting on it (ignoring surrounding bodies that exert forces). Such diagrams help us to focus only on the body (under consideration) and on the forces required to formulate the equation of motion for that body.

Probe question

Have you observed a sprinter at the start of a race?

She wants forward reaction to be optimized in order to kick-start. She also needs to ensure that normal reaction is minimum possible.

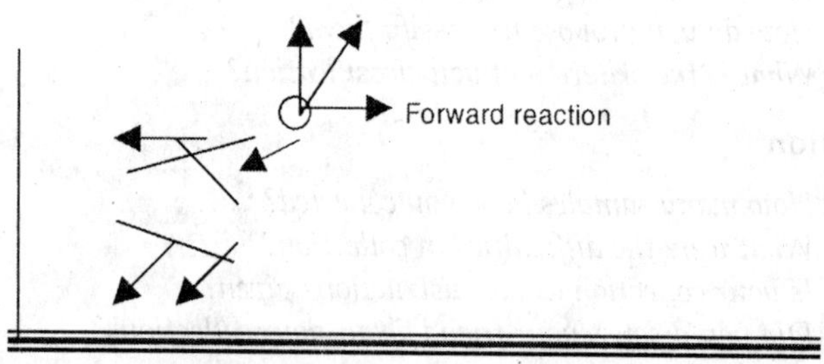

If normal reaction is maximum the body is in equilibrium. While if forward reaction is maximum acceleration is maximum.

A player in air has always one force acting on her i.e., her own weight. Hence at that moment whatever action she does, the reaction together with her weight determines resultant. Whenever action in air is poised at a point distantly located than the center of mass a turning effect is perceptible.

The free body diagram by no means suggests that no force acts on the body. It suggests that there is no need to consider external influence once all forces on the body are considered for finding the equation of motion.

Let us analyze the case of the box on an inclined plane

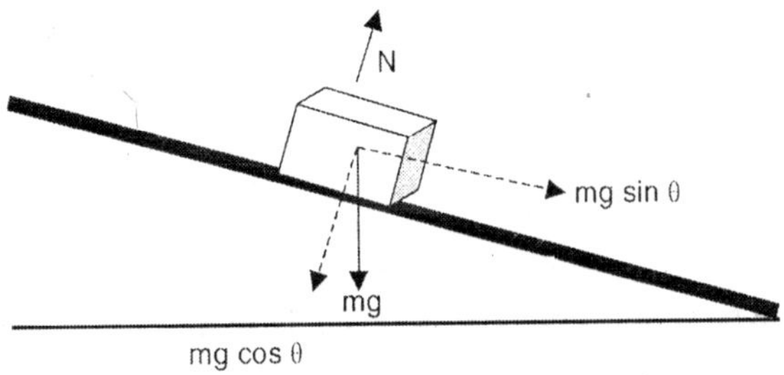

Assume that the plane is smooth (no friction between box and the plane). The plane makes an angle θ with the horizontal. The only force appears to be acting on the box is mg., the weight of the box. For finding equation of motion we need to consider all the forces acting on the box only (ignoring the effect of surroundings).

The downward force exerts a push on the plane given by mg cos θ and a pull towards the slope given by mg sin q. Since there is no motion happening due to mg cos θ, there must be a balancing force to it. We denote it by N. The box slides down the plane hence mg sin θ is the force causing the motion. The acceleration produced by it is along the surface of the plane and its magnitude is (mg sin θ)/m or simply g sin θ.

Practical use of g sin θ

The wonderful result in the form of above formula enabled Galileo to estimate g.

With this principle it is very easy to reduce the effect of gravity to our convenience by the use of inclined planes.

Evaluation

For θ = 10° calculate the effective value of gravity. Is it twice for θ = 20°?

1. Is it possible to increase the effective value of gravity? If yes how? If no why? Give reasons.

2. If surface is perfectly horizontal will effective gravity be zero?

Assignment: Show that the effective weight of the box lying on the floor increases when we push it and reduces when we pull it.

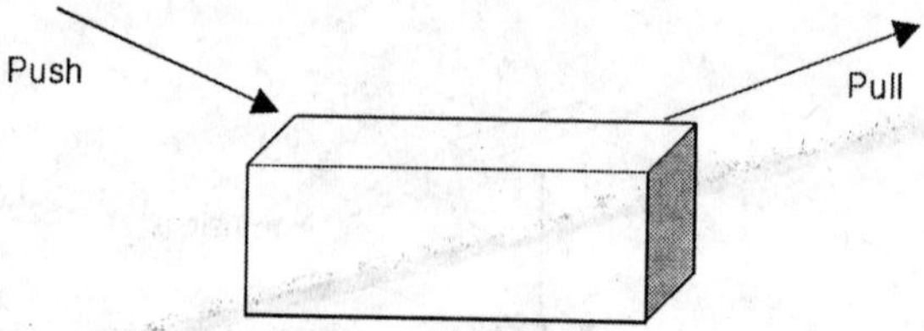

Under what conditions the opposite is true?

Module 5

On the vision

(Level X: age group 15+)

After going through this module, pupils will be able to understand that the vision of eye depends on several factors, the intensity and frequency of light that our eye receives determines the colour and brightness of the light.

Let us focus two beams of light (say red and blue, obtained from two sources A and B respectively) on a small area surrounding P on the white screen as suggested in the figure.

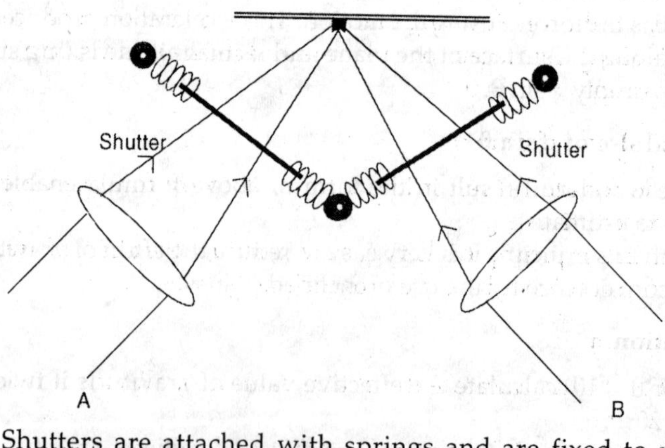

Shutters are attached with springs and are fixed to rigid supports. Further these have openings, which can allow light to pass through when there is no movement of the shutters. But essentially these are independent and they can be made to move along the line so that adjusting the spring lengths we can alter the frequency of opening for the passage of light. When a viewer looks at P the region appears to be of the colour that the light it receives at that instant.

When only one shutter operates it blocks the beam periodically and so flickering appears on the screen. Monitoring the blocking frequency enables to match the brightness of the two colours.

Play with colours: Use colour filters and a light source whose intensity can be varied.

1. Allow a particular colour light to fall on a white screen placed in a dark room. Increase the intensity of light in the room. How is the change in earlier colour?
2. Do the same activity-replacing screen of a different colour. Record your observations.
3. Focus two colours on the same spot on the screen. Record the colour. Now change the intensity of one of the colour from almost zero to a large value. Record the observations.
4. Investigate the role of environment colour on the vision.

Evaluation: Nature manifests in more than 10000 shades. Does it mean that so many colours exist?

1. Leaves of same plant at different locations usually have different colours. Assign the reasons.
2. Has mixing of colour any effect on the wavelength of light?

Assignment: Visit your garden and record colour of leaf of a particular plant. Visit next in winter and summer respectively. Is the observation similar? Correlate it with thickness of leaf, water content in the leaf and surrounding environment. You will find composition has also major role to play in colour perception. Find it out from resource available.

What was purported? The write up intends to elucidate concern for environment from a physicists' point of view. Nature or environment never discriminates from what angle we view it. It is as it is. The modules and projects suggested here are by no means exhaustive to understand the environment. We can explore it from still more different ways and make our best efforts by which we can maintain its vivid and diverse yet friendly outlook towards living being in general and human beings in particular.

Our effort while investigating need to be appreciative of and realizing as to what principles and mechanism the nature employs in order to preserve its cohesive nature and its obsession for symmetry

Let us deliberate now: Though the philosophy of science lies in its inherent struggle to explore and understand the nature yet the basis and strong point of science is its ability to predict-to tell what will happen in a feasible experiment / a hypothetical experiment or an experiment that can never be done under certain given conditions. Thus we need to contrive situations for designing experiments that would enable to touch upon each and every aspect of our endeavor and to uncover mysteries that nature abounds in.

Once we predict sometimes on the basis of some experimentation, again we need to establish the validity or tenability of the prediction. Science progresses thus. Quite many times with new insight we wonder how wrong our perceptions were over the years. A small but compelling example from environment and akin to latest theory of physics-quantum mechanics will be illustrative of this notion.

Quantum mechanics wards off the notion of certainty. It talks of probability and chance of happening an event. Fortunately for us uncertainty amplifies when number of successive events is large. Feynman cites. Suppose we have some uncertainty at some stage due to an inaccuracy in measurement. At every successive stage the uncertainty adds up and ultimately its dimension may be such that it is noticeable at classical domain. He recalls that when you stand nearby base of the dam where water falls over the dam (or better near a water fall). Every now and then a drop will land on your nose. But its precise position is indeterministic. Even a little wiggle in the flow at earlier time amplifies and conspicuous at landing of the next drop landing at different location on us.

Teaching Environmental Education

The Multiple Intelligences Approach

MRIDULA RANADE

Environment has become a focus of our concern today, and providing environmental education to children is now a critical need. Considering the urgency of the situation, the infusion model used earlier (Some environment related activities or paragraphs are added to chapters in other subjects) has had to be discarded by curriculum planners. Today's need demands that environmental education should be taught as a separate subject.

The main emphasis of environmental education is to acquaint students with environment related issues and problems. They must also be able to peruse environmental problems, understand modern-day concerns related to the environment, and be able to analyse, evaluate, and equip themselves to resolve these problems. Thus the environmental education curriculum is based on the following three core aspects [NCERT, 2007]:

- Learning about the environment
- Learning through the environment: implying a systematic exploration through a variety of activities
- Learning for the environment by developing a genuine concern for, and sensitivity towards its protection and preservation

Thus, in teaching environmental education, teachers need to focus, not only on knowledge, but also on generating awareness, developing the right attitudes, values and skills, and promoting healthy behaviour towards the environment among students at all levels of school education. By implication, learning opportunities should not remain limited to the classroom alone but extend much beyond it.

Many teachers find themselves ill-prepared to deal with this *new* subject. Often, they display a negative attitude towards the perceived overload of teaching yet another subject.

Using methods and techniques of teaching that grab and retain the interest of the students in a subject and lead to effective learning should be the hallmark of teaching any subject at any level. Unfortunately, this is not the case in most classes. The expository lecture method is the predominantly used method in most classrooms. It is a well-known concern of educational planners that EE, if taught through the usual method, will not lead to fulfilment of the objectives of teaching environmental education.

To overcome this problem, NCERT [2007] has suggested a large number of transactional modalities, which include:

- Narration of events, experiences and stories
- Assignments and projects
- Field trips and visits
- Establishing eco-clubs
- Field studies and surveys
- Brainstorming and quizzes
- Role play and drama
- Lectures and demonstrations
- Discussions
- Case studies

All the above transactional modalities need to use an open-ended problem-solving approach in devising class work so as to promote awareness about the environment.

Environmental education offers tremendous opportunity in using innovative teaching methods and techniques. These will not only help in effective learning of the subject, but will also help in the all-round development of all students, and in developing their interest in learning in general. This opportunity should certainly not be wasted by the teachers.

Even when teachers are aware of the need to use innovative and varied approaches in teaching, their limited repertoire of methods and techniques hampers them. It is therefore necessary to provide them with a framework, which can help them to generate teaching ideas with ease and also to understand the educational benefits of using them. One useful framework of thinking about teaching is provided by Dr. Howard Gardner's theory of Multiple Intelligences.

Multiple Intelligences: Theoretical Background

In order to be able to reach all students, every teacher needs to firmly believe that all students are capable of learning. It is then important for the teacher to be equipped with as many teaching/ learning strategies as possible to reach those students who do not seem to learn well from traditional teaching methods. Our schools, which primarily measure verbal and mathematical skills, frustrate a lot of students who have less aptitude in these areas. This leads them to believe that they are intellectually inferior to their high-scoring classmates. However, such low-scoring students could be very successful in endeavours that require other aptitudes, such as mechanical, artistic, musical and interpersonal skills. By recognizing and building on students' varied strengths, a teacher can help them to succeed. Understanding these individual differences and how students learn differently due to these differences is a vital step in providing quality education. The theory of Multiple Intelligences propounded by the Harvard psychologist, Dr. Howard Gardner [1983, 1993a, 1993b, 1993c, 1995, 1996, 1998, 1999] provides a very useful perspective to understand learning in terms of individual differences and provides significant insights, guidelines and "rules of thumb" to the teacher to design her lessons so as to reach every student in the class. It enables one to see beyond the narrow field of academic excellence and appreciate the talents and contributions of the students in other areas. Gardner's theory celebrates the way students learn and respond in a variety of different ways, and encourages teachers to respect, value, and nurture that diversity.

Gardner initially [1983; 1999a] proposed and defined seven intelligences, as follows:

1. Logical/Mathematical intelligence
2. Verbal/Linguistic intelligence
3. Visual/Spatial intelligence
4. Musical/Rhythmic intelligence
5. Bodily/Kinaesthetic intelligence
6. Interpersonal intelligence
7. Intrapersonal intelligence

Logical/Mathematical Intelligence: It is the intelligence most commonly associated with scientific and mathematical thinking. It implies the ability to use deductive reasoning, to think logically, to detect patterns, to investigate issues scientifically and to carry out mathematical operations. Learners high in this intelligence are always curious about the world around them, ask lots of questions like to do experiments and can make connections between pieces of information.

Verbal/Linguistic intelligence: Verbal/Linguistic intelligence implies the ability to use words and language effectively to express oneself and to remember things. These learners have highly developed auditory skills. They think in words rather than in pictures.

Visual/Spatial intelligence: Visual/Spatial intelligence implies the ability to perceive the visual. These learners tend to think in pictures and need to create vivid mental images to retain information. They enjoy looking at charts, maps, pictures, videos, slide shows or movies.

Musical/Rhythmic intelligence: Musical/Rhythmic intelligence consists of the capacity to recognize and compose musical pitches, tones, rhythms, and patterns and to use them for performance or composition. It also involves the ability to appreciate music. Musically inclined learners think in sounds, rhythms and patterns. They immediately respond to music either appreciating or criticizing what they hear. These learners are often extremely sensitive to environmental sounds.

Bodily/Kinaesthetic intelligence: Bodily/Kinaesthetic intelligence implies the ability to control body movements and handle objects skilfully. Learners with high bodily intelligence have a good sense of balance and eye-hand co-ordination. They express themselves through movement. Through interacting with the space around them, they are able to remember and process information.

Interpersonal intelligence: Interpersonal intelligence involves the ability to recognize the intentions, feelings and motivations of others and thus to see things from other people's point of view. Learners with high interpersonal intelligence can relate well to other people and are likely to work well with others.

Intrapersonal intelligence: Intrapersonal intelligence involves the ability to be aware of one's inner state of being through reflection, to understand oneself- to know one's own strengths and weaknesses, dreams and relationships, and use that information to regulate one's own life.

More recently, Gardner [1998] has nominated additional candidate intelligences, of which Naturalist intelligence is of great relevance in teaching/learning of environmental education. In fact, it is also known as Environmental intelligence.

Naturalist intelligence: Naturalist intelligence involves demonstrating "expertise in recognition and classification of the numerous species - the flora and fauna" of one's environment." [ibid. p. 115]. It involves the ability to understand and work effectively in the natural world *[Daniels, 2004, p.208]*.

The first two forms of intelligence (Mathematical and Verbal) are typically the abilities that contribute to strong performance in traditional school environments and to producing high scores on most IQ tests or tests of achievement. However, according to Gardner, the other intelligences are not commonly stimulated in schools and need to be given more attention and an important place in the teaching-learning process.

The Multiple Intelligences Approach to Teaching-Learning

The theory of Multiple Intelligences (MI) has proposed the existence of at least 7 distinct intelligences, which could be viewed as different mental representations, or intellectual languages, which help an individual to learn from and respond to his surroundings. Since every individual has varying amounts of each of these intelligences, each individual could have a unique intelligences profile. When applying the theory of MI in Education, the focus is on identifying, nurturing and helping the students to use their unique combination of intelligences in the act of learning. If a student's predominant intelligence is used to learn a subject, he/she can be more positive about learning and can learn better. In a single class then, we have students who have different predominant intelligences, and to be able to reach every student, we must be able to address the different intelligences.

In order to do this, we can apply the information and insights of MI theory to teaching-learning, such that a variety of intelligences are stimulated in the regular classroom during the teaching of every learning unit.

Use of Multiple Intelligences Approach in Teaching Environmental Education

Following is a list of methods/activities/techniques that can be used to stimulate each type of intelligence, along with examples wherever necessary. The list of ideas provided below is not exhaustive for the particular intelligence, and a teacher can always find more ideas. Also, a single teaching idea can stimulate various intelligences. Hence, the following list is only meant as a useful guideline.

Used as a checklist while planning any lesson, it can provide a smorgasbord of ideas for teaching.

1. Stimulating Logical/Mathematical Intelligence

- Present the content/laws/statements in the form of mathematical formulae. E.g.: Use of formulae to explain birth rate, death rate, population explosion, etc.
- Quantification of content. E.g.: Providing information in terms of numbers, percentages, ratios, etc.
- Provide scope to solve mathematical problems. E.g.: Calculate death rate, percentage of pollutants in water, calories in a meal, etc.
- Use Socratic questioning. This involves asking students a series of questions in such a way that the students are led to finding the answers themselves. E.g.: Why are certain legal provisions made by the government with respect to the environment?
- Use of Inquiry Training Model of teaching [Joyce, 1980]: This model uses discrepant events (events those are contrary to one's expectations) based on those principles the teacher wishes to stress or bring out. The events are presented to the students and they discover the desired principle themselves, through a series of questions put to the teacher, in such a way, that the teacher can only provide "Yes" or "No" answers. E.g.: To make students learn about poisonous and non-poisonous snakes and to logically reason out a situation, following discrepant event can be used:

The Snake Bite Mystery

A retired lawyer went to live in a village. The villagers warned him about some very poisonous snakes found in that area which could kill a man instantly.

One evening, the lawyer took his dog, a Doberman, for a run in the fields. A snake bit his dog, and immediately afterwards bit him. The dog began to howl. The lawyer died on the spot, but nothing happened to the dog. How can you explain this?

[Answer: The snake was non-poisonous; the lawyer had a heart attack due to ignorance and fear of snakes.]

- Use of logical problem solving exercises, puzzles and games. e.g.: Providing opportunity solves various problems related to the environment, Game of 20 questions to identify a plant or animal.
- Providing opportunities for classification and categorization. E.g.: Classification of animals or plants on the basis of various criteria.
- Use of flow charts in teaching: E.g.: Sequential development of Bio-geo-chemical cycles, food chains, etc.
- Getting students to design scientific experiments to test hypotheses related to environmental issues.
- Encouraging students to generate a variety of questions about the environment (and of course to find answers).

2. Stimulating Verbal/Linguistic Intelligence:

- Use stories or read interesting anecdotes/information in class to explain content.
- Use appealing quotations related to the content.
- Tell verbal jokes relevant to the content.
- Use games such as "spelling-bee" for difficult-to-spell words.
- Explain etymology of terms in the content. E.g.: Hydrolysis is Hydro (water) + lysis (break up).
- Provide assignments that involve interviewing people. E.g.: Interviewing housewives about their family's eating habits, use of water/electricity, etc.
- Organize elocution competitions, large and small-group discussions on environment-related issues.
- Conduct brainstorming sessions in class on topics such as "Ways to reduce water/electricity/plastic bag consumption."
- Encourage students to read books related to the environ-ment. E.g.: The book, "An inconvenient truth" by Al Gore is a must-read by all students. (It is also a visual treat)
- Assign writing activities for homework, such as writing essays, autobiographies, poems, skits, captions, keeping observation journals on topics related to the environment.

- Involve students in word games such as crossword puzzles, anagrams, on environment-related topics
- Provide opportunity to students for extemporaneous speaking in class on a variety of environment-related topics.
- Help students to develop and use Mnemonics, Acrostics to memorize content.
- Encourage students to use word processors for writing assignments.
- Involve students in publishing class newspaper on environment-related topics.

3. Stimulating Visual/Spatial Intelligence

- While teaching, represent content visually through the use of relevant charts, graphs, maps, diagrams, pictures, photographs, figures, transparencies, etc.
- Prepare visually rich slide shows on the content or use other available computer software to supplement classroom teaching.
- Encourage students to draw, sketch, paint, construct models, dioramas, collages, sculpt, or use computer-assisted design software to represent environment-related information. E.g.: Various habitats, cyclic changes in environment, etc.
- Use bulletin boards or exhibit corners for displaying students' work and collections.
- Get students to draw mind-maps or concept- maps [Novak, 1990, 1991] before starting a unit (helps to understand their previous knowledge and misconceptions if any) and after teaching (as a revision exercise).
- When and wherever possible, provide opportunity to students to use lenses, microscopes, telescopes, and binoculars for learning.

4. Stimulating Bodily/Kinaesthetic Intelligence

- Use explanatory actions while explaining concepts
- Device classroom games involving movement, such as dumb charades, passing the parcel for a quiz, moving around in class to find a pair, blackboard-based games requiring students to come up to the blackboard, etc.
- Provide students the opportunity to handle material, and assign hands-on activities/experiments, such as develop-ing

saplings, planting trees, preparing vermiculture pits, cooking in a solar cooker, testing the purity of water, etc.

- Take students on field trips. E.g. To a biogas plant, rainwater harvesting unit, etc.

5. *Stimulating Musical/Rhythmic Intelligence*

- Provide opportunities for content-related choral chanting, singing rap-songs, etc.
- Encourage students to link new content to old tunes and sing the same
- Encourage students to compose new melodies and sing songs related to environmental concerns.
- Play content-related recorded sounds (E.g. bird calls, examples of sound pollution), mood music, background music or songs in class.

6. *Stimulating Interpersonal Intelligence*

- Use cooperative learning methods [Cooperative Learning, Web page]
- Provide scope for interactions in class, through activities such as "pair and share", peer-teaching, group brainstorm-ing and discussions, group projects, etc.
- Initiate formation of environment clubs.
- Encourage students to plan and do community work in groups.

7. *Stimulating Intrapersonal Intelligence*

- Connect content to personal experiences of students
- Ask thought-provoking questions and provide one-minute reflection time during class to encourage students to examine personal opinions, choices, aversions, attitudes or values.
- Use well-designed self-learning packages or computer-assisted instruction for study of certain topics.
- Assign quiet deskwork.
- Provide a variety of options for home assignments.
- Encourage students to set personal goals with respect to environmental issues. E.g.: Reducing one's own electricity or water consumption.
- Encourage students to keep personal journals about their environment.

8. Stimulating Naturalist Intelligence

This is the most important intelligence that needs to be stimulated when teaching *EE*.

- Encourage students to carefully observe nature. The teachers can give observation-proforma, or students can be asked to prepare their own.
- Encourage collection of natural objects by students for display in class (ensuring that they do so without disturbing the environment)
- Ask students to classify plants, animals, rocks, soil, etc. on the basis of various criteria.
- Take students on field trips or outdoor activities in the midst of nature. Taking some classes under a tree in suitable weather is also a good idea.
- Encourage students to care for plants/ garden /animals in class (if possible) or at home.

Research of Use of Multiple Intelligence (MI) Approach in Teaching Environmental Education

The *MI* approach and the various ideas outlined above were used in teaching a unit of environmental education to a sample of 45 B.Ed. student-teachers from SNDT College of Education, Pune, in a M.Ed.-level research conducted under the author's guidance. The efficacy of this approach in terms of achievement in the unit was tested using a pre-test post-test experimental design, and student-teachers' reactions to this approach were also analysed.

The title of the research was: "A Study of the Effectiveness of the Use of Multiple Intelligences Approach in Teaching- Learning for a Topic in Environmental Education in the B. Ed Course".

The unit, "Population Explosion from the B.Ed. *EE* syllabus of SNDT Women's University was taught using the *MI* approach. Various activities based on all the eight intelligences were planned through a detailed content analysis of the unit. Some examples are:

Use of Advance Organizer, active games such as passing the parcel to solve puzzles and ball game in a ring as part of a quiz activity, circle activity to explain the concept of "carrying capacity" of the environment, story and joke on global warming, extempore speeches by students on causes of population explosion, use of mnemonics and analogy, map-reading, census information provided through graphs, singing of poem on "effects and measures of population explosion", use of appropriate newspaper cuttings, use of graphic organizers for teaching, visually enhanced slide show on a part of the unit, "Consequences of population Explosion," use of quotations with an impact, transparencies, essay writing on topics such as "If you are in the committee for planning population education", group discussion on the topic, "As a teacher, ways of creating awareness about population explosion," pair and share activity on the topic "measures to control overpopulation," etc.

Student teachers' predominant intelligences were identified using a *MI* inventory. This information was used while teaching, by assigning appropriate activities according to student-teachers' predominant intelligence.

Student-teachers' reactions to *MI*-based teaching were obtained through an opinionnaire regarding the impact of the *MI* approach.

Findings

Important findings of the study are as follows:

- Significantly greater achievement was seen in post-test (0.01 level of significance in t-Test) as compared to pre-test as a result of teaching through *MI* approach.
- The opinions of student-teachers about *MI* approach were very positive.
- They felt motivated while learning.
- The slide show helped them to remember content better.
- They got a chance to express their ideas and opinions. Games, jokes and music, which are rarely used in teaching, were found to be very effective.
- They learnt several new and effective methods and techniques of teaching, which they were eager to use in their own teaching.

Conclusion

From the research conducted using the *MI* approach for teaching EE, it is clear that apart from leading to better learning, the approach is really well appreciated by the learners, even when they are adults. Younger learners will definitely enjoy the approach even more, and learning *EE* will not seem a chore anymore.

Due to its multifarious advantages, the author strongly recommends the use of this approach in teaching any subject, but especially environmental education. At the same time, she foresees a lot of objections from the teachers regarding the use of this approach, such as lack of time, resources, too many students in class, too much planning time, discipline problems, etc. However, with creative planning, a little foresight, and plenty of determination, most of these problems can be overcome. Many teachers who have used *MI*-based teaching have been richly rewarded with high student motivation, interest in learning, greater enjoyment in learning, increased responsibility, homework completion and quality of homework, improvement in cooperative learning skills of students, reduced discipline problems and higher achievement *[Campbell, 1991; Baldes, 2000; Geimer, 2000; Janes, 2000; George, 2001; Ranade, 2006].*

Environmental Awareness Among Students

A Survey

RAJARSHI ROY AND ANJANA PAIRA

In the hue and cry over the need to become more sustainable in our brief tenancy on this unique and miraculous planet, it is all too easy to ignore the voices of those who can contribute a lot about what it is like to live sustainable. Environmental factor is of prime concern of the day almost in all walks of life. Environmental education, which contributes to consciousness towards numerous dimensions of environmental awareness and obviously of consciousness about protection of the environment, need to be explored. Today's' students of higher learning institutions in general and the students of Pharmacy (Survey made), in particular, after completion of their study, suppose to be incorporated in the workforce of tomorrow. But what is their attitude towards environmental awareness? To what extent the curricula, they are undergoing, developing and helping them to imbibe the very attitude towards environment? The chapter attempts to explore the attitude of the very segment of students group following an empirical approach.

Irrespective of levels, types and forms, according to modern educational psychology, students hold the central position in the formal system of education. Actually the entire system of education run for the betterment of students in various dimensions.

Human Propensities—The Basic Requirements

The basic requirements for survival of any species are termed as propensities. A list of human propensity includes food, shelter, health and safety, commonly known as survival needs propensities, apart from education, employment and at the present day, possibly the various forms of agro and industrial development, which, in the post-modern society, shifted towards development of information technology and knowledge-development for the sake of maintaining life style (commonly known as developmental needs) and security.

Of course, man doesn't survive only on rice or bread. Human needs go beyond the purely physical aspects and are immersed in social, economic and environment as well. We do require meaningful employment and job satisfaction, environment, leisure and some affective human qualities like respect, care and affection. Deprived of these, a person may languish just as truly as if deprived of food and water.

Most of our physical needs demand access to natural resources, which includes *land, water* and *air*, which, with the aid of radiant energy from the sun, generate plants and animals. The so-called nonrenewable resources such as minerals and fossil fuels are also needed for human survival and development. All these resources are present on a thin layer of the earth's surface, which is commonly termed as *environment*. Actually it is the environment within which we live. Therefore it is considerably clear that the link remains among the environment, human beings and, their needs *[Roy, 2006]*.

On the other hand, technology is the applied field of science, which provides knowledge to satisfy human needs (*and sometimes, human greed too, at the cost of environment*). Education, Science and Technology provide knowledge and thereby help the human beings to produce dramatic improvements to enrich human propensities and needs. Right now, we are in a landmark of human history, accompanied with enhanced intelligence and creativity *[Roy, 2004]*. Consequently, we are changing the basic components of our environment by adding synthetic chemical products and by-products and thereby changing the *hydrosphere* and *atmosphere*.

Sustainability of Development

The popular definition of sustainable development is to meet the need of the present without compromising the ability of the future generations to meet their own needs *[Roy, 2005[a]]*.

It is a fact that consideration of human needs presumes that human beings must actively seek ways to improve the quality of their life. This further reveals that education- irrespective of its content areas, is a value-loaded connotation. It is accepted without any doubt that improvement of social and economic status of the human beings is needed. Development must continue to be promoted in both industrialized and less developed societies; however, there should be a balance between the utilization pattern of natural resources and economic growth. Economic and social development are always welcome, but not at the cost of renewable and non-renewable natural resources. Such forms of development, which considers the environment and its protection must last on this planet for a long, long time if not ever, be termed as *sustainable development*. Increased support to environmental protection will ensure ecological balance and ultimately ensure sustainable development.

Environmental Education in India possesses a significant contribution from its history. Our epic *Isho Upanishad* said long ago, *"...this universe is the creation of the supreme power and is meant for the benefit of all; Individual species must therefore learn to enjoy its benefits by regarding themselves as a part of the system in close relationship with other species; therefore let not any one species encroach upon the right of others."*

These thoughts are represented in the rituals of the people of this land since the Indian civilization came into existence, and since then, our norms, customs values, mores and over all, culture developed in such a way that follows the worship of nature and its various components, and thereby ensure preservation of the environment. However, this philosophy was attacked since the end of last century with the propagation of exotic-philosophies. As a result, the policy of education got boost from exotic agencies in such a way, which hindered the preservation of environmental resources. Being in Sanskrit, the *Upanishadic* thoughts have remained a close look far from us not only on account of the language barrier, but also due to the lack of good environmental communicators among those who know the *Sanskrit language*.

Purpose of Environmental Education

The purpose of environmental education is to provide the individual and social groups sufficient scope so that they should acquire awareness and knowledge, develop attitudes, skills and abilities, and participate in solving real-life environmental problems. The perspective should be integrated following an interdisciplinary approach, and should be holistic in nature. The important objective of environmental education is therefore not to introduce a new subject but to evolve a new approach to education to integrate the concept of preserving environment with the existing content of a subject-discipline. Therefore it may be assumed that environmental education is an approach, which is expected to provide the necessary methodology to integrate the consciousness about environment (both in applied and basic/ theoretical aspects) with engineering, social sciences, ethics, law and other allied disciplines, so that the knowledge will be holistic.

Environmental Education and Development

Our environment determines our lifestyle. Development in contemporary civilization also depends upon the environment. The younger generation, especially students of higher education who are supposed to be the future leaders and decision makers may opt for changes in their life styles. Indications are prominent in this context around us, from which one can easily realize the trend of changes. These changes will certainly be some determining factors in the renewal of development, especially with respect to products as well as demands of all types of industry, agriculture and thereby the economy. Higher educational institutions are in general, and the faculty members absorbed therein in specific, have major responsibilities in shaping the above-mentioned changes, both directly and indirectly. Students at higher educational institutions should be well equipped in this mission so that they can encounter the problems of environment in one hand, and on other hand, can impart consciousness about environment among the masses that comprise their environment and society. Therefore education and awareness about environment is essential, and to meet the needs, there should be provision of a sound environmental education, irrespective of levels (however, with special emphasis at the university level). While attending tertiary education, students will be able to develop their philosophy of life in tune with environment, which will serve them as a context for the decisions and actions during active life and actual field of work.

Though it is essential to transfer the knowledge and skills about the environment and environmental-hazards (most of which are man-made), which is not enough. So far as the taxonomy of educational objectives is concerned, it comprises three domains viz. cognitive, affective and psychomotor (also known as conative), (incorporating intellect, behavior and skills, respectively). The affective domain needs to be given priority for developing a wide range of soft skills viz. positive attitude, feelings, interest, commitments, ethical values and responsibilities with respect to protection of and improvement of environment with due consideration given to future generations. This should be the prime task of higher education- to nurture and generate planners and implementers of future with environmental awareness, as well as appropriate methodology to be accorded to environmental education.

Technical Education vis-a-vis Environmental Education

Technical (as well as technological) education differs from rest of the education gamut so far the nature of students' development is concerned. It is often argued that while in the other segments of education, the basic objective of educational instruction is to develop theoretical knowledge; the central emphasis in technical and technological education is to develop certain specific skill among the students, apart from knowledge *[Harten, 1991]*. It is to be mentioned here that skill cannot be imbibed in isolation *[Roy, 2002]*. The basic philosophy of skill-development stresses on the principle that any theory (or the theoretical knowledge) should be followed by appropriate practice. These are considered under 'cognitive' and 'psychomotor' domain of educational objectives, respectively, under various sequential sub-domains *[Simpson, 1972]*. However all these activities, i.e., developing the level of knowledge in the specific subject area and competency over certain specific skill will go in vain until and unless the student is having a strong positive attitude and interest towards the subject of study. Infact, effectiveness and acquisition of knowledge by the student largely depend upon sequel of factors and variables.

Students' attitude towards environmental pollution monitoring and control is one such major factor, possessing tremendous impact over the society, even after the completion of study. As such, interest towards certain dimension of environmental awareness possesses a direct relation over the attitude of the individual as well as protection of environment.

However, at the present juncture of time, attitude of the pharmacy students towards environmental issues are still unknown. Health hazards, [a substantial numbers of which are directly related to environmental hazards], need to be overcome through medicines and drugs, produced and manufactured by pharmaceutical industries. In the very phase of producing the drugs and medicines, what feeling and attitude the management of such plants exhibits? In other words, to what extent the 'future management' of such industries and plants are developing awareness and concern about environment?

This basic question needs to be answered by the present study.

Objective and Methodology of the Study

It attempts to explore the attitude and feeling of the engineering students towards environment, pursuing undergraduate degree programme in pharmaceutical science and engineering discipline. Their attitude towards related issues are also analyzed. Sample incorporates randomly selected eighty undergraduate students studying bachelors programme in pharmacy in three pharmacy colleges in eastern regional states. It is worthmentioning that all the respondents are enrolled in courses, approved by AICTE.

Given here the definition of the key terms, on which the present study hinges on.

Attitude: It is a psychological factor having some similarity with traits and interest. Attitude is a reflection of personality. It may be considered as a manner, mode of response of an individual towards a thing, idea, person, object or a situation. Attitude is chained with stimulus in the following way:

Stimulation → Sensation → Perception →
Habit → Traits → Interest
Set of mind → Goal → Motivation
} Attitude

It denotes *"...some total of man's inclination and feelings, prejudices or preconceived notions, ideas, fear, threats or convictions about any specific topic"*.

Here the word *attitude* denotes the feeling and tendency of the respondents towards the 'environmental pollution monitoring, control and related issues'.

The standardized attitude scale towards 'Environmental Consciousness', which was used for the study, includes twenty items, placed in a five point Likert's scale. Both positive and negative items were placed in the scale in a haphazard manner. The scale was standardized one, with a reliability coefficient of 0.842.

Data, obtained through the attitude scale where by nature objective. Therefore, simple statistical approach was adopted to tabulate and to treat collected data, however the same was supplemented by qualitative interpretation.

Analyses and Interpritation

I. *Awareness about hazards caused by pharmaceutical and allied industries*

It appears from the response pattern of our sample group that cent percent of our respondents strongly opposed that for a student of pharmacy, it is not essential to be aware about environmental hazards caused by pharmaceutical and allied industries. On contrary, it may be assumed that the sample group strongly feels it essential to be aware about environmental hazards, those are caused by pharmaceutical and allied industries.

II. *Need for including components for environmental awareness in curriculum*

Responding towards an item stating *whether curriculum needs to incorporate a paper on 'environmental pollution monitoring and control' or the like,* it is observed that majority of the respondents [65%] strongly feels that curriculum for pharmacy needs to accord a paper on 'environmental pollution monitoring and control' or the like. Following the trend though differs in terms of degree of agreement; rest 35% of the respondents also agrees to incorporate a paper of similar kind in the existing curriculum.

III. *Need for emphasizing 'environmental pollution, monitoring and control' in B. Pharm. Courses*

As the analysis of response reveals, as many as 32.5% of the respondents strongly feels the need to accord more emphasis over 'environmental pollution, monitoring and control' (EPCM) in B. Pharm. courses. 43.75% of the respondents feel the need, however not to the extreme degree. On the other hand, 6.25% of the respondents oppose the view. Rest of the respondents [17.5%] tends to be neutral towards the very issue.

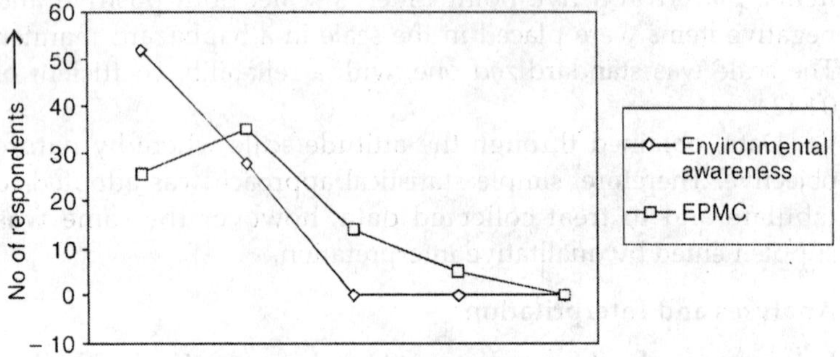

Fig. 1 : *Attitudes towards curriculum*

IV. *Whether any paper on B. Pharm should equip the students to follow appropriate technology to control or to minimize the pharmaceutical plant waste?*

It is interesting to note that grand majority of the respondents [68.75%] strongly support the very issue stating that any paper on B. Pharm must equip the students to follow appropriate technology to control or to minimize the pharmaceutical plant waste. This group is followed by 18.75% of the respondents who just support the very issue. On the other hand, 7.5% of the respondents opposed the issue, to whom, as if, that it is not the prime objective of a course on pharmacy. 5% of the respondents remain neutral towards the very issue.

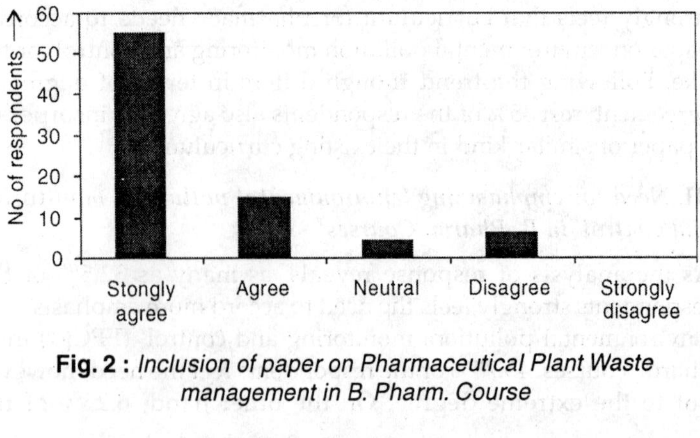

Fig. 2 : *Inclusion of paper on Pharmaceutical Plant Waste management in B. Pharm. Course*

V. ***Whether in practice, pharmaceutical industries cause environmental pollution?***

Though it is a negative one, however the very item is opted with strong agreement by 20% of the respondents. Just half of the total respondents [50%] are also agreed to the very issue. Rest 30% of the respondents seems to be strongly disagreeing with the very item.

VI. ***Apart from courses on pharmacy, should topics related to environmental consciousness be incorporated in the other courses also?***

Responding towards the very item, a grand majority of the respondents [70%] agreed towards the statement and though less however 18.75% of the respondents expressed their strong agreement towards the issue. It is only 11.25% of the respondents, who seems to be indifferent towards this issue.

VII. ***Is there any possibility of water pollution, if any [unknown] chemicals mix with water?***

The item, being an indirect one, helps to pool the data in relation to environmental awareness of our sample group of respondents. While responding towards the very item, grand majority [83.75%] of the respondents reported in an affirmative manner with varying degree of agreement, which reflects their awareness about the component of environments. The rest of the respondents remain neutral towards the very question.

VIII. ***Does natural resources like air, land, water, etc., needs preservation and control?***

At the time of responding towards the very direct question, grand majority of the respondents [93.75%] expressed their consciousness towards environment with varying degree. However rest remains undecided over the very issue.

IX. ***Does courses on environmental pollution monitoring and control are at all helpful to protect our environment?***

With their frank and open response, majority of the respondents [81.25%] applauded that courses on environmental pollution monitoring are not at all helpful to protect our environment. However, 18.75% of the respondents report in a reverse fashion, with different degree of agreement towards the very statement.

X. *Whether knowledge about environment is sufficient enough to protect the environment?*

Responding towards the item, as much as 75% of the respondents reported that knowledge about environment is not sufficient enough to protect the environment. Rest of the respondents found opting other options with almost equal proportion of agreement.

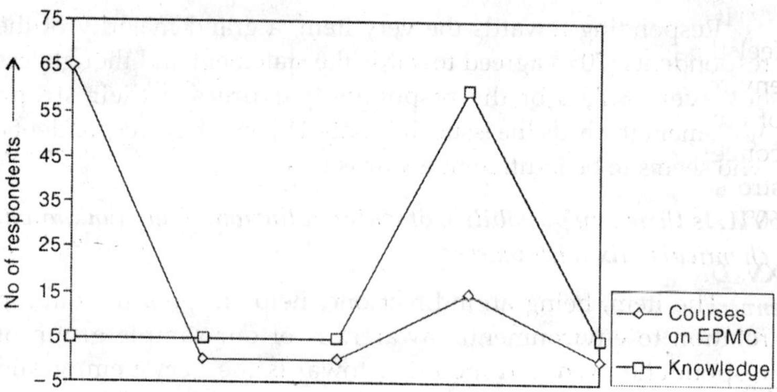

Fig. 3 : *Need to protect environment through EPMC*

XI. *Whether the expenditure involved treatment of effluents from pharmaceutical industries are nothing but wastage?*

In response, grand majority of the respondents [88.75%] strongly negates the statement. A very few proportion of the respondents [11.25%] agrees towards the statement.

XII. *Apart from gaining knowledge and skill, whether there remains any scope to develop skill and positive attitude towards environmental pollution monitoring and control through various short courses?*

While responding towards the query, grand majority of the respondents [98.75%] reports that skill and positive attitude towards environmental pollution monitoring can be developed through various short courses. To others, it is difficult to develop skill and positive attitude towards environmental pollution monitoring and control through short courses.

XIII. ***Should environmental education be introduced in formal education system since at the very primary level?***

Pattern of response towards the item reveals that around one-third of the respondents are in favour of the very statement with varying degree, where as rest remain undecided over the issue.

XIV. ***Does mass media need to play substantial role to enhance environmental consciousness among the mass?***

It is interesting to note that cent percent of the respondents feel that mass media need to play substantial role to enhance environmental consciousness among the mass, for the protection of environment. So far the extent of acceptance of the issue is concerned our sample group bifurcated. While 40% of them strongly hold that mass media need to play substantial role, rest 60% just accepting the view.

XV. ***Does theoretical courses better options to enhance environmental consciousness?***

A grand majority, while responding towards the very item, reports that theoretical courses may not be the better option to enhance environmental awareness among the students, however needed.

XVI. ***Does environment possess any substantial role for development?***

As the pattern of response appears, sent percent of the respondents strongly favored the very item, to whom, environments possess any substantial role for development.

XVII. ***Should students in formal courses be given an opportunity to be actively involved in organization, meant for environmental problems and issues?***

While responding towards the item, cent percent of the respondents accept the view. Grand majority of them strongly favored the statement.

XVIII. ***Perception of the respondents about the environmental awareness of their classmates***

Broad classification of response pattern reveals that while two-third of the respondents accept the statement with varying degree, 20 per cent of the respondents remain undecided, followed by rest 5% of the respondents who negates the view.

XIX. ***Is it practically possible to follow environmental ethics?***

While analyzing the response towards the very item, it was observed that around one-fourth of them strongly favored the statement, followed by another quarter, who just accept the view. Rest quarter negates the view while others remain neutral. This pattern of response reveals that though it is easy to talk about environmental consciousness, but it is not so easy to practice environmental ethics.

XX. ***Can environment satisfy human greed?***

90 per cent of the respondents are with the opinion that environment can satisfy human need but not human geed.

TABLE 1: Mean Attitude Score of Gender Groups towards Environmental Awareness

N	M	SD	Midpoint	Interpretation
Male	84.727	4.54	60	+ ve
Female	85.00	5.20	With scale range	+ ve
Total	84.8125	4.62	$20 \rightarrow 100$	+ ve

The above table reveals that the sample group possess strongly favourable attitude towards environmental consciousness. Among them, the female group possess more favourable attitude compared to their male counter group.

However, result obtained over t-test reveals that this difference is not significant at any standard level. As such it may be termed that irrespective of gender, the undergraduate students of pharmacy possess favourable attitude towards environmental consciousness.

POST–SCRIPT

With a view to enhance the environmental awareness as well as to up-to-date the subject-specific knowledge of the undergraduate-students of pharmacy, it is essential for the planners and implementers of technical education system to arrange appropriate scope within the curriculum so that those who will be in job or in service in pharmaceutical and allied industries can also contribute their share for the protection of the environment.

Once the function of environmental education is to evolve a environment-conscious society, to develop awareness, to help social groups and individuals to acquire an awareness of, and sensitivity to the total environment and its allied problems as also to help social groups and individuals to gain a variety of experience in, and to acquire a basic understanding of the environment and its associated problems, therefore, curriculum of B.Pharm. should include sufficient components in this direction. Development of values and feelings of concern for the environment, and the motivation for actively participating in environmental improvement and protection needs to be enhanced in this process among the technocrats and scientists, who are ultimately supposed to be hastened in the work-force in course of time. Therefore, the planners and implementers of the system of Technical Education need to think of the strategic programmes since now to protect our precious environment in the coming days.

Technology-Rich Environments in Teacher Education

NILI MORE AND IDA HEILWEIL

The current study accompanies a four-year program for teacher education, emphasizing interdisciplinary learning in technology rich environments, as part of lifelong professional development. The theoretical framework of our study is based on three interrelated ideas: constructivism, activity-based learning and distributed cognition. The aim of the study is to investigate the impact of intensive exposure to ICT environments, on the student-teachers both as learners and as teachers. A positivistic approach using a survey filled in four occasions throughout the four years of study was used to achieve both a broad coverage and an in-depth inquiry of the research aims.

Analysis of the data indicates that learning in a technology rich environment has a positive impact on attitude toward technology and promotes teaching in such environments, although a long-term experience time is needed for that.

The Backdrop

Ever since the Israeli Ministry of Education launched the "Tomorrow 1998" program in 1994 to computerize the entire educational system in Israel by providing computers to all schools (one computer for ten students) and appropriate training to all in-service teachers, colleges of education have tried to develop programs that train pre-service teachers to teach in technology rich environments. However, in the last decade research shows that novel teachers complain that they do not feel prepared to integrate technology in their classes since their experience as learners in such learning environments was very limited *(Mor, 2001)*.

Context of the Study

The current study accompanies a teacher education program aiming to promote the expected change in teaching and learning. This program emphasizes interdisciplinary learning in technology rich environments, as part of lifelong professional development beginning in the teacher training stage. In this program the emphasis is on the use of Information Communication Technology (ICT) for learning, teaching and constructing a learning community for student teachers, teachers and teacher educators. Students, co-operating teachers and teacher educators learn together in professional learning communities, where each one is a teacher and a learner simultaneously. The purpose of this study is to examine the role of ICT in facilitating collaborative learning in the new professional community.

The study includes 48 teacher trainees who participated in this program towards their B.Ed. degree (October 2001- July 2005). The aim of the study is to investigate the impact of a constructivist experimental teacher education curriculum, including e-learning and exposure to ICT environments, on the students' attitude towards the use of computer technologies in teaching. This program is enacted in a complex, technology-rich space designed specifically for teacher-trainees taking their first steps in lifelong learning and e-learning. It includes a variety of interconnected ICT components of two types:

1. Information tools (internet sites, data resources, online tasks, e-libraries)
2. Communication tools (discussion forums, dialogic journals, synchronous chat rooms, e-mail). The leading principles of the program are: constructing theoretical understandings via activity-based learning, engaging students in constructing rich technology-based learning environments for their own learners, enhancing learning through multi-channel environments via hypertext and multimedia, and inviting reflection on self learning experiences.

Objectives of the present study are as follows:

- To investigate the impact of exposure to ICT environments on the students both as learners and as teachers

- To check whether learning in a technology rich environment promotes teaching in a technology rich environment

Theoretical Framework

Recent studies of ICT environments in teacher education focus mainly on the difficulties in establishing such environments *(Wedman & Diggs, 2001; Schaffer & Richardson, 2004).* "The United States Office of Technology Assessment (1995) reported on technology in teacher education and noted significant limitations, including:

1. Faculty do not model technology use;
2. Students learn about technology — not with it;
3. Field experiences for pre-service teachers are not designed to model the use of technology, and
4. Technology is isolated from the main curriculum and pedagogy of teacher education.

Collectively, these limitations point out the failure of teacher education programs to develop, implement, and sustain technology-enhanced learning environments. Put another way, it is unlikely these limitations will be overcome unless such environments become characteristic of teacher education programs." *(Wedman & Diggs, 2001).*

An Israeli research *(Mor, 2001)* reinforces the above findings. Participants of the research (295 student teachers) learned in a novel, technology learning environment and reflected on their experiences as learners through individual and group processes preparing themselves to teach in technology rich learning environments. However, they did not change their conception of learning and their traditional teaching conduct as a function of experiencing this novel learning environment. This can be explained by the fact that only one course was taught in such en environment throughout the students' four years of study and there was no extensive model of the suggested environments in real life. Very rarely were the student teachers exposed to learning or teaching in a technology rich learning environment both as learners (in college) and teachers (in the training schools). Thus student-teachers learned about such environments but did not function in them; they did not have a model. Furthermore, their training schools, in most instances, neither supported nor accepted the suggested novel approach. The conclusion Mor (2001) reached was that in such a context neither a cognitive nor a behavioural change could occur. The findings of the study give rise to the belief that if more space and time were devoted to the experience in the teacher training process, and if the opportunity to experience the new mode of learning both in the training courses in the college and in the practicum in the training school were given, both cognitive and behavioural changes will take place and the change in teachers' conception of learning may occur.

The teacher-training program is based on theoretical analyses of learning within ICT supported environments focusing on three interrelated ideas: constructivism, activity-based learning and distributed cognition.

Constructivism emphasizes four principles that should be applied to technology-based learning environments *(Savery & Duffy, 1995)*: learning is an active and engaged process; learning is a process of constructing knowledge; learning is focused on thinking skills rather than working on the "right answer the teacher wants"; learning involves "social negotiation". Learners create their own knowledge and understanding through active engagement with realistic tasks in authentic contexts using actual tools, and since there are many learners, there may be a multiplicity of understandings, though these will be moderated through social discourse. Learning is seen as the process of 'assimilation, augmentation and self reorganization of incomplete mental structures *(Soloway, 1997)*, and is considered to be most effective where learners are pro-active in and control the construction of their own explanations *(Philips, 1997)*. This theory, as it implies, rests on the assumption that learners can more readily understand and assimilate new things if they are provided a context in which they can explore the new information and construct the meaning. Learners go from passive receivers of information (behaviourism) to active construction agents. There is an emphasis on process rather than specified outcomes, and in these circumstances, it is likely that learning outcomes will be less predictable and may vary from learner to learner *(Von Glaserfeld, 1996)*.

Inspired by activity theory, several recent theorists have focused specifically on active and engaged learning processes in technology-based environments. Jonassen and Rohrer-Murphy (1999) propose that teachers develop learning strategies that support: interaction with and manipulation of the exploration environments constructed; strategic search through these environments; intentional attempts to achieve cognitive objectives; engaging in dialogue with other learners and with instructional systems; articulating what has been learned and reflecting on the processes and decisions that were part of the process; generating assumptions, attributes and implications of what has been learned and 'extending' the information.

Jonassen (2000) recommends using "computer applications as cognitive tools". He refers to tools such as databases, semantic networks (i.e., concept maps), and live conversation environments as Mindtools, because they are "computer-based tools developed to function as intellectual partners with the learner".

The contribution of the distributed cognition approach is in its emphasis on the distributed nature of cognitive phenomena across individuals, artefacts and social structures. It casts learning environments as spaces in which participants "self-organize" into functioning communities with a general goal of supporting each other in their learning. Specific roles of group members are not assigned but rather emerge from the interaction of the whole. This approach led Wilson and Ryder (1998) to describe technology-based environments as Dynamic Learning Communities (DLCs), generally characterized by distributed control and autonomy of community members who share new knowledge through high levels of dialogue, interaction, and collaboration and by performing flexible learning activities (such as a shared goal, problem, or program) that provide a common focus and incentive to work together.

The above conceptual framework has been applied to e-learning curricula by designers of e-learning environments *(e.g., Wilson, 2001a, b)* who take advantage of Internet tools to incorporate a number of supports for community and social cohesion into academic courses, including: meaningful and authentic exercises; extended opportunities for collaboration; user-friendly communication tools; tools for organizing, evaluating, and publishing knowledge; effective means for resolving disagreements and making group decisions; and respect for individual members. Needs more explanation: how are all the mentioned above better in a technology rich environment As Jones (2003) notes, the above vision of e-learning environments shows that, to a large extent, the tools, educational theories and pedagogic constructs already exist. However, as a whole, teachers are as yet insufficiently trained to construct such environments in their classrooms or to lead the necessary curricular change in their schools.

In order to achieve the construction of CSCL environments by teachers, teacher education programs have been encouraged to include technology as a pervasive part of teaching *(e.g., Queitzsch, 1997)*. This limited (why limited?) recommendation initially resulted in an 'add-on,' instrumental approach to technology in pre-service teacher education *(Zhu & Yan, 2001)*, which does not sufficiently prepare teachers to switch from the traditional, expository mode of teaching to the facilitation of DLCs, nor does it prepare them to participate in such communities for their own lifelong learning, or to take advantage of web-based materials for the preparation of teaching and assessment materials. An 'add-on' approach does not prepare future teachers to act as change agents who understand the big ideas behind the technological change.

In response to this criticism, writers on curriculum reform in teacher education *(e.g., Vrasidas & McIsaac, 2001)* demand not only that technology be an integral part of teacher preparation programs, but that teacher educators prepare prospective teachers in constructivist ways using technology, provide them with opportunities to think like experts in making instructional decisions, select media for appropriate use, structure learning activities, and employ sound pedagogical strategies in real-life contexts. Mor (2001) claims that teachers ought to experience first-hand learning in a technology rich environment in order to be able to conduct teaching in such environments. Sherry and Gibson (2002) describe the path that teachers should take to transform themselves from learners to change agents. This path includes the following phases: teachers should experience the task of learners, teachers should act as adopters, teachers have to practice working as co-learners, teachers should try to be reaffirmers or rejecters, and then teachers can act as change leaders. This description leads us to the belief that in modelling expert behaviour to students, the instructor needs model all of the above-mentioned professional roles.

To summarize, theory and research indicate inter-woven relationships between the wide exposure to learning environments and ICT and the impact they have on student teachers. The present study examines the extent and the quality of the impact of those environments on 48 aspects.

Research Design and Procedures

This study was based on quantitative methodology (positivist or normative) since it enables to identify two major features of the normative paradigm. The first is that human behaviour is seen as essentially rule-governed, and the second is that the methods of natural science are adopted *(Cohen and Manion, 1994)*.

Participants: The participants of this study are 48 pre-service students who were chosen randomly to participate in a special program for teacher training during the years 2001-2005. All students in this program were invited to take part in this research and they all agreed to participate. They are all female in gender and the average age is 21.86, ranging from 18 to 36 (standard deviation 2.73). Twelve participants specialized in early childhood education (K-2nd grade), fourteen specialized in special education (K-12th grade) and twenty-two specialized in elementary education (1-6th grade).

Research Tool: The main tool used for the quantitative research was a questionnaire used in a previous study *(Ropp, 1997)* that investigated attitudes of students towards computer technology. The instrument was altered slightly to meet the needs of the population of this study. It was translated to Hebrew and a double blind method was used in an attempt to eliminate subjective bias. The survey contained three sections:

(*a*) Personal information,
(*b*) Personal use of computers, and
(*c*) Attitude toward the use of technology.

The first section of the survey gathered demographic data from each respondent. Items addressing such issues such as age, gender, and skill level regarding computers were included. The second section requested specific information about the respondents' skills regarding their use of computers. A scale was provided to guide the responses for these 18 questions. This scale provided four options regarding how frequently the respondent used the specified technology:

(*a*) Know very well,
(*b*) Know fairly well,
(*c*) Know a little and

(*d*) Don't know.

The final section of the survey addressed the respondents' attitudes regarding how they feel about computer technologies in teaching and learning. A scale was provided to guide the responses; the range of the scale extended from 1 to 4 (completely disagree) with a total of 30 questions addressed.

The Cronbach Alpha for this survey was 8816.

Procedure: The researchers adopted quantitative paradigm in the attempt to find possible answers to the research questions. A survey questionnaire was filled in by the entire population of students who participated in the program on four different occasions – first week of their first year (October 2002), last week of their first year (June 2003), last week of their second year (June 2004) and last week of their fourth and last year (June 2006) of their studies. Statistics were used to analyze the data provided by the filled out questionnaires to detect processes of change throughout the four years of the research.

The quantitative data underwent a free varimax factor analysis with orthogonal rotation and a one-way ANOVA analysis, which enabled the identification and characterization of the various types of learners in the group and yielded three factors accounting for 61% of the total variance. In the attempt to examine whether the participants of this study went through a change during the four years of their studies concerning the three factors, a one-way ANOVA that compared the four measurements concerning the scores of the factors, was conducted. This will be discussed in detail in the findings section.

RESEARCH FINDINGS

The Four Measurements

Analysis of the questionnaires, filled out by all students in four occasions, using a free varimax factor analysis with orthogonal rotation, yielded three factors accounting for 61% of the total variance. Table 2 presents the factor loadings.

The first factor will be referred to as "the attitudes towards computer technology" and its high score shows the positive attitudes of the participants towards integrating computer technology in the teaching and learning processes. The second factor will be referred to as "the contributions of computer technology

TABLE 2 : Factor Loadings

Sl. No.	*Statement*	*Factor 1*	*Factor 2*	*Factor 3*
1.	Computers are as important as books It is essential to provide each learner with a computer	.73 .62		
2.	I feel very comfortable working in a computer technology environment	.85		
3.	Every student in college must take a computer application course	.72		
4.	Computer technology enables learners to become active learners	.65		
5.	The school program should be changed to integrate more technology	.65		
6.	I feel at ease when teaching in a rich technology environment	.82		
7.	I am willing to use computer technology in my teaching	.63		
8.	The computer can efficiently replace "time consuming" activities	.60		
9.	If computers are not used in school, the learners are deprived of basic skills	.60		
10.	Computer technology will enable students to become better teachers		.55	
11.	Teaching in a computer technology environment will improve my learners' attitude towards learning		.63	
12.	Computer technology will help me manage and organize learning in class		.73	
13.	Using technology in schools will help learners to better understand the impact technology has on their lives		.52	
14.	Using technology is mainly for problem solving activities		.47	
15.	Using computers in class will reduce the standard of learning			.59
16.	Using computers arouses pressure			.61
17.	Using computers in my work only means extra work for me			.66
18.	Anything done with the computer I can perform as efficiently without it			.62
19.	Using computer technology requires teachers to dedicate more time and effort			.64
20.	Computer technology will not improve the attitude of learners to a the school subjects			.58

to learning" and its high score shows the participants' beliefs concerning the pedagogical benefits and contributions of computer technology to learning and teaching and its ability to improve abilities and achievements of learners through its use. The third factor will be referred to as "the cost of technology integration" and its high score reflects the participants' assumptions concerning the perceived cost of using computer technology in learning and teaching.

In order to determine the reliability of each of the three factors the Alpha Cronbach coefficients were computed and revealed values of .83, .78 and .89 for the first, second and third factors respectively, indicating satisfactory level of reliability. For statistical analysis, three measures were computed by the mean score of the items included in each factor. The score ranges from 1 (the lowest) to 4 (the highest).

In order to examine the relationships between the three factors, Pearson coefficients were computed. The factor of "cost of using ICT" was negatively correlated to "attitude towards ICT" ($r = -0.32$, $p < .001$) and to the "contribution of ICT to learning" ($r = -0.44$, $p < .001$). The "attitude towards ICT and "contribution of ICT to learning" were positively correlated ($r = 0.72$, $p < .001$). These correlations indicate a satisfactory content validity of the measures.

In the attempt to examine whether the participants of this study went through a change during the four years of their studies concerning the three factors mentioned above, a one-way ANOVA was conducted to compare the four measurements concerning the scores of the factors. The first measurement was taken in the beginning of first year, the second measurement was taken in the end of the first year, the third measurement was taken in the end of the second year and the fourth measurement was taken in the end of the fourth and last year of their studies.

Table 3 presents the means and standard deviations of the three factors in each of the four measurements.

The ANOVAs revealed a significant affect of the time of the measurement on the factor of "cost of ICT" ($F(3,150) = 158.12$, $p < 001$), a significant affect of the time of the measurement on the factor of "contribution of ICT" ($F(3,150) = 33.34$, $p < 001$) and a significant affect of the time of the measurement on the factor of "attitude towards ICT" ($F(3,150) = 19.17$, $p < 001$) Post hoc

TABLE 3 : Means and Standard Deviations of the Three Factors in Four Measurements

		Attitude towards technology	*Contribution of ICT to learning*	*Cost of using ICT*
Beginning of first year (I)	Mean	3.00	2.96	3.21
	SD	0.50	0.59	0.55
End of first year (II)	Mean	2.85	2.56	3.08
	SD	0.59	0.70	0.65
End of second year (III)	Mean	3.21	3.00	1.98
	SD	0.46	0.51	0.47
End of fourth year (IV)	Mean	3.68	3.63	1.37
	SD	0.27	0.38	0.24

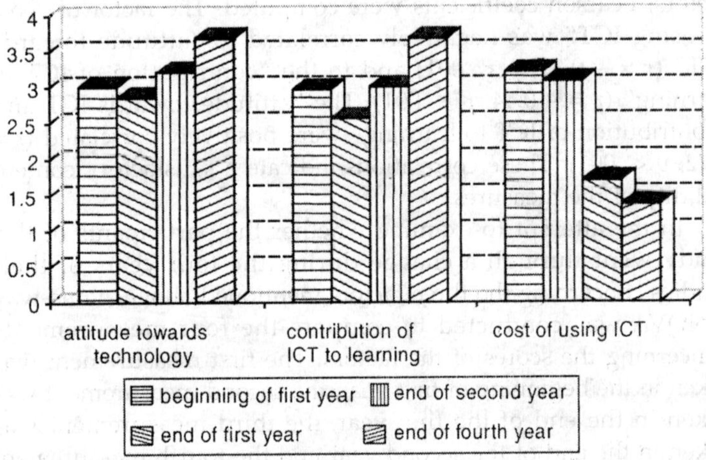

Figure 1 : *Means of the three factors in four measurements*

comparisons among the four measurements, using Scheffe test, conducted on each one of the factors, produced the following results: The level of "attitude towards computer technology" falls from the beginning of the first year to the end of the first year, increases between the end of the first year to the end of the second year and continue to increase between the end of the second year to the end of the fourth year. The level of "contribution of ICT to learning" shows a similar tendency-falls from the beginning of the first year to the end of the first year increases between the end of the first year to the end of the second year and continue to increase to the end of the fourth year. Thus, in both factors the changes followed a U pattern. However, the level of "cost of using ICT" decreases systematically from the beginning of the first year to the end of the fourth year.

Conclusion: The attitudes of the participants towards computer technology decrease slightly between the beginning and the end of the first years i. However they increase in the end of the second year and are highest in the end of the fourth year.

The beliefs of the participants regarding the benefits and contributions of ICT to learning and teaching decrease between the beginning and the end of the first years i. However they increase in the end of the second year and are highest in the end of the fourth year.

The perceived cost of integrating ICT in teaching and learning is at its highest point in the first measurement – the beginning of the first year. However, there is a decline in the end of the first year, the end of the second year and reaches its lowest point in the end of the fourth year.

Discussion: The findings of the current study indicate a two-stage change in student-teachers attitudes towards technology and in their use of ICT. Phase 1 : First year- deterioration of beliefs in ICT. Phase 2 : Years 2-4 -increase of beliefs in ICT. During the first year of the program there was a shift of participants' belief in technology towards the negative direction. This can be explained in various ways:

- An overriding impact of technology, the new component in the learning environment,
- Incubation time needed
- Absence of technology in the "real" education-system surrounding participants, which neither supports nor reinforces the new model practiced,
- Resistance to change

During the second, third and fourth years of the program there was a gradual shift in student-teachers' attitudes and beliefs towards the positive direction; they used digital tools more intensively in both learning and teaching.

Findings: The findings of the current study show that

- Studying in a technology rich teacher education program has an impact on the participants
- Learning in a technology rich environment promotes teaching in such environments (aim 2)
- Long term is needed for incubation of and penetrating into the digital environment; thus it's important not to stop using technology in teaching and learning after a short while, even if it seems difficult and not contributing in the beginning.

Conclusions

Attitudes towards ICT change for the better after a long term and massive exposure to ICT

- Experience as a learner promotes use of ICT as a teacher.
- Students use the computer as a mindtool both personally and professionally
- Significance of the study
- This study assists
- Learning to incorporate ICT in teaching.
- Enhancing the use of computer technology in Israel's educational system.
- Promoting teachers' tendency towards lifelong learning through routine use of ICT for personal and professional updating via e-learning.

Suggestions for Further Research

- To repeat the research with a wider and a more heterogeneous population
- To check more case studies of all 4 types of students
- To perform a similar study with in-service teachers in their professional development.

Environmental Education for a Sustainable Future

MAGANLAL S. MOLIA

There are four principal objectives of the chapter, first, it seeks to heighten national recognition of environmental education as one of the crucial elements of any effective effort to achieve sustainable development in Australia - an informed community is a critical prerequisite to a sustainable future. Too often in the past, responses to environmental problems have not properly harnessed the enormous potential which complementary educational activities have to bring about better environmental outcomes.Environmental education has been an integral component of some effective government programs, as is the case with the Natural Heritage Trust currently being implemented by the Federal Government. However, there has never been a strategic national attempt to translate our national and international written commitments about the importance of environmental education into a coordinated plan of action. This article marks the commencement of that process by placing environmental education unambiguously on the list of essential national endeavours towards sustainability.The second objective of this article is to stimulate debate amongst stakeholders about what directions, and specific measures Australia can take in order to make tangible improvements in environmental education activities, and bring about better environmental outcomes as a result.The article aims to illuminate the state of environmental education in Australia in a way which is helpful not just to providers of environmental education, but to stakeholders working outside the field. In doing so, it is intended that the community will be better informed to form a consensus on how we can improve the national environmental education effort.Engaging external stakeholders in this process of stocktaking and re-orienting of government educational programs will help to ensure that Commonwealth activity is more complementary to environmental educative needs and activities in the wider community.Finally, the article seeks to challenge other sectors to review and further develop their own environmental education activities.

The Importance of Environmental Education

1. Environmental Education in the Global Context.

The 1997 UNESCO Statement 'Educating for a Sustainable Future: A transdisciplinary vision for concerted action' states:

'It is widely agreed that education is the most effective means that society possesses for confronting the challenges of the future. Indeed, education will shape the world of tomorrow.' (1997: 13).

For the foreseeable future, sustainable management of the environment will be one of the greatest challenges confronting the world. Over the past 30 years, the international community has been confronted with a wide range of transboundary environmental problems which involve more than one country in terms of being responsible for the problem, dealing with its impact, and ultimately providing solutions.Climate change, loss of biodiversity, declining fisheries, ozone layer depletion, and trade in endangered species, are only a few of the major environmental threats which have led to a global cooperative response.Worldwide recognition that these problems reflect a need for global commitment to sustainability culminated at the Earth Summit in Rio De Janeiro in 1992 when 150 nations (including Australia) endorsed the Agenda 21 document, which provides a framework for sustainable development strategies at all levels.Agenda 21 remains the basis of internationally agreed courses of action towards sustainable development. Chapter 36 of Agenda 21 on Promoting Education, Public Awareness and Training focuses on the role of education in environmental decision making. In it, world leaders asserted that:

> 'education is critical for promoting sustainable development and improving the capacity of people to address environment and development issues. ... It is also critical for achieving environmental and ethical awareness, values and attitudes, skills and behaviour

> consistent with sustainable development and for effective public participation in decision-making.'

There is also an acknowledgment of the importance of education in achieving success in other Agenda 21 priority areas such as meeting basic needs, capacity building, environmental data and information, and environmental science.

2. *Domestically*

For Australia, the Agenda 21 framework, and education's key role, are vital to resolving our domestic environmental challenges, and also to achieving sustainability on a global scale.Many global environmental threats pose potentially major adverse consequences for the Australian environment-ozone depletion is an obvious example. Others, such as climate change, require substantial changes in the way our economy and society utilises energy and natural resources.In addition, we face significant challenges with respect to those environmental problems which are essentially domestic. According to Australia State of the Environment 1996, a number of issues provide grounds for serious concern.The most pressing of these issues are the loss of biodiversity and the continued destruction of habitats across Australia. In addition, river systems and groundwater supplies continue to be depleted at unsustainable rates in many parts of rural Australia, with major environmental consequences like algal blooms, rising salinity, and declining aquatic ecosystems. High rates of land clearance and vegetation loss, and the poor quality of our soils (and their slow rates of formation), make land degradation a problem of national proportions. In our cities, loss of remnant vegetation continues apace, air pollution is perceived as a major threat, while stormwater and sewage and other waste disposal continue to have substantial adverse impacts on biodiversity and water quality. Invasive plants and animals also pose a serious and increasing threat to native ecosystems in rural, urban, and marine environments.Governments at all levels are working to meet these and other difficult environmental challenges. Through the Natural Heritage Trust in particular, the Commonwealth is providing an unprecedented degree of financial support to support a wide range of projects which respond effectively to the threats which have been identified as of greatest national concern.

3. The Contribution of Environmental Education.

Australia's ability to meet environmental threats at home and abroad is inextricably linked with the priority it places on effective environmental education.Environmental issues are frequently complex and contested. Research, invention, innovation and adaptation are all required. None are possible, let alone likely, without a clear understanding of the ecological and policy issues and linkages involved. Without a firm, educated basis of knowledge and understanding, progress on environmental issues becomes haphazard, uncertain and unlikely.We recognise the need to do more, we know many current environmental problems have solutions, but we often lack the information and understanding we need to effectively assess current environmental management practices, and plan for the future. The knowledge, values, skills and tools we need to meet environmental challenges are all sourced from formal and informal education.In addition to providing us with the environmental literacy required to address threats to our natural capital, effective environmental education also enables us to integrate ecological thinking into social and economic planning - which is essential to achieving sustainable development.An educated understanding of environmental issues also reduces the sense of helplessness which might emerge in the face of environmental challenges. In a fast-moving world of competing priorities, it is all too easy for governments, businesses, and individuals to turn away from medium and long-term problems (a category into which many environmental threats fall) and focus exclusively on the short-term. Without the empowerment and capacity to address problems, which environmental education provides, a short-term focus is all the more likely.

The Nature of Environmental Education

Defining Environmental Education.'Environmental Education' is used in this Discussion Paper in its broadest sense to encompass:

1. raising awareness;
2. acquiring new perspectives, values, knowledge and skills; and
3. formal and informal processes leading to changed behaviour in support of a sustainable environment.

The Term 'Environmental Education' Has Various Connotations

It has sometimes been interpreted narrowly to relate only to the scientific aspects of environmental problems. Its placement therefore among the disciplines of formal education has been most prominently in science and geography.Yet these traditional disciplines do not necessarily capture the wide range of aspects which a holistic education about environmental matters should incorporate. Public policy, electoral politics, economic, and even diplomatic factors are just some of the many cross-disciplinary linkages which should be integral to environmental education.In contemporary international discussion, the term 'education for sustainability' has been used by some to reinforce that the issues with which environmental education deals cut across and engage traditional disciplines and areas of study. It must be a transdisciplinary process.The widely accepted definition of 'sustainability' is that proposed by the Brundtland Commission in 1987: 'Sustainable development is that which meets the needs of the present without compromising the ability of future generations to meet their own needs.'A detailed vision of what education for sustainability might mean in practice is likely to be the subject of continuing discussion. But the following principles are likely to remain basic to its operation.

Principles of Environmental Education

1. *Environmental Education must involve everyone*

Because of its very nature and importance, environmental education cannot be confined to any one group in our society. It is a responsibility for everyone - government, industry, the media, educational institutions, community groups - right down to the level of the individual.

2. *Environmental Education must be lifelong*

Information about environmental problems is forever improving, as we learn from our past experiences and mistakes. As we develop and apply better environmental technologies, the ability of society and individuals to respond effectively also improves.In order to move closer to achieving sustainable development as a nation, all Australians need to continually refresh the knowledge and skills which they apply to the environmental challenges we face.Just as workplace learning and retraining are essential to continued productivity, the same is true of environmental education, whether in formal or non formal settings.

3. Environmental Education must be holistic and about connections

In order to address environmental challenges, we need people who think broadly and who understand systems, connections, patterns and causes. The challenges themselves frequently have social, scientific, cultural, economic and ethical aspects, all of which must be considered for their effective management. Specialist discipline-based knowledge, while contributing critically, is no longer adequate by itself - holistic appreciation of the context of environmental problems is essential.Meeting this need presents a dilemma to the formal education systems over whether environmental education should be taught as a separate subject or incorporated into one or more particular subject areas. The right answer may vary from situation to situation, depending on what is most practical - suffice to say, a much stronger re-orientation of all relevant areas of formal education towards issues of sustainability is required.Equally important is the need to establish better communicative links between those people working on, or learning about, similar or related environmental issues, but who come from different professional or disciplinary backgrounds. Better grounds for communication and partnerships are also required between formal and non formal education settings, and between various groups with competing interests on environmental issues.

4. Environmental Education must be Practical

One of the most fundamental defining characteristics of effective environmental education is that it must lead to actions which result in better environmental outcomes, not simply the accumulation of inert knowledge or impractical skills.This is ultimately the yardstick by which we are able to measure the effectiveness of our efforts in environmental education.

5. Environmental Education must be in Harmony with Social and Economic Goals

Effective environmental education must also encourage the pursuit of environmental goals in harmony with other powerful and legitimate social and economic goals - it should not be taught in a vacuum, or simply equip people to pursue an agenda on the margins of society.Environmental education needs to incorporate this reality by providing. people with the knowledge, understanding and capacity to influence mainstream society in a way which progresses environmental objectives along with other legitimate social and economic objectives.

The Components of Environmental Education.The evolution of environmental education has required closer and renewed investigation into learning processes. It has become customary to define the components of learning relevant to environmental sustainability. These are sometimes described, misleadingly, as 'stages'. Even though they may seem to follow a natural sequence and be discrete in themselves, people's encounter with issues of sustainability can begin and develop from any of these components. They should be seen as cyclical and interactive, with periods focused on reflection, research, development and action.

These components, which apply equally to formal and informal education, are adapted from the international edition of Teaching for a Sustainable World, edited by John Fien, 1996 (Introduction xxvi-xxvii).

Awarness Raising—'How Does it Matters?'

Market research into environmental issues consistently confirms what educators have long held as a first principle of operation: start from where the students (or consumers, farmers, industrialists, citizens, decision makers and so on) are. What is it that matters to them most at this point in time? What do they want to achieve? How do these attitudes relate to environmental issues? These are the starting points for any useful process of problem solving as well as meaningful and enduring learning.Awareness raising is not just a matter of shaping attitudes; it must also be about the development of knowledge. Is this view legitimate? What information supports it? Is that information relevant and reliable?It is anticipated that from these initial steps of establishing and confirming the personal relevance of environmental issues, there will be an evolution to understanding of issues on a larger scale: personal, local, regional, national and global.

Shaping of Values—'What Aught to be Done?'

Without appropriate and helpful underlying values and attitudes, environmental education is bound for failure. These values include:

- respect for and appreciation of the interdependence of all life forms and the resilience, fragility and aesthetic qualities of the natural environment
- appreciation of the dependence of human life on the finite resources of the earth
- appreciation of the role of human ingenuity and creativity in ensuring survival and in the search for appropriate and sustainable progress
- Because of the way in which environmental education may challenge accepted practices and beliefs, it is an area of some contestation. For this reason the process of developing values has a controversial aspect. Thus the following values are also most important:
- a sense of balance and fairness to all in deciding among conflicting priorities
- an appreciation of the importance and value of individual responsibility and action.

Developing Knowledge and Skills—'How can Something be Done About It?'

At its heart capacity building means acquiring relevant knowledge and skills, a process often seen as the conventional function of any type of education.It has been noted that the types of knowledge needed to participate effectively in environmental education are wide ranging and not confined to any particular discipline. Some of the areas of knowledge which environmental education must deal with however are:

- the planet earth as a finite system
- the resources of the earth, particularly air, soil, water, minerals, their distribution and their role in supporting living organisms
- the nature of ecosystems, their health and interdependence within the biosphere
- the dependence of humans on the environmental resources for life and sustenance

- sustainable relationships within the environment
- the implications of resource distribution in determining the nature of societies and the rate and character of economic development
- the role and values of science and technology in the development of societies and the impact of technologies on the environment
- the interconnectedness of present political, economic, environmental and social issues, and
- processes of planning, policy-making and acting to solve problems.

The skills which should be acquired include capacities to:

- define and explain fundamental concepts such as environment, ecological systems, community, development and technology and being able to apply them to specific situations using a range of relevant resources and technologies
- analyse problems, and frame and investigate relevant questions
- assess and evaluate differing points of view
- develop hypotheses based on balanced and accurate information, engage in critical analysis and careful synthesis, and test new information and personal beliefs, explorations and experiences against these hypotheses
- communicate information and points of view effectively
- develop partnerships and the foundation for cooperative and consensual action
- develop strategies for action, including locating appropriate resources, and means for their implementation.

Making decisions and taking action—'What to do?'

Environmental education is not a passive process. In response to the new levels of awareness, knowledge and skill, and on the basis of evolving values and attitudes (all suggested above), it is about changing behaviour, whether one's own or as part of larger community changes.As mentioned above, this is one of environmental education's defining characteristics. It is, above all, practical in the sense that some result should and must come from it if our futures are to be as we would wish.

The Evolution of Environmental Education.A model developed in the Netherlands (Caring for the Earth: A Strategy for sustainable living IUCN,UNEP, WWF 1991) suggests a series of stages in the evolution of environmental education. The four stages suggested are:

Reactive: providing particular products and programs in response to limited demand. Education is often instigated by isolated individuals, specialists, voluntary organisations, or the information/community relations/education units of some government agencies. Education aims at reducing ecological ignorance.

Receptive: in which organisations include environmental education objectives in their policies and planning. School curriculum development bodies become involved, but programs are implemented without reference to work elsewhere in the education field. Objectives emphasise changing knowledge and attitudes.

Constructive: in which programs and objectives are more thoroughly implemented. There is wide dissemination of developments, links are made across sectors. There is community participation and objectives are oriented towards sustainable living.

Pro-active: in which the culture of all organisations is defined in terms of ecologically sustainable living supported by comprehensive, lifelong environmental learning integrated within education systems, industry, social organisations/neighbourhood groups and government.

It can be argued that environmental education in Australia is generally in the second stage described by this model with some evidence of progress towards the third. Further substantial action is required to take us towards the fourth stage.

Criteria to help guide efforts to develop environmental education at the national, regional and global levels.

Whereas it is a fact that biological and physical features constitute the natural basis of the human environment, its ethical, social, cultural and economic dimensions also play their part in determining the lines of approach and instruments whereby people may understand and make better use of natural resources in satisfying their needs.

Environmental education is the result of the reorientation and dovetailing of different disciplines and educational experiences which facilitate an integrated perception of the problems of the environment, enabling more rational actions capable of meeting social needs to be taken.

A basic aim of environmental education is to succeed in making individuals and communities understand the complex nature of the natural and the built environments resulting from the interaction of their biological, physical, social, economic and cultural aspects, and acquire the knowledge, values, attitudes and practical skills to participate in a responsible and effective way in anticipating and solving environmental problems, and in the management of the quality of the environment.

A further basic aim of environmental education is clearly to show the economic, political and ecological interdependence of the modern world, in which decisions and actions by the different countries can have international repercussions. Environmental education should, in this regard, help to develop a sense of responsibility and solidarity among countries and regions as the foundation for a new international order which will guarantee the conservation and improvement of the environment.

Special attention should be paid to understanding the complex relations between socio-economic development and the improvement of the environment.

For this purpose, environmental education should provide the necessary knowledge for interpretation of the complex phenomena that shape the environment, encourage those ethical, economic and aesthetic values which, constituting the basis of self-discipline, will further the development of conduct compatible with the preservation and improvement of the environment; it should also provide a wide range of practical skills required in the devising and application of effective solutions to environmental problems.

To carry out these tasks, environmental education should bring about a closer link between educational processes and real life, building its activities around the environmental problems that are faced by particular communities and focusing analysis on these by means of an interdisciplinary, comprehensive approach which will permit a proper understanding on environmental problems.

Environmental education should cater to all ages and socio-professional groups in the population. It should be addressed to:

- the general non specialist public of young people and adults whose daily conduct has a decisive influence on the preservation and improvement of the environment;
- particular social groups whose professional activities affect the quality of the environment; and
- scientists and technicians whose specialised research and work will lay the foundations of knowledge on which education, training and efficient management of the environment should be based.

To achieve the effective development of environmental education, full advantage must be taken of all public and private facilities available to society for the education of the population: the formal education systems, different forms of non formal education, and the mass media.

To make an effective contribution towards improving the environment, educational action must be linked with legislation, policies, measures of control and the decisions that governments may adopt in relation to the human environment.

Goals, objectives and guiding principles for environmental education.The goals of environmental education are:

- to foster clear awareness of, and concern about, economic, social, political and ecological interdependence in urban and rural areas;
- to provide every person with opportunities to acquire the knowledge, values, attitudes, commitment and skills needed to protect and improve the environment;
- to create new patterns of behaviour of individuals, groups and society as a whole towards the environment.

The categories of environmental education objectives are:

- Awareness-to help social groups and individuals acquire an awareness and sensitivity to the total environment and its allied problems.
- Knowledge-to help social groups and individuals gain a variety of experience in, and acquire a basic understanding of, the environment and its associated problems.
- Attitudes-to help social groups and individuals acquire a set of values and feelings of concern for the environment and the motivation for actively participating in environmental improvement and protection.

- Skills-to help social groups and individuals acquire the skills fro identifying and solving environmental problems.
- Participation-to provide social groups and individuals with an opportunity to be actively involved at all levels in working toward resolution of environmental problems.

Guiding Principles

Environmental education should

- consider the environment in its totality - natural and built, technological and social (economic, political, cultural-historical, moral and aesthetic);
- be a continuous lifelong process, beginning at the pre-school level and continuing through all formal and non formal stages;
- be interdisciplinary in its approach, drawing on the specific content of each discipline in making a holistic and balanced perspective;
- examine major environmental issues from local, national, regional and international points of view so that students receive insights into environmental conditions in other geographical areas;
- focus on current and potential environmental situations while taking into account the historical perspective;
- promote the value and necessity of local, national and international cooperation in the prevention and solution of environmental problems;
- explicitly consider environmental aspects in plans for development and growth;
- enable learners to have a role in planning their learning experiences and provide an opportunity for making decisions and accepting their consequences;
- relate environmental sensitivity, knowledge, problem-solving skills and values-clarification to every age, but with special emphasis on environmental sensitivity to the learner's own community in early years;
- help learners discover the symptoms and real causes of environmental problems;
- emphasise the complexity of environmental problems and thus the need to develop critical thinking and problem-solving skills;

- utilise diverse learning environments and a broad array of educational approaches to teaching/learning about and from the environment with due stress on practical activities and first-hand experience.

Priorities for Environmental Education in the Community

In recent years, environmental education has expanded in scope and its methods have become more diversified. This expansion has, nonetheless, been accompanied by some insecurity about its place and nature.There is a strong sense among those directly involved that, following a period of rapid growth (most apparent in some sectors in the last decade), the most urgent need is for consolidation, coordination and integration.What follows is a list of suggestions of things which providers of environmental education can do to enhance our collective national effort. It is not intended to be an exhaustive list, but rather a range of options which providers might consider if they have not done so already - in many cases educators have gone beyond the suggestions below.

IN GOVERNMENT

Federal Government

There is a need at the Commonwealth level to foster new linkages between departments so that environmental education activities being pursued by different federal agencies are part of a coherent whole-of-government effort.Environment-related activity has become commonplace in a wide range of Commonwealth departments, but greater linkages and coordination are required to ensure that these activities incorporate the potential of education to facilitate positive environmental outcomes.The means by which the Environment and Heritage Portfolio can improve its educational activity and the activities of other Commonwealth agencies is treated separately in the previous section.

State and Territory government departments

Where they have not done so already, State and Territory governments should develop and implement an environmental education strategy. Such strategies should recognise and develop the educational possibilities in program activities.State governments might also consider designating staff with explicit responsibility for environmental education. In designing and implementing program activities, such staff should ensure access to and use of specialists in the field of environmental education.States should also foster linkages and partnerships with the various actual and potential providers of environmental education - including other State/Territory agencies along with external educators.

Local Government Bodies

The provision of elected representatives and staff in Local Government with education and training about environmental matters is a major precursor to sustainability at the local level. Designating staff in local authorities with explicit responsibility for environmental matters is another positive step. Councils can help to educate their local communities by demonstrating best practice initiatives in land management and in the treatment of waste/sewage.Councils also have the opportunity to recognise and develop the educational possibilities associated with local environmental strategies, campaigns and practices. Councils should recognise the opportunity to involve the community in the formulation and implementation of such activities, and to build partnerships based on sustainability with local providers of formal and informal education.

Formal Education Providers

Though these sectors are not administered by the Federal Government, there is a need for increased levels of national consistency and coherence in all of them.

Early Childhood Learning

Early childhood learning facilities can make a positive contribution by establishing or extending programs focused on environmental education for sustainability. A 'whole centre' approach is optimal - where, for example, the policies, programs, building and grounds functioning and maintenance all reflect a concern for environmental sustainability.The use of play and other materials which have an environmental focus is to be encouraged, as should environmental awareness and sustainable practices among parents at home, parent-managed committees and parent-operated play groups.

School Education

Schools are in a position to ensure a place for environmental education in every relevant curriculum area at each level of schooling. They can make sure that environmental education draws on cross-disciplinary information, skills and experiences and has a practical action-based focus. School teachers should receive environmental education in their training, and in subsequent professional development opportunities, where it is relevant to the material being taught.Access to more courses which have an explicit focus on environmental education needs to be a choice available to all senior students. Schools should provide quality materials that attend to nationally agreed priority environmental issues, and ensure that environmental policies and practices are effectively implemented, monitored and, as necessary, updated.Schools should move from generalised awareness of problems to teaching and learning about accurate, objective and substantive details within many of the key learning areas. Increased content knowledge and well informed action is urgent and rests on improved teaching. Opportunity also exists for schools to draw on the support of community facilities (public and private) for access to enterprises that demonstrate the principles of ecologically sustainable development in action.

Higher Education

Universities and colleges have the scope to establish departments or centres with staff positions (such as professorial status) focused on issues of environmental sustainability. Such opportunities have not been taken up on enough campuses.Higher Education institutions also need to provide students with the maximum practicable flexibility to customise course programs to suit the multi-disciplinary requirements of a thorough environmental education.A 'whole institution' approach to good environmental practice should be promoted across the higher education sector in order to raise environmental awareness across entire campuses.

Vocational Education and Training

Vocational Education and Training facilities should enhance their contribution to environmental education by ensuring that competencies based on sustainability are included in the design of all training packages and other course offerings. They can also ensure the general public availability of a comprehensive range of specific environmental courses in areas such as renewable energies, natural and cultural heritage management, land and marine conservation and restoration, and waste management/ resource recovery. Vocational education and training should also model good environmental practice at all sites of provision, and they should provide practical field experiences and training by working in partnership with conservation organisations, community groups and appropriate government agencies.

WORKPLACES

Business and Industry

Businesses can contribute by practicing and promoting good environmental management which integrates conservation with development, production and distribution processes. Companies have an opportunity to assist with the process of community education and awareness-raising by finding, developing and marketing cost-competitive environmentally friendly products and processes. Internally, companies can ensure that designated staff with responsibility for, and expertise in, environmental management are an integral component of their human resources structure. Such staff should be given the resources and managerial support to communicate the necessary technical and conceptual information required to foster better environmental awareness and performance company-wide. The implementation of comprehensive and credible environmental management systems is also a way to foster continual environmental improvements, and educate the workforce in the process.Externally, companies are in a position to participate in appropriate partnerships with other organisations (including community groups) to foster increased knowledge about environmental problems, and build greater capacity for resolving them. This may involve support for educative materials relevant to the business sector, support for conferences dealing with environmental concerns, or financial or in-kind support for grass-roots community projects in environmental monitoring and remediation. Companies can also promote activities directed at sustainability in representative professional, business and industry associations.

Peak Bodies

Peak bodies representing industry, agriculture, labour and other sectors can help foster the adoption of environmentally responsible practices in the Australian workplaces by adopting comprehensive policies which incorporate a commitment to principles of sustainability.Environmental education should feature prominently among the training programs, workshops and conferences conducted by peak business organisations and unions. Peak bodies should also foster environmental performance by showcasing examples of workplace-related good environmental practice through awards, and by publicising success stories in their publications.

NON-FORMAL EDUCATION SETTINGS

The Media

The Media has a particular responsibility for advancing environmental education in our community, because of its pre-eminent role in the distribution of information in our community. In terms of editorial content in news bulletins and current affairs coverage, it is important for reporters to be either cognisant of, or inclined to become so, about environmental aspects of stories covered. This depends to a degree on the priorities of the newsroom culture, so a commitment from senior editors is vital.Programming decisions are also important-documentaries and feature stories which heighten an appreciation of natural heritage, and an awareness about environmental problems, are among the most powerful educative tools.The Media (particularly television) is also in a powerful position to educate the public about environmental matters through community service announcements-often in partnership with community groups and government agencies. This requires a donation of air-time or column-space, which should be seen as a worthwhile investment rather than a cost, if for no other reason than the improvement it can make to public perceptions about the particular broadcaster or publisher.

Environmental Interest Groups and Organisation

A central function of any effective environmental interest group should be to promote the importance of environmental education as widely as possible, and to contribute to that process as far as possible. In order to maximise an NGO's effectiveness in this regard, human and financial resources need to be devoted to education, and the educative knowledge and skills base of the group needs to be continually renewed.Environmental NGOs have the opportunity to collaborate with other community groups, formal and informal educators, governments, and individual businesses where appropriate, on projects which increase appreciation of environmental problems, and commitment to their resolution in a sustainable way.

Other Community Organisations

Every community organisation in Australia can make a positive contribution to environmental education, irrespective of their primary function. Whether it be a Scout Troop, a Church Parish, or Meals on Wheels, community groups can make a positive contribution by incorporating environmental sustainability into their decisions and activities.By fostering a concern for local natural and cultural heritage, through decisions about material use and recycling, equipment purchases, and facility maintenance, community organisations can help to encourage effective participation in environment management in the wider community.Where possible, community groups (especially service organisations) should look to forge productive links with other groups specifically devoted to environmental monitoring and repair, such as the Australian Trust for Conservation Volunteers, Landcare groups, and environmentally related government programs like Bushcare, Waterwatch and Coastcare.Each of these activities is a substantial contribution to the overarching effort.

The Home

The possibilities for environmental education in the home environment are virtually endless. Almost every decision which householders make about purchasing, consuming and disposing presents an opportunity to improve environmental performance. Given the enormous range and number of decisions made in the average household, adults and children should constantly be looking for ways to teach each other how to make more environmentally friendly choices.In addition to looking to ways to re-use, recycle, and reduce waste in the home through choices at the supermarket and decisions about waste disposal, households can also contribute to local ecosystems - for example through decisions made in the garden. By planting native trees and shrubs, and using alternative means to chemicals where possible, householders can ensure that their impact on the local ecology is as small as possible.

Conclusion

The foundations of sustainable development are built on the way we think, the values we hold and the decisions we make. It cannot depend on just the technology available to us, the nature of our environment, or the policy instruments at our disposal. A public which is educated about the need for sustainable development is essential to achieving sustainable development.Though the responsibility for environmental education is a shared one, the Federal Government has an important role to play in terms of national leadership, coordination, and acting as a catalyst for positive educational initiatives in a wide range of community settings. The Commonwealth Government has acknowledged the importance of environmental education in international commitments like Agenda 21, and in national commitments such as the National Strategy for Ecologically Sustainable Development, the National Greenhouse Strategy and the programs of the Natural Heritage Trust. However, until now, actions have failed to adequately reflect these commitments to environmental education.Similarly, in the community, there is not enough appreciation of the nature and importance of environmental education. People also tend to understand environmental education too narrowly, in terms of formal educational settings such as schools.And while there is an enormous amount of effort going into environmental education activity in a wide range of sectors, the activities lack the coordination required to maximise effectiveness.

Some Pedagogical Issues on Environmental Education in India

SANAT KUMAR GHOSH

Indian wisdom has always perceived human beings as an integral and central constituent of nature. Man's desire for a long, healthy, enlightened and joyful life has made him invoke the forces and elements of nature, usually in a deified form, to bless him and his progeny. Logically, therefore, loving, understanding, fearing and befriending nature, not conquering, exploiting or defiling it, was a general way of living in ancient India. The following wish occurring in the *Rigveda* unambiguously proved this man-nature relationship:

> *For us who are governed by the Great Cosmic Order,*
> *May the breeze blow sweet and pleasant,*
> *May the rivers flow sweet and pleasant,*
> *May the plants be sweet and pleasant,*
> *May the night and dawn be sweet and pleasant,*
> *May the dust of earth be sweet and pleasant,*
> *May the upper regions, our Father, be sweet and pleasant,*
> *May the tree be sweet and pleasant,*
> *May the sun be sweet and pleasant,*
> *And may our cattle wealth and speech be sweet and pleasant.*
>
> — *Rigveda 1.90. 6-8*

The scripture vividly describes the five elements that constitute this universe and provide the life support for man and animal and the base for all form of vegetation and all forms of human activity.

International Initiatives

Now it is being increasingly realized all over the world that living a harmonious and healthy life on this planet is man's greatest need.

S/he has nowhere else to go to. Understandably therefore, humanity needs a new relationship with nature, a healthier bond between the 'self' and the 'surroundings', a new set of cultural values and a 'paradigmatic shift' in the global vision of earth-man relationship. The two 'Earth Summits', the first one held in Stockholm, Sweden, in June 1972 and the second one held in Rio de Janeiro, Brazil, in 1992, discussed manmade global warning and the depletion of bio-diversity. Declarations of far reaching consequences were made at these Summits. In the international context, the Report of the Club of Rome in early seventies of the last century strongly advocated the environment factor. But the remedy prescribed, i.e.,' No-Growth' was a bitter pill. It was followed by the Report of the Independent Commission on International Development Issues under the chairmanship of Willy Brandt, 'North-South: A Program for Survival' (1980). The Brundtland Commission Report (1987) really looked closely and critically at the contemporary environmental issues. This Report also provided an explanatory link between Third world poverty and global environmental deterioration. It also generated intellectual awareness of a new type of growth, i.e., 'Sustainable Development'. The World Summit on Sustainable Development (WSSD) held in Johannesburg in 2002 had also the same theme.

Indian Scenario

In India too, in spite of her long tradition of environment friendly society, environmental issues are attracted serious attention with the global contend and it has been felt that our education had to respond appropriately to this crying need of the time. The National Policy on Education, 1986 (renewed in POA, 1992) stated: "There is a paramount need to create a consciousness of the environment. It must permeate all ages and all sections of society, beginning with the child. Environmental consciousness should inform teaching in schools and colleges. This aspect will be integrated in the entire educational process." Accordingly, the National Curriculum for Elementary and Secondary Education: A Framework (1988) presented the NCERT's (National Council for Educational Research and Training) view: "The school curriculum should highlight the measures for protection and care of the environment, prevention of pollution and conservation of energy." In consonance with these documents, the environmental study was made an independent subject at the primary level and topics related to environment were suitably infused with different science and social science subjects at all stages of school education. Books under a `Reading to Learn' series were brought out to highlight a number of environment related subjects and concerns. Emphasis was also laid on teacher orientation-cum-training in the subject and a number of training modules were developed by the NCERT.

The Hon'ble Supreme Court of India's directive to develop a model syllabus of Environmental Education (EE), as a compulsory subject in a graded manner, for the entire school stage was welcomed. In the detailed discussions that followed it was noted that National Curriculum Framework for School Education *(NCERT, 2000)* has already made recommendations of far-reaching consequences with regard to EE for different stages of school education. Significant initiatives undertaken by the state level agencies in revising their curriculum and syllabus including EE over the years were also highlighted. It asserts the Fundamental Duties *(Article 51 A of part IV A of the Indian Constitution)* to protect and improve the national environment including forests, lakes, rivers, and wildlife and to have compassion for the living creatures.

One of the General Objectives of Education, it mentions, "understanding of the environment in its totality, both natural and social, and their interactive processes, the environmental problems and the ways and means to preserve the environment." Following these, a subject, the Art of Healthy and Productive Living, along with Language and Mathematics, has been introduced at the level of Classes I and II. All the three Subjects are to be woven around the immediate environment of the young learners and integrate environmental concerns as well. In Classes III-IV, Environmental Studies becomes a separate subject. In Classes VI to X, Environmental Education (EE) has been integrated suitably in Social Sciences, Languages and Science and Technology. At the higher secondary level, besides integrating topics related to environment in various subjects appropriately, Conservation Education and Disaster Management Education have been included as potential subjects of choices along with the traditional subjects. In the Vocational Education stream, EE and Rural Development have been suggested as a part of the General Foundation Course at this stage. Supporting all these issues, the Curriculum Framework, 2005, has also stated, "For the primary grades, the natural and social environment will be explained as integral parts of languages and mathematics. Children should be engaged in activities to understand the environment through illustration from the physical, biological, social, and cultural spheres. The language used should not be gender-sensitive. Teaching methods should be in a participative and discussion-oriented mode."

The Environmental Education Concern

Despite these initiatives, it has been felt that although a fair amount of information about the environment is being given through textbooks, it has not been succeeded to generate a concern that may lead to effective action for conserving and further improving the environment. In such a field of global concern, it may not be so important to know as to feel and be motivated to act. Therefore, the further course of study in EE should emphasize the emotional and attitudinal aspects of the learners' personality along with the requisite cognitive component most of which is available in different subject textbooks, in any form. Thus, it is argued, a value based, action oriented course of EE would lead from knowledge to feeling and finally to appropriate action. This alone would bridge the wide gulf between the avowed intent and the actual implementation of a program that concerns the present and future of the entire humanity on earth.

As regards the present model of environmental education, a concern has been expressed that the integrated or infused model, though used in almost all the countries of the world, is fragmented and therefore, not necessarily tested in examinations. It is not given the importance it deserves as a serious, structured separate entity that a student must learn as one of the core topics in the curriculum. It only generates some incidental awareness of phenomena related to environment, but the primary concerns for teaching and evaluation invariably remain the content of sciences or social sciences. The concern aspect of knowledge and the feelings associated with it that would result in concerted efforts for environmental protection. Consequently, the degradation of "self and the surroundings" continues unabated. This has resulted in a demand for developing a graded, action oriented, value based course in environmental education for all the classes/ levels of schooling in such a way that it can addresses the general environment concerns properly without adding to the curricular load.

The new syllabus of environmental education being proposed here would aim at generating among young learners an awareness of and sensitivity to the total environment in a holistic manner and the problems associated with it. It would also equip the future custodians of the earth with the requisite knowledge of the total environment, natural and social, the problems associated with it and the necessary skills for solving these in a positive and sustainable manner. The processes and strategies suggested would help develop positive attitudes, social values and strong concern for sustainable development and further improvement of the environment. While learners would appreciate local wisdom through traditions and customs, they would also discover their linkages with both national and global concerns. In effect, the course would prepare them to initiate and carry on practical initiative at the individual, the group and the community level for solving environmental related problem and moving toward a life of perfect harmony with their social and natural environment.

Aims and Objectives of Environmental Education

According to Nevada Conference of the International Union for the Conservation of Nature and Natural Resources (1970), "Environmental Education is a process of recognizing values and clarifying concepts, in order to develop skills and attitudes necessary to understand and appreciate the interrelatedness among man, his culture and his bio-physical surroundings. Environmental education also entails practice in decision making and self-formulating a code of behavior about issues concerning environmental quality". Thus, the goal of EE emphasizes on attitude and skill development rather than merely concept development, which is quite different from other academic disciplines.

The Tbilisi Conference (1977) elaborates the goals of environmental education as follows:

1. To foster clear awareness of and concern about economic, social, political and ecological interdependence in urban and rural areas;
2. To provide every person with opportunities to acquire the knowledge, values, attitudes, commitment and skills needed to protect and improve the environment;

3. To create new patterns of behavior of individual, group and society as a whole towards the environment.

Specific Objectives—Identified in India

- To create awareness among the students about the environment and its problems;
- To enable students to acquire the basic knowledge about the environment;
- To enable students to understand the environment and its relationship with man;
- To create a positive attitude among the students towards the environment;
- To develop skills among students with a view to solving environmental problems;
- To create a sense of responsibility towards the environment;
- To get themselves feel the urgency for ensuring appropriate actions to solve environmental problems.

Environmental Education Curriculum in Formal Education

Primary Stage

Teaching of language and mathematics have been inter-woven around children's immediate environment in Classes I and II and no separate textbook for environmental studies has been prescribed for these classes. In Classes III - V, separate textbooks for environmental studies have been provided. Eenvironmental education has been further reinforced under the Art of Healthy and Productive Living (AHPL) for which a single teachers' handbook has been developed by NCTE for Classes I to V. The contents and concepts covered in these books include the following:

1. Familiarization with one's own body;
2. Awareness about immediate surroundings;
3. Need for food, water, air, shelter, clothing and recreation;
4. Importance of trees and plants;
5. Familiarization with local birds, animals and other objects;
6. Interdependence of living and non-living things.
7. Importance of cleanliness and sanitation;
8. Importance of celebration of festivals and national days;

9. Awareness of sunlight, rain and wind;
10. Caring for pet animals;
11. Awareness about air, water, soil and noise pollutions;
12. Need for the protection of environment;
13. Knowledge about the sources of energy;
14. Importance of the conservation of water resources and forests; and
15. Indigenous and traditional knowledge about the protection of environment.

The textbooks lay emphasis on raising awareness levels and sensitizing children about environmental concerns. Emphasis has also been laid on the need to organize learning in local specific contexts, which will provide more meaningful experiences to children. Aspects of indigenous knowledge have also been introduced. There are references and suggestions for conducting activities in and outside the classroom. The NCERT textbooks for environmental studies generally take a comprehensive view of the natural, physical, social and cultural environment.

It is evident that the textbooks represent relevant ideas commensurate with the age and developmental level of children so as to provide them the necessary understanding about their immediate environment. However, there is a scope for inclusion of more activities to enable children to translate environmental awareness into effective behavioral action.

Upper Primary Stage

The contents of upper primary textbooks present an extension and elaboration of the concepts introduced at the primary stage. The textbooks in Rajasthan and Madhya Pradesh (Classes VI-VIII) and in Karnataka (Classes V-VII) contain environmental concepts by and large in the textbooks of science and social science. The textbooks of Karnataka for Class V in the subjects of science, social science and language have environmental ideas infused with these subjects. The state of Orissa deals with the environmental concepts and concerns in its textbooks of science and geography. These are also included in a single textbook of History and Civics in some other states. The NCERT textbooks of Science and Technology, and Social Sciences have incorporated such concepts in the textbooks.

Major Concepts of significance Dealt within Textbooks

1. Adaptation process of living beings in environment;
2. Natural resources;
3. Water cycle;
4. Food chain;
5. Importance of plants and trees in keeping the environment clean;
6. Classification of plants;
7. Role of plants and animals in maintaining environmental balance and soil conservation;
8. Ecosystems;
9. Necessity of clean air for healthy living;
10. Animals and their characteristics;
11. Effects of environmental pollution and the consequences of air pollution - greenhouse effect, ozone layer depletion and increase in carbon dioxide;
12. Role of micro-organisms in the environment;
13. Dependence of the community on the environment;
14. Basic knowledge about the earth and its atmosphere;
15. Physical features of the country;
16. Population and environment;
17. Care and protection of livestock;
18. Necessity of wildlife protection;
19. Impact of deforestation;
20. Impact of industrialization on environment; and
21. Role of civic society in protection of the environment, personal and public property including monuments.

Although most of the content areas of environmental education have generally been covered in the curriculum, still there is a need for inclusion of more individual and group activities and project works in order to promote both the affective and conative domains of environment learning. Co-scholastic activities including organization of plays, cultural programs, debates, mock parliament, discussions and community activities may help further in achieving the objective.

Secondary Stage

The concepts of environmental education have been provided in the textbooks of secondary (IX-X) sciences and social sciences in all the states. In most of the states, there are three textbooks, namely, Science Part-I (Physical Science), Science Part-II (Biological Science) and Geography, while in Karnataka, one textbook deals with Science (Physics and Chemistry), the second with Science (Biology) and the third with Social Sciences. The textbooks deal with environmental concepts both at concrete and abstract levels. The major concepts covered are:

- Bio-sphere;
- Greenhouse effect;
- Ozone layer depletion;
- Use of fertilizers and pesticides;
- Wildlife protection;
- Soil chemistry;
- Management of domestic and industrial waste;
- Pollution of noise, air, water and soil and control measures;
- Ecosystem;
- Management of non-degradable substances;
- Edible and ornamental plants;
- Sewage disposal and cleaning of rivers;
- Nuclear energy;
- Radiation hazards;
- Gas leak;
- Wind power;
- Bio-energy; and
- Environmental laws and acts.

Environmental concepts also extend to subject areas like languages and social sciences, which reinforce learning and internalization of all such concepts. The NCERT textbooks of Science and Technology, and integrated Social Sciences, however, provide a wide view of EE, highlighting various environmental problems and suggesting a variety of projects and community related activities to resolve environmental issues.

Higher Secondary Stage

This is the stage of diversification. Students opt for either the academic stream or the vocational stream. The treatment of concepts becomes deeper and more discipline oriented. Certain concepts of environmental education occur in different subjects and the books provide only restricted views of these.

Since the content caters to the demands of the concerned subject as an independent discipline, a comprehensive view about environmental education is not available in the textbooks. Majority of the concepts are found in the textbooks of Biology, Chemistry and Geography, which are optional subjects. Students opting for any one of these subjects would accordingly benefit in different aspects of environmental education, while others would remain deprived of this advantage. There is need for identifying the core content to be evolved on the basis of the concepts included within environmental education at the secondary level.

Considerable variation in the presentation of content has been noticed in the different textbooks. The topics constitute isolated entities and the focus has thus got diffused.

The coverage of environmental education concepts in the textbooks of various subjects includes:

1. Environment and sustainable development;
2. Atmospheric pollution-global warming, greenhouse effect, acid rain, and ozone layer depletion;
3. Water pollution-international standards of drinking water, importance of dissolved oxygen in water, bio-chemical oxygen demand and chemical oxygen demand;
4. Land pollution - pesticides;
5. Ecology;
6. Strategy for control of environmental pollution - the management of waste and green chemistry;
7. Economic growth and development, current challenges of economy, poverty and environmental degradation;
8. Importance of protecting the environment;
9. Environment and behavior - reducing environmental stresses;
10. Understanding life on earth - world climates, natural vegetation, soil, water, drainage system, transport and communication;
11. Natural hazards and disasters (earthquakes, cyclones, floods, droughts and landslides) and their management;
12. Population and biotic community;
13. Eco-system and species;
14. Conservation of natural resources including wildlife conservation;

15. Growth of human population and its effect on environment;
16. Economic importance of trees;
17. Damage to environment by overexploitation of natural resources;
18. Impact of ill planned industrialization;
19. Scientific management of sewage;
20. Alternative automobile fuel;
21. Conservation of energy and alternative sources of energy - solar, geo-thermal, wind and biomass; and
22. Role of government and community in conservation of environment and the environmental laws.

The review of the environmental themes in the textbooks at different stages of school education reaffirms that textbooks, by and large, have environmental concepts included in them.

Higher Education and Research

There are many disciplines in higher education, which also cover some areas of environmental concepts mentioned earlier. A separate course on Environment Science (Environmentology) has been introduced as a counterpart of environmental Engineering Course. Areas of study in such courses may be grouped under the broad following heads:

- Environment Planning and Resource Development;
- Environmental Impact Studies;
- Ecological Disturbances and Environmental Degradation with national, international and global perspectives;
- Investigation of various Pollutants and Exotic Agents;
- Planning and Management of Solid and Liquid Wastes, Collection and Transportation for different localities;
- Materials Re-cycle and Re-use;
- Instrumentation in Environment Studies, etc.

Professional Courses

At the professional level, the major aim of environment education is to develop specialized knowledge and technical skills on environmental issues.

Lawyers are increasingly assuming an important role in protecting environment. Appropriate course structure to be designed to enforce the existing environment laws but also to create awareness of the need for enacting modern laws against environment degradation.

Society requires a service on "Preventive and Social Medicine" from a medical practioners. Thus, a certain amount of content in the area of environment or in the style of Medical Environment should be incorporated within this course with modern outlook.

In all branches of Engineering appropriate environmental issues related to the discipline concerned have already been introduced in creating, modifying and developing the environment of mankind. Environment Engineering as a separate full-fledged course has already been introduced as a modern course of study.

Environmental Education is now an essential component of all types of Teacher Education Courses. Teachers have the main responsibility to transmit the environment related proper knowledge, concept, skills and attitude to the next generations and to develop a culture of environment protection.

Teaching-Learning Methodology of Environment Education

As regards the modalities of introducing EE, the following alternative approaches may be suggested:

Allowing the state governments to prepare their own syllabi based on a framework provided by the NCERT with each state ensuring that the syllabi cater effectively to all the eco-zones of the concerned state;

Providing the states with separate syllabi for EE prepared by the NCERT;

Formulating a broad framework for EE for schools, which would help them, plan their own detailed syllabi and strategies.

A large number of transactional modalities have been suggested which include:

- Narration of events, experiences and stories;
- Assignments and projects;
- Field trips and visits;
- Establishing eco clubs;
- Field studies and surveys;
- Brain storming and quizzes;
- Role play and drama;
- Lectures and demonstrations;
- Discussions;

- Case studies;

All the above transactional modalities/strategies need to use an open-ended, problem-solving approach in devising class work so as to promote knowing about, feeling for, loving and protecting the environment. A graded, action-oriented, value based course in environmental education for all classes/levels of schooling is to be formulated without adding to the curriculum load.

Environmental Education Teaching Methodology

An Example

A five-step teaching method can be adopted, namely,

(i) Warming up, (ii) Exploration, (iii) Conceptualization, (iv) Consolidation and (v) Extension, for teaching environmental education at the school level to promote cognitive, affective and psycho-motor dimensions of learning output of young learners. This is a mixed method of formal (I to iv) and informal (v) teaching –learning process. The method is described below with an example:

Unit: Endangered Animal Species (For a period of approximately 50 minutes)

Activity 1 (Warming up: 5 minutes)

Purpose

- To stimulate students' interest in Endangered Animal Species of the World;
- To activate students' background knowledge;
- To introduce students to vocabulary that will help them to successfully complete the lesson.

Procedure

1. Write the phrase "Endangered Animal Species" in the black-board, and ask the students what they think about it.
2. As students volunteer their responses, write key words from their reactions on the blackboard. If the students are unfamiliar with the concept of endangered species, relevant information to be provided by adding some key words about the concept.
3. Ask students if they can name some of the reasons behind

some of the animals being endangered. List the reasons on the blackboard.

Activity 2 (Exploration: 25 minutes)

Purpose

- To have students explore some of the reasons that animal species become endangered;
- To allow students to practice listening, speaking, reading and note-taking about the concept in a meaningful way;
- To give students the opportunity to use key vocabulary and characteristics of the concept of the lesson.

Procedure

1. Distribute the Summary Chart of the Endangered Animal Species, one to each student and tell them that they are going to learn about the problems facing each of the endangered species listed in the sheet.
2. Put students into pair, and give one case history to each pair of students.
3. Explain the task to the students that they are to work in pairs using the information in the case history to find the relevant information they need about their assigned species.
4. Students read the case histories in pairs, consult themselves and make notes in the appropriate boxes on the Endangered Species Summary Form.
5. Have pairs take turns giving their Summary Reports to the class. As students listen, they attempt to complete their charts with the information being reported. Encourage students to ask for repetition and clarification if necessary.

Activity 3 (Conceptualization: 15 minutes)

Purpose

- To provide students with opportunities to use appropriate vocabulary in a meaningful way;
- To allow students to explain the concept in his/ her own terminology;
- To reinforce vocabulary and key concepts associated with the lesson;

- To give students the opportunity to be successful in asking further questions, giving personal observations.

Procedure

Tell the students that they are going to have whole class discussion and they may use the notes they made on the Summary Sheets for the purpose.

Conduct a whole-class discussion session centering on the following (probable) questions:

1. What are the main reasons that Asian Elephants are in trouble?
2. Which animals are the big threats to Kagus?
3. What are some of the problems that have caused Rhinoceros to become endangered?
4. Why the Leatherback Sea Turtle has become endangered?
5. Which species are in trouble because of habit destruction?
6. Which species are endangered because people like to collect them for various purposes?
7. Name some plants, which have become endangered like animals.

Activity 4 (Consolidation: 5 minutes)

Purpose

- To conclude the formal lesson;
- To provide an opportunity to discuss the relevance of the lesson;
- To apply the new knowledge in the real life.

Procedure

1. Ask students once again to name some reasons that some animal species become endangered.
2. Ask students to name other endangered animals or plants including causes of their threat.
3. Ask students to collect further information from Internet resources.
4. Ask students to summarize the whole discussion in their own languages.
5. Ask students about the significance of the lesson as perceived by the students.
6. Make an exit discussion.

Activity 5 (Possible Extensions of the Lesson)

Purpose

- To extend the knowledge in the real world;
- To fill up the gaps of theoretical knowledge;
- To make students inquisitive to the problem of our environment.

Procedure

1. Have students do a mini-survey on endangered animals and plants in their locality. Students can interview of 10-20 senior people asking the names of the specimens which were frequently found in the locality 20-30 years back but now rarely found or never found and causes of its extinction. A report can be developed on the basis of the information collected.
2. Students and civil society jointly can organize an awareness program through exhibition of photographs, seminars, discussions on endangered specimen in the locality.
3. Students with the civil society can chalk out a plan for preservation of the endangered specimen in the locality.

Conclusion

"Creating a society of motivated citizens committed to conservation, preservation and protection of the environment and striving towards a life in perfect harmony with nature," is the global mission that could be achieved through nurturance of young minds by developing an awareness of and concern about the environment and its associated problems. In this process the learners will develop the requisite knowledge, skills, attitudes, motivation and commitment to work individually and collectively towards a better man-nature relationship. This is actually not a new concept to the Indians. Traditionally, Indian wisdom has always perceived human beings as an integral and central constituent of nature. Our desire for a long, healthy, enlightened and joyful life had been made us invoke the forces and elements of nature, usually in a deified form, to bless him/ her and progeny, loving, understanding, fearing and befriending nature, not through conquering, exploiting, defiling or abusing it. The present situation of environmental degradation has been evolved with the western concept of development, which has been spreading throughout the globe. Thus, in spite of its very complex form, the goal, preservation of environment, could be achievable, if appropriate pedagogical methods are evolved and designed for the purpose.

The EE is equally important in the non-formal and informal sectors of education too, if not more than the formal system of education. For developing a desired culture among the common people of all sectors, rural or urban, literate or illiterate, rich or poor, optimum scope of both the non-formal and informal education systems required to be strengthened. In reality, to provide education to rural people, on environmental problems or for that matter on any issue on environment, is an extremely difficult task as it is associated with the economic, social and cultural conditions of the people. Inequality spectrum is most crucial in determining as to who can adopt any novel method for environment protection. In this very broad scenario, the scope for the weaker section to adopt any environment protection issue, say, any alternative energy scheme and accrue benefit from it is rare, especially, when it concerns with the financial involvement. The traditions and perceptions play very important roles in the behavior pattern of human beings in general. These are deeply rooted in the way of life, particularly in the rural life. In the urban areas also almost the similar scenario is noticed particularly in the slums. Even among the vast array of educated people in the middle and upper strata of the society, working in private and public offices, industries and business houses, running their own business and firms, etc., are not so aware about the serious problem of environmental degradation, though they read newspapers, journals or leaflets, view telecasts or films or visit different places, fairs, festivals etc. Use of plastic bags is a simple example of such problem. It is not so easy to motivate all section of the society for environmental protection unless the strong non-formal and informal systems of education are also evolved for the purpose along with the formal system. The matter is urgently knocking our doors demanding immediate sensible actions, otherwise, we will be held responsible for any forthcoming disaster due to man-made environmental upset. Time is ticking away.

Environment Education

An Indian Perspective

FAISAL ZIA SIDDIQUI AND TAUSEEF Z. SIDDIQUI

To overcome the environmental problems such as global warming, ozone depletion, deforestation, loss of biodiversity, protection of oceans and fresh water resources it is necessary to make the people aware about its consequences and schools, colleges and universities are the best place for imparting Environmental Education (EE). In India more than 90% states have now developed some type of environmental education guidelines and course curriculum at the level of schools, colleges and universities. The UGC has made it compulsory to all the universities and colleges in India to introduce a compulsory paper of environmental studies at undergraduate level as per the directives of the Hon'ble Supreme Court of India. (UGC DO No. F.131/2000 (EA/ENV/COSI) 24 July 2002).

Environmental Education: Indian Scenario

Environmental Education (EE) programmes in India gained momentum during the last three decades. In a country like India with vast geographic area, richness and uniqueness of ecosystems, and diversity of socio-cultural environment, most of the EE programmes do not address issues of the entire country. Therefore, development and implementation of EE perspectives to cover location/region-specific concerns would require specific strategies. The ultimate goal of EE is to bring about changes in attitudes and behavior patterns of citizens and enable them to act and react wisely in situations involving environmental quality.

Environmental education means the educational process dealing with man's relationship with his natural and man-made surroundings, and includes the relation of population, pollution, resource allocation and depletion, conservation, transportation, technology and urban and rural planning to the total human environment. Environmental education may also be defined as a process for developing skills and attitudes necessary to understand and appreciate the inter-relationships between man, his nature and his biophysical surroundings.

It is obvious from these definitions that environmental education takes a holistic approach and as such it is inherently interdisciplinary in nature. Environmental education has been a failure to prepare citizens who are more responsive to environmental problems. The main reason for this is cited to be the lack of sound national strategies for environmental education. Most environmental education strategies only focus at awareness level (which tends to be ineffective in changing behavior) and thus fail to instill ownership and empowerment in learners. Environmental education gets least priority because other immediate development issues become more pressing for the government.

Barrier, Constraints and Drawbacks

The widespread practices for the promotion of environmental education in India have been unsuccessful through the years in many ways. Unfortunately, to-date the subject of environmental education is linked with the subject of Environmental Studies', which focuses on providing students with scientific facts and figures on global environmental problems. It addresses environmental issues from a viewer's point of view by identifying the primary sources and proposing corrective measures needed to redress the symptoms, for example, ozone depletion and global warming. Therefore, students end up knowing what is wrong with the planet but can in no way understand what should be done by 'them' as individuals, neither can they see or join how to become responsible for the environmental problems and hence, understand how they need to help solve issues by changing their own lifestyles.

Some schools think that students only need to be given information on environmental problems which will sensitize them to nature and once they have been empowered with data they will be able to take up the cause of the environment. They make student take up campaigns to save the endangered and rare species or start awareness campaigns on a host of issues like control of vehicular pollution. All these efforts are creditable however; there is no knowing whether the students learning all this will be able to take the right decisions about the planet with its wealth of life forms. Misplaced in most of these are clear-cut norms and methods of living sustainably and in tune with the earth. The need of the hour is initiating cultural changes that are necessary to make the shift to more ecologically sustainable lives.

Above all, the techniques adopted in EE have not helped people realize that individuals can bring about an optimistic change and need to improve their own surroundings and communities by becoming accountable and proactive, 'community minded' society.

The main problems in environmental education that India is facing can be summarized as follows:

Curriculum Load

There is a tremendous pressure from parents and community that school curriculum has become very heavy and is responsible for development of stress among students and thereby affecting their normal development. The problem of curriculum load is a complex one and has its roots in many related issues.

Preparation of Teachers

Pre-services preparation and In-service training of teachers are major problems in implementation of environmental education curriculum. Given the huge number of teachers and geographical character of the country, management of in-service programmes is indeed a challenge.

Methods of Assessment

The present assessment/evaluation system in science education is a major bottleneck in bringing improvement in the education system of our country. Unfortunately, what is not relevant to examination is not considered relevant in teaching and learning. Framework of assessment used is not conducive to the development of problem-solving skill among the pupils – given the fact that instruction is mainly assessment-driven in India. Further, assessment of practical work is not attached much importance–resulting in utter neglect of practical work in impart of education.

The way environmental education is being dealt with in schools in India therefore, needs to be completely revamped and clearly-defined methods should be laid out for easy applicability in schools, bearing in mind the following aspects which have to be the foundation of this change:

- To work more towards a cultural change that leads us ultimately into living more sustainable lives.
- To venture ecological education a core subject of our education and also includes environmental perception into the other subjects.
- To transform thinking patterns that the earth is ours for the taking. We have to understand more about the nature of this finite earth and then work out ways and regulate ourselves to live sustainably and in harmony with it.
- To become more community minded citizens.

Framework for Analysis of Environmental Education

Environmental education is learner-centered, providing students with opportunities to create their own understandings through hands-on, minds-on investigations. Learners are engaged in direct experiences and are challenged to use higher-order thinking skills. Environmental education supports the development of an active learning community where learners share ideas and expertise, and prompt continued analysis. Environmental education provides real-world contexts and issues from which concepts and skills can he learned.

Environmental education recognizes the importance of viewing the environment within the context of human influences, incorporating an examination of economics, culture, political structure, and social justice as well as natural processes and systems. The goal of environmental education is to develop an environmentally literate community. Through comprehensive, consistent programs, learners explore how feelings, experiences, attitudes, and perceptions influence environmental issues.

They become knowledgeable about natural processes and systems and gain an understanding of human processes and systems. Learners are able to explore and analyze environmental problems and issues using a variety of techniques. They also use basic science and math skills and discover the nature of unfairness. They develop a sense of their rights and responsibilities as citizens, are able to understand the ideals, principles, and practices of citizenship in our democratic republic, and they gain the skills necessary for responsible citizenship.

A knowledgeable, skilled, and proactive community is a key to resolving the environmental issues that promise to become increasingly significant in the next century. While our schools play a major role, cultivating environmental literacy is a task that neither begins nor ends with formal education. Many parts of our society shape attitudes toward and knowledge about the environment-family, peers, religion, community, interest groups, government, the media, etc.

Environmental education often begins close to home, encouraging learners to understand and build connections with their immediate surroundings. The awareness, knowledge, and skills needed for these local connections and understandings provide a foundation for moving out into larger systems, broader issues, and a more sophisticated understanding of causes, connections, and consequences.

Environmental education fosters skills and habits that people can use throughout their lives to understand and act on environmental issues. It emphasizes critical and creative thinking skills along with other higher level thinking processes that are key to identifying, investigating, and analyzing issues, and formulating and evaluating alternative solutions. Environmental education builds the capacity of learners to work individually as well as cooperatively to improve environmental conditions.

For each environmental issue there is not just one right answer or solution—there are many perspectives and much uncertainty. Environmental education cultivates the ability to recognize uncertainty, envision alternative scenarios, and adapt to changing conditions and information.

Knowledge, skills, and habits of mind translate into a civil society that is better able to address its common problems and create lifestyles that are more in tune with the earth.

Underlying Principle

There is far too much confusion today, in India, on the subject of environmental education, with regard to both its content and the manner in which the subject is taught. Trained resource persons should come in and help the schools teach the subject since most school teachers are not formally trained or have little experience to teach this subject. It is clear that on the subject of environmental education, most city schools and educationists need some definite direction with clearly spelt out goals and methods as described below:

We must accept the present system of education and the limitations that it faces. To accept ground-reality that environmental education has also failed in India and consequently, understand and document the reasons for this adversity.

To bear two important points in mind while thinking of environmental education, a) we should be clear as to what outcomes we are looking for in environmental education and b) to try and formulate a strategy plan that will ensure that environmental education is taught in the correct manner and achieves the set goals. Environmental education should impart knowledge that allows one to live a sustainable lifestyle and provide practical solutions that can be adopted by individuals in their day-to-day lives. Schools should become grounds for learning about sustainability.

To adopt a multi-pronged approach to tackle the different aspects of disseminating environmental education successfully.

We must improve Teacher Training Courses by incorporating new modules like environmental education so that the new generation of teachers is better equipped to teach the subject. Moreover, the biggest obstacle facing environmental education in India is that teachers are not armed with any successful models of environmental education Practices that focus on sustainability and can be emulated and replicated. No models have been assessed, documented or compiled into a single manual for easy reference by teachers, though there are many successful prototypes of environmental education in India that have been tried and tested by educational institutions.

Therefore the immediate task is to develop a comprehensive, scientifically accurate, technically sound and easily replicated models of environmental education programs and projects that can be adopted by the schools. It is vital to document and highlight these successful models of environmental education, which can help future generations to lead more sustainable lives.

The topic of environmental education is being deliberated upon by the Supreme Court of India. NCERT and even State Education Boards across the country are coming together with EEists and experts to arrive at a consensus on various issues pertaining to the teaching of this subject. As the matter proceeds in the Supreme Court, the confusion becomes even more apparent. In an affidavit submitted to the Supreme Court almost all the State Education Boards have stated that they have dealt with environmental education through the infusion method i.e. introduced it through the other subjects. The Supreme Court vetoed the infusion method and directed NCERT to prepare a clearly defined syllabus and lay out a policy for all Education Boards to follow.

The surest way to ensure a positive change in the way environmental education is taught in schools is by developing good Teacher Training Course Material for educators across the country. Hence, the dire need to conduct a study on the 'Best Practices of environmental education focuses on 'sustainability' in the country and document these successful models. The documentation can be then compiled into a Teachers' Manual, which can then be printed, published and distributed throughout the country by NCERT.

It is firmly believed that environmental education needs to be a subject through which children are actually taught to 'change their lives' and 'live more sustainable lifestyles'. This is not an easy task for schools but the way forward would be to:

1. Explore different ways in which one can adopt sustainable means in different areas of ones lifestyle by making schools grounds of sustainable practices.
2. To investigate if any schools or educational institutions have introduced such models of environmental education, which have been successful through the years and document the same?
3. To document the best practices of successful models of sustainability since these have been tried and tested by the schools.
4. To disseminate the information so that it can be replicated and taught by schools, teacher training colleges and all institutions all over the country in urban areas.

To quote some examples of best practices of sustainability in schools:

- **Waste Management in schools** - for e.g. separation of wet and dry garbage and vermicomposting.
- **Improving Energy Efficiency in schools** - for example, Methods to prevent the wastage of electricity in schools using renewable and non-conventional energy sources like solar panels and solar cookers.
- **Water – Conservation techniques** - for example, Rain water harvesting.
- **Growing organic food** - for example, City farming project with vermicomposting and minimal external inputs and establishing school nurseries.
- **Soil Regeneration** – for example, making soil with kitchen waste and preparation of rich nursery soil to add to degraded soil.
- **Transport** – for example, Innovative methods to ensure minimum use of fuel per school.
- **Practicing the 3 R's of Reduce, Re-use and Re-cycle** - for example, Paper saving techniques, using colours from natural materials for art work in schools such as using flower petals and leaves for colouring and vegetable colours instead of lead-based paints.

SYLLABUS FOR ENVIRONMENTAL STUDIES IIIRD YEAR DIPLOMA IN ENGG. (Civil/Electrical/Instrumentation/Mechanical/ Architecture/DDC/DDH)

COURSE NO : BCE-320 PDS/WEEK-01
SESSIONAL MARKS : 10 TOTAL MARKS : 50

- Unit-I Introduction to the Environment
- Definition, scope and importance, Need for public awareness. Natural resources and associated problems, Ecosystem - its components and energy flow.
- Unit-II Causes and Impact of Environmental Degradation
- Factors affecting environmental degradation. Global warming, Acid rain, ozone depletion, deforestation and desertification. Population explosion.
- Unit-III Types of Pollution-I
- Types of pollution, Classification, sources and effects of Air and Water pollution. Type of control methods.
- Unit-IV Types of Pollution-II

- Classification, sources and effects of Land, Solid/ Hazardous Waste and Noise pollution. Type of control methods. Role of an individual in prevention of pollution
- Unit-V Management of Environment and Sustainability
- Concept of Sustainable Development, Environment Management System (EMS)/ISO 14001,Environmental issues related to the specific discipline.

As per the instructions of UGC and AICTE, The University Polytechnic under Faculty of Engineering & Technology, Aligarh Muslim University introduced the course in "Environmental Studies" in the curriculum of Final Year Diploma in Engineering (All branches) from the session 2004-2005. However rather than following the similar syllabus framed by UGC and AICTE, the important topics were selected and a new concise syllabus was developed which has been successfully implemented for the last three years.

But the confusion still remains among the students of Civil and Architecture who are already studying a course in Environmental Engineering in their 2nd year. Therefore, the members who were involved in the preparation of the Environmental studies syllabus at the National level were contacted to know their views on the following points:

1. If a course in environmental engineering is already running does the institution have to still introduce the course of environmental studies?
2. Can the existing syllabus of environmental engineering be modified to cover all the important topics of environmental studies?
3. Can any one of the above courses be dropped from the curriculum?

The response is still awaited from them.

Competencies and forms of learning

Competence-oriented educational concepts focus on output, whereas the conventional syllabuses, traditional method of learning and didactic approaches focus on input: the later raises the question about which subjects people should study. By contrast, the output apporach asks what problem solving strategies, concepts and abilities for social action they should have. It is only logical to think about these lines. After all, it does not help much to define only what children and youth should be taught and not to define what should be learned, and then children and young people and their parents-as well as the educational administration—can demand that this knowledge, these skills be imparted. Another advantage is that the learning content can be freely selected. When skills acquisition, as opposed to retrievable school knowledge, is important, student's choices of content and their acquisition of skills, thereby preventing the mere accumulation of 'inert knowledge' (Weinert, 2000).

In Indian perspective, the medley of constructive, free choice and traditional approaches should be adopted. The blending of all these approach which focuses on more on problem based learning (PBL), this concept of Problem Based learning where the common people can think and take up the environmental issues in a more pragmatic sense and can think critically in that context. This approach can act as a catalyst and play a crucial role in imparting Education for Sustainable Development (ESD) in a more amicable and fruitful manner, there must be an interrelationship between the different sections of the society, just take an example when a student comes into his/her house infused with all the tools and knowledge of envirnomental issues and he/she obviously watches

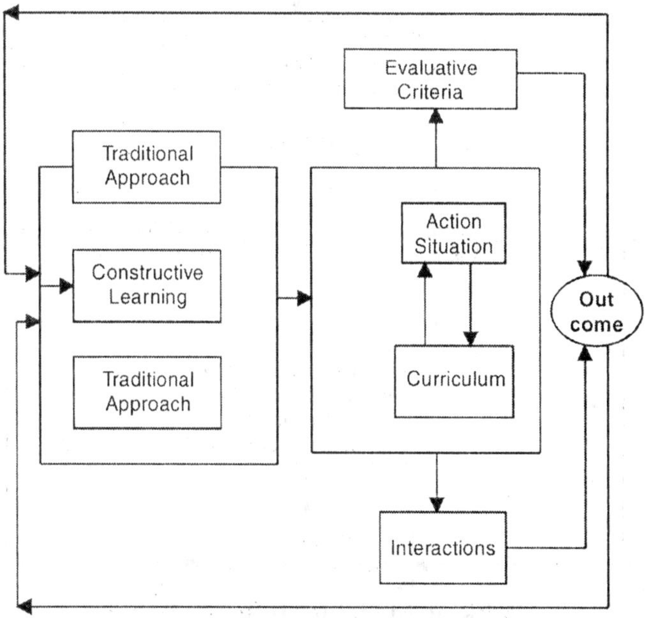

her/his parent activities and in any case the parents are not having the knowledge about environmental concepts and issues, they through away the waste, which directly effects the thinking and wont of the children, as children are usually make their parents as their role models, and if they see them doing these type of activities they usually think on the same road and will never become an environmentally literate citizen in practical manner.

Over the last decade there has been a meteoric change in our country in the field of Environmental Education (EE) and a lot of initiatives are taken by the private players, government and NGOs in this context and they doing a commendable effort in this field in shaping the citizens of tomorrow into a literate green citizens, citizens of sustainable thinking.

Development of working model for informal and formal Environment Education

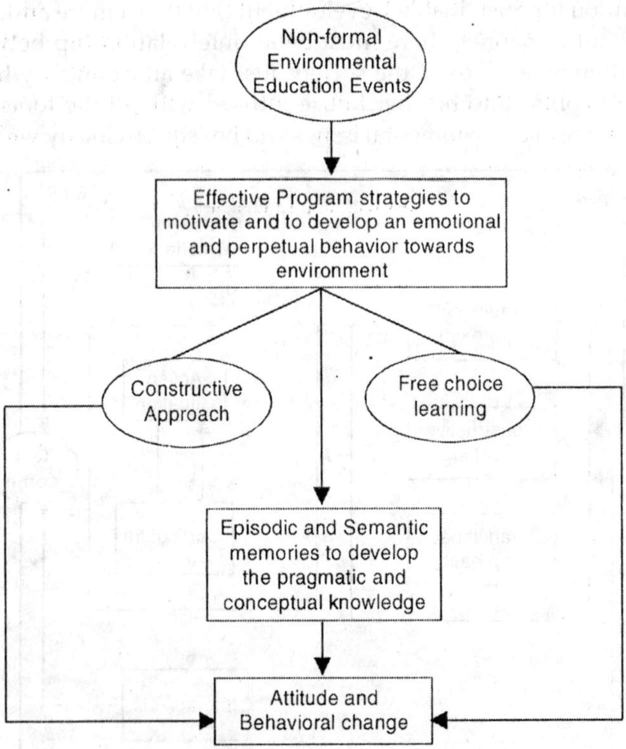

Working Model for Informal Sector

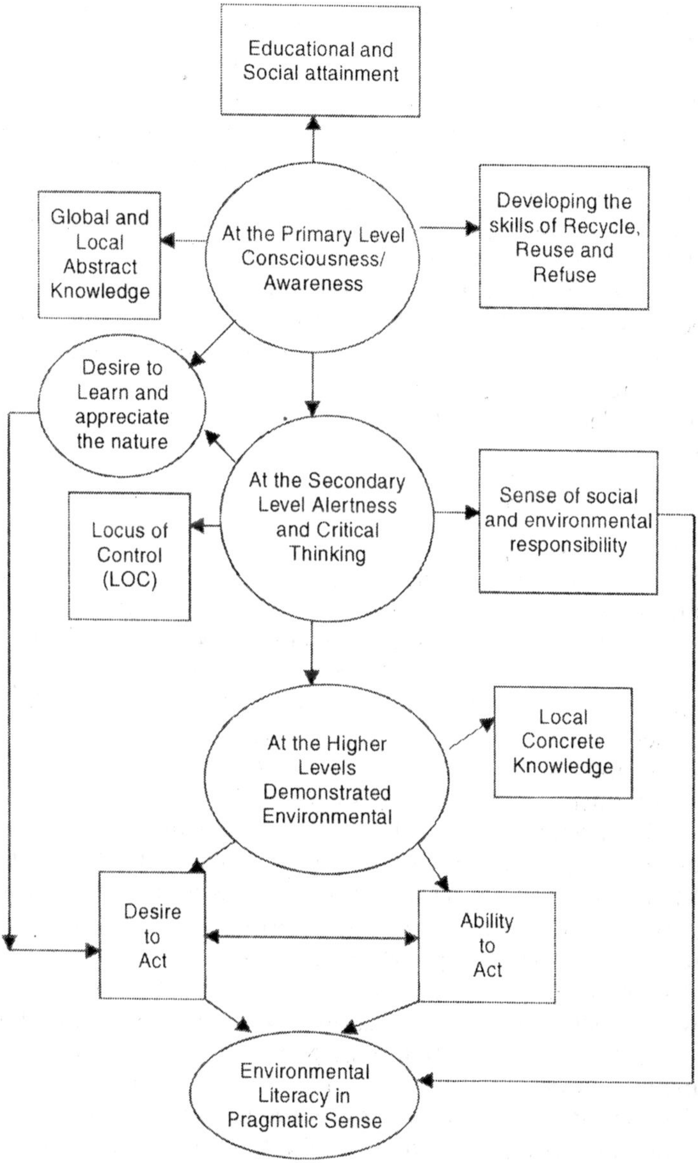
Educational and Social attainment
Global and Local Abstract Knowledge
At the Primary Level Consciousness/ Awareness
Developing the skills of Recycle, Reuse and Refuse
Desire to Learn and appreciate the nature
At the Secondary Level Alertness and Critical Thinking
Locus of Control (LOC)
Sense of social and environmental responsibility
At the Higher Levels Demonstrated Environmental
Local Concrete Knowledge
Desire to Act
Ability to Act
Environmental Literacy in Pragmatic Sense

Components of the Model

Definitions of environmental education and education for sustainability (for example, UNESCO, 1978; Sterling, 1992; UNESCO, 1993) imply that it is a process (rather than a fixed goal), which attempts to create an environmentally responsible population that contributes to sustainable development, and consists of a number of discrete (but related) components. These environmental components include information, awareness, concern, attitudes/beliefs, education and training, knowledge, skills, literacy and responsible behaviour.

In order to design a 'working model' of environmental education numerous components are involved. There are different phases of ones education that is at primary level, secondary level, and higher level. There are different approaches, which are analysed in the present model and are explained in the subsequent sections.

1. At the Primary Level

The students of class (1st to 5th) are in their immature phase and the school administration must focus perpetually in developing the students a more educational and social attainment towards studies and telling them the basic principles of Recycle, Reuse, Recover and Refuse. The teachers should try to give them the basic and abstract knowledge of both Global and Local environmental issues, which indirectly helps the students to develop the tinge of Consciousness/Awareness about the environment and its significance in their lives and surroundings.

Children have always had an immediate interest in the trees, bugs and birds outside their classroom in this early phase of their lives. Teachers have traditionally used the outdoors as a way to make science come alive and to bring together a variety of disciplines, such as math and social studies. Teachers report that environmental education captures their students' attention more readily than many other topics. Given the widespread concern over academic achievement in Indian schools, especially in science and math, environmental education holds great promise for boosting the quality of learning in our classrooms at this early stage and hence the first part of the proposed model solely focuses in developing a desire to learn and to appreciate the nature.

2. At the Secondary Level

The students of class grade VIth to Xth are in their transition phase of their educational spectrum. They are having a sense of social and environmental responsibility and the teachers must focus in that area, as to how to motivate and inspire the students in that context, also to groom them to think critically and creatively towards the issues of sustainable development and to develop an understanding towards both global and local environmental issues. The perpetual focus must be towards developing a sense of 'Locus of Control'. Locus of control (LOC) is a general concept, which can be applied in any context to individual's perception of their ability to bring about change through their own behaviour. If the individual believes that events or outcomes of situations are the direct results of his/her actions, he/she has an internal Locus of Control. In a meta-analysis of research on environmentally responsible behaviour, Hines et al. (1987) found that an internal Locus of Control is likely to effect/change and can have an ever-lasting impact on the students' attitudes and behaviour of the students. Students with an external Locus of Control do not try to bring about change because they thought they are helpless and are unable to do any thing.

3. At the Higher Level

This category includes a wide range, the undergraduates, graduates, postgraduates and lastly the student in higher secondary. At this juncture of their lives they are pragmatically and theoretically very sound pertaining to the issues of environmental education, the only area which needs to be worked upon is of giving the concrete and in depth knowledge of the local issues, to inspire them and to develop in them the desire to act according to the situation, a demonstrated environmental action needs to be taken by them.

Perception of environmentally responsible behaviour as the social norm may cause social pressure on individuals to conform; 'If a social norm for environmentally responsible behaviour existed, more students might behave responsibly, even if they do not have strong attitudes about environmental protection' (Newhouse, 1990). In other words, environmental behaviour may be influenced by what students believe is 'the doing thing'. Traditionally, environmental education has been as concerned with promoting "responsible environmental behaviour" as it has been with teaching children about the environment. However, there is no consensus among parents or the community at large on what constitutes environmentally responsible behaviour or to what extent schools should encourage students to take action on behalf of an environmental cause. The field should place its emphasis on building environmental knowledge, not on promoting a particular kind of behaviour.

The present model of formal education is especially designed in terms of Indian context but can be replicated in other developing countries as well; it can also be helpful for the teachers, regulators and policy makers to form a strategy towards environmental education.

Strategies for Promotion of Environment Education

EE has obtained momentum but has not been able to make the quantum leap towards preventing, stopping and reversing environmental degradation. Some of the reasons given below may help explain the situation and describe the stumbling blocks for environmental education in the region.

The problems of environmental education are universal in nature and directly related to the complex problems of development process, persistent poverty, growing population and environmental degradation.

Environmental themes are widely integrated into formal education courses. Yet we do not know how effective they are in real-life situations, or if formal education is the best way to achieve a sustainable society, a society that meets the needs of the present generation without compromising the needs of future generations. Research is necessary to provide the answers.

Numerous NGOs and other organizations are involved in the field of environmental education. Any organization can boast that it is successfully undertaking environmental education related activities. Nevertheless, there is also duplication of activities and competition among different organizations. When this is so, then it is necessary to determine their status and synergize their strengths in promoting environmental education in the region.

Finally, merely raising awareness is not enough to promote environmental education. Environmental education must go beyond awareness rising. It must inspire interest and encourage people to pilot-test new ideas and then, based on their evaluation, adopt them as integral parts of their lives. For this, more projects and actions are required to provide role models for successful environmental education efforts.

Networking and Building Collaborations and Partnerships

Networking with experts, educationists and researchers in the field of Sustainable Practices and/or environmental education so as to identify different successful models of environmental education that are being practiced or can be put into,practice by schools/ institutions across the country that focus on sustainability. For example, the best model that addresses important environmental issues like

I. Water conservation,
II. Efforts for the conservation/restoration of flora-n-fauna or any efforts improving neighbourhoods, or efforts that brings in a sense of respect for nature
III. Waste management, efforts at reducing consumptive patterns of individuals, essentially practice of the 3R's
IV. Energy conservation,
V. Soil regeneration and growing food
VI. Community service with regard to the environment.

Studying the Identified Successful Models of Environmental Education

Studying the identified sustainable models, one each for the different environmental issues of (i) water conservation, (ii) efforts for the conservation/restoration of flora-n-fauna or even any efforts at improving neighborhoods, or efforts that bring in a sense of respect for nature (iii) waste management, efforts at reducing consumptive patterns of individuals, essentially practice of the 3 R's (iv) energy conservation, (v) soil regeneration and growing food (vi) community service with regard to the environment by gathering primary data and preliminary material. The models can be spread far and wide across India but each must be studied in detail so as to get an insight into the models unique features and characteristics. The models should also be judged for easily replicability by other schools and teaching institutions.

Site Visit

The site at which the chosen models are being practiced should be documented in great detail with the use of photographs. Observations of the techniques, materials, resources, costs and people involved can be closely documented to gain a better understanding of the rationale, methodology used and in what manner it has been effective, including how successfully the students are implementing it, how motivated they are as well as how have the people in the locality reacted to that model and if they been empowered to use the model as well. In short getting as much information as possible in order to assess the model's viability and applicability, especially in urban areas.

Compilation of All Documented Material

Compiling all the documented material in readiness for its dissemination is the most important and the final stage. All the best practices should be compiled with visual aides to enable the models to be easily replicated and put into practice. The methodology can be made as simple as possible as easy comprehension. The final document can then be printed into a Teachers' Handbook for schoolteachers or Manual cum Guidebook for the Teachers' Training Colleges. The Manual or Handbook can also be supplemented with audio-visual presentations for example, a slide show or CD.

As we are entering in next millennium its essential for our experts to review the EE materials, this will help in closing the gap between what environmental scientists know and what the public and students needs to know. Current environmental education and training programs are stressed on controlling, remediation or clean up environmental problems. Therefore, teachers need continuing awareness, EE and related training programs to keep up with the complexity of environmental problems and technologies and strategies to reduce environmental risks. Because more than 90% of the world population growth and much of the economic growth expected in the next 40-50 years will be in developing countries it's important that EE must made a priority.

Conclusion

Though various measures have been initiated by various governmental and non-governmental agencies to promote and foster environmental education, the overall achievement has not been satisfactory so far. Existing environmental education programs only generate awareness and sensitivity but do not focus at the skill and attitude levels. School children do not get opportunities to develop skills to analyze and evaluate local, regional, or national environmental problems or issues. Thus, it seems that the existing formal education programs have failed to inculcate a sense of ownership and empowerment in school children.

As in all other areas, education and awareness raising efforts are critical in shaping people's perception, attitudes, and behavior towards environmental concerns. These efforts enable individuals to appreciate better environmental policies, legislation and regulation, and foster individual responsibility toward sustainable resource management and development.

Documenting successful models and best practices of environmental education with a focus on sustainability will be beneficial for schools, educators, researchers in the field and environmentalists since the teachers yet do not know how to go about imparting environmental education. It would also help NCERT provide resource material as per the National Policy. However, the biggest beneficiary and greatest victor in due course will be planet earth!

Imagine if all the sustainable models of environmental education are put into practice by millions of students all over India, it becomes a part of their lives and brings forth an attitudinal change - well that will be a revolution of sorts!

Lastly, it can be concluded that though the existing environmental education programs do not seem to be satisfactory, the future looks promising. Moreover in planning to develop school curricula on conservation education at the national level. It is hoped that these steps will bring desirable results in the future in sustaining precious natural resources of India.

> *If you are planning* for a year - sow rice* for ten years - plant trees* for a hundred years - educate people A Chinese Proverb.*

> *"Let us sum up by recalling the new Panchsheel of the new millennium, that we should launch: (a) Child centred education; (b) Woman centred family; (c) Human centred development; (d) Knowledge centred society; and (e) Innovation centred India."*

This mandate will help lead India into a knowledge society. The future India would develop into a learning society with scientific temper.

Tending of Diversity through A Robust Core Curriculum

Gender, Socio-economic Status, and Ethnicity as Components of Environment

Bruce Joyce, Marilyn Hrycauk, Walter Hrycauk and Emily Calhoun

This chapter renders the case study of a school division that built a core primary grade literacy curriculum built on current research on the teaching of literacy and studied the effects on the diverse students that it serves in its 15 elementary schools. The emphasis is on Kindergarten and Grade one curriculum, but the effects on student learning have been studied, at this point, through grade five. As such the report apparently not related to environmental education, however helps deduce how curricula act as an influential factor to infuse knowledge. Teachers may equip themselves through the study while dealing with environmental education.

Approaches to Accommodating Dating Diverse Student Populations

Generally, there are three approaches to meeting the needs of diverse student populations. In common, their emphasis has been on increasing the extent to which sub-populations have access to education that enables high achievement.

- The first emphasizes inclusion: Ensuring that various types of diverse students are not deprived of full participation in the mainstream schooling process and that equity in educational opportunity is achieved.

- The second emphasizes the development of program variations to support the development of students with ethnic, socioeconomic, or social/psychological characteristics that are different from the "mainstream" population.
- The third, the one discussed and reported here, builds on current research on the teaching of literacy and emphasizes the development of a robust core curriculum that has room for the development of the talents of nearly all students.

We have no intention of pitting the three approaches against one another. Inclusion is important. There are many natural forces that separate students from one another. Prominently, neighborhood differences in demography can generate inequalities related to socioeconomic status [SES] and ethnic differences, differences that can have a lifelong effect. [Use WASH DC example?] As difficult as it is, we need to seek ways to reduce the effects of *de facto* segregation and other forces that generate exclusion and inequality.

Targeted initiatives are important. We need to continue the search for ways of helping students whose characteristics make them candidates for low academic, social, and personal achievement. Efforts of developers like the SIMS group at the University of Kansas are vital. They are particularly so because large-scale initiatives to target students hampered by low socioeconomic environments have, on the whole, been very unsuccessful, as have many programs that serve students with mild or moderate learning disabilities. Interestingly, gender can be very important in the literacy areas. In many school districts, males lag seriously behind females from primary levels through high schools and, in the United States, college, where 60 percent of the enrollments are females and, once there, they outperform males on average. The strength of the core curriculum is important. First, the core curriculum (in this case the literacy curriculum) serves all students. We do not need to make the assumption that it is perfect—or does a good job with the mainstream students but not such a good job with others! And, we can wonder, does a robust curriculum pull all students, not just mainstream students, into higher levels of achievement through instruction and building a culture of higher achievement?

In Northern Lights we made a serious overhaul of our K-2 curriculum. In previous papers we have reported the considerable improvement in student literacy learning that has resulted on average *(see: Joyce, Hrycauk, and Calhoun, 2001; Hrycauk, 2002; and Joyce, Hrycauk, and Calhoun, 2003).* Here we concentrate on the effects on diverse populations.

We begin with a description of the curricular changes and its rationales, proceed to the provisions for staff development and the study of implementation, and then to the evaluation of student effects, including effects on the diverse populations served by the school division. These populations include genders, SES differences, students diagnosed as having learning disabilities, and ethnic differences (especially the progress of aboriginal students. While we have been able to report general effects on student learning, a recent change in provincial regulations now permits us to report data by SES and ethnicity.

The Northern Lights School District

The division is in northern Alberta and spans pver 200 km. with a geographic area of 14,800 square kilometers. Schools are located in the major towns of Cold Lake, Bonnyville, and Lac La Biche (these three have populations of about 6000), the villages of Glendon and Plamondon, the hamlet of Casden, and the rural areas of Ardmore, Ion River, and Wandering River. The division operates a school on 4 Wing, a major air force installation near Cold Lake.

With respect to the student population, there are about 6000 students. The genders are about equal. Students with mild to moderate learning disabilities comprise about 11 percent of the student population and about 8 percent are of interest here, because the diagnosed disabilities theoretically affect learning to read and write. Students whose parents identify them as aboriginal make up 28 percent of the population (1675 students). Of these, 230 are first nations persons who live on reservations and have "status rights," Including the rights to treaty benefits and to inherit land. Sixty-two students are first nations students who do not live on reservations and do not have status rights. Metis students have some aboriginal ancestors. There are 976 students or 16 percent of the district student population. There is one Inuit student—origins are in the artic areas of North America.

Historically, student achievement might be described as Canadian/US normal. Over the last decade, and before, "standard" test results have been relentlessly average.

Desiging the Curriculums

Here we will concentrate on the rationale for the K-1-2 curriculums. Because there have been controversial issues about the design and implementation of formal kindergarten programs because of issues about whether formal instruction is developmentally appropriate, we will allot somewhat more space to the kindergarten questions. However, issues over how to teach grade one and two students to read have been argued heatedly (as "phonics" verses "whole language" and the rationale for the curriculums we developed cuts across a number of those issues. Our purpose here is simply to try to provide the reader with an understanding about what the curriculums looked like and why.

What is Developmentally Appropriate?

For years, the term "developmentally-appropriate" has been the dominating phrase in discussions about kindergarten. Not only professionals but also laymen have come to use the phrase, partly because it was popularized by a leading psychologist who was also a columnist on child psychology for a popular magazine *(Elkind, 2001, 1987)*. To educators and laypeople alike, the term makes intuitive sense. "Of course, we would hope that schooling would make contact with the student's developmental level." However, the term got infected with "polar opposite disease." Again and again, the position was (and is) expressed that kindergarten-age students are not developmentally ready to learn to read. And, the picture drawn of teaching reading to young children is often of the worst kind of meaningless drill and practice with flashcards representing abstract words or sounds, even with made-up rather than real words. The use of that horrific picture raises a second and confusing question: Is the problem being raised one of developmental readiness or an aversion to a miserable curriculum? The mantra of developmental readiness has become so entrenched that even a panel of the leading scholars of reading curriculum, charged with making a comprehensive analysis of research on reading, dismissed the idea of kindergarten readers without even a nod toward relevant research *(Snow, Burns, and*

Griffin, 1998). They began their interpretations of research with grade one, apparently because the idea of teaching reading earlier was resoundingly dismissed by the experts. The polarization — putting a "play school" orientation against a harsh curriculum — is disseminated to the public regularly. The title of an April 2005 article in the San Diego Union-Tribune, "Kindergarten or 'Kindergrind' is an example. And the article reports that teachers scaled back literacy goals developed by school officials after a two-year conflict on the grounds of developmental readiness confounded by the idea that if you teach reading you do so harshly. For many decades San Diego Unified has been one of the least-troubled of the nation's large school systems, but a quarter or more of its students cannot read effectively as they graduate from the primary grades. But its kindergarten teachers construed an upgrade of their emergent literacy emphasis to be necessarily a move toward a harsh and rote curriculum *(Gao, 2005)*.

As we write, the position papers of national organizations continue to come from a "developmentally inappropriate" perspective (IRA, 1998; IRA and NAEYP, 1998). Some experts even question whether having "full day" kindergarten is too much, let alone a curriculum in reading (Natale, 2001). And, with all the controversies surrounding the United States No Child Left Behind initiative, kindergarten was notable chiefly by its absence. As in the Snow investigation, the National Reading Panel simply assumed that reading in kindergarten was not a live proposition (National Center, 2000).

The categorical rejection of a formal literacy curriculum in kindergarten is odd for several reasons. In the United Kingdom, year one students, who are the same age as kindergarten students in the United States, appear to learn to read with about the same success (and degrees of failure) as first grade students in the United States who are a year older. Also, one of the most respected scholars of early reading in the United States has presented an extensive argument *(Durkin, 1966)* for beginning early and her rationale is essentially unquestioned by other scholars. Further, in a longitudinal study, Hanson and Farrell (1995) found that the effects of a reading curriculum in kindergarten could be seen in the academic achievement of twelfth grade students. Finally, the "father" of the idea of Kindergarten, Fredrich Froebel emphasized the need for a rich environment that would pull students into inquiry and development; neither a free-play school in a play-only environment nor a rough-edged curriculum.

From our perspective the real issue is whether a systematic reading curriculum can be developmentally appropriate.

By the way, we are acquainted with some really fine emergent literacy classrooms. In them, there are rich classroom libraries — collections the children can pore over and ask the teacher to read selections aloud. Interesting field trips are mined for new language, tied to real experiences. The science-learning center is a place for observation and experimentation. The students may not learn to read, but they surely grow in cognitions and language development. Unfortunately, when the developmentally appropriate theory is taken to mean staying within what the students bring to school rather than enriching their development, the result is what Mike Schmoker characterized as the "Crayola Curriculum" *(Schmoker, 2001)*.

Curriculum Design

Important for our early literacy curriculum was the emergence of the Picture Word Inductive Model from the tradition of the language experience frame of reference with the addition of concept formation and attainment models of teaching *(Calhoun, 1999)*. The Picture Word Inductive Model designs cycles that begin with photographs of scenes whose content is within the ability of the students to describe. For example, photographs can be of aspects of the local community, or they can take students around the world with photos of scenes they can relate to- a picture of a boy in Nepal is an example. The students take turns identifying objects and actions in the picture. The teacher spells the words, drawing lines from the words to the elements in the picture to which they refer, creating a picture dictionary. The students are given copies of the words and they identify them using the picture dictionary. They proceed to classify the words using the well-tested inductive model of learning, noting their similarities and differences. The teacher selects some of their categories for extended study. Both phonetic features and structural characteristics are studied. The teacher models the creation of titles and sentences, and the students create same, dictating them and learning to read them. The students gradually learn to assemble titles and sentences into paragraphs about the content of the picture. The picture word cycles (inquiries into the pictures) generally take from three to five weeks.

A major assumption underpinning the curriculum is that students need to become inquirers into language, seeking to build their sight vocabularies and studying the characteristics of those words, trying to build generalizations about phonetic and structural characteristics.

Our image of a nurturant curriculum appears to differ widely from what many people imagine would be the shape of a curriculum for young children and which image causes those people to shy away from formal literacy instruction for kindergartners. We believe that the developmentally-appropriate issue is confounded by aversion to a harsh and rote curriculum. For our part, we did *not* imagine students with workbooks, alphabet flash cards, or letter-by-letter phonics drills. We imagined an environment where students would progress from their developed listening/speaking vocabularies to the reading of words, sentences, and longer text that they had created, where they would examine simple books in a relaxed atmosphere, where they would begin to write with scribbling and simple illustrations, where they would be read to regularly and where comprehension strategies would be modeled for them through the reading and study of charming fiction and nonfiction books. If the work of childhood is play, we imagined the students playfully working their way into literacy. We wished to create an environment where students would learn to read in a joyful fashion. From the literature on early reading, we identified several dimensions of learning to read *(see, Calhoun, 1999)*:

- The development of sight vocabulary. At first, this would come through the analysis of pictures (a large picture, 24 by 30 inches or more, would be the basis of study for three to five weeks. Imagine the students studying a picture of a woman holding a child in a market in Kuala Lampur. The students identify items and actions: "banana," "smile" "cars," and so on. These words are printed and spelled by the teacher with lines going from the words to the objects in the picture. Thus the words are within the students' listening-speaking vocabulary. Additional words are studied as the teachers' shares nonfiction and fiction books about markets around the world. Students visit these settings through their own exploration and reading of tradebooks.

- The inductive study of words. Students classify words, discovering phonetic and structural characteristics. They learn that the language is comprehensible — that words are almost always spelled the same, an onset in one word is likely to sound the same if it begins another word, that rimes have a lot of regularity, that adding "s" to *banana* and *smile* will create a plural, and taking "s" from *cars* will get you a single *car*.
- Wide reading at the developed level. At the beginning, students can engage at the picture level (see below) and, gradually can deal with caption level books as they learn how meaning is conveyed by the authors. They also learn to generate sentences from the words they have shaken out, at first dictating them "The woman is holding the boy." And paragraphs are created from the sentences. The teachers' model sentence and paragraph making. And, of course, the teachers read to the children regularly.
- Regular (several times daily) writing. At first they may just illustrate a word with a drawing. Gradually, students' progress to writing picture-related sentences and paragraphs.
- The study of comprehension strategies. Although most of the research on comprehension is with older students, the search for meaning begins early and the modeling of comprehension strategies (explicit instruction in the literature) is important from the beginning (for greater detail, see, Calhoun, E. 1999, Joyce, Hrycauk, and Calhoun, 2003).

Implementation and Student Learning

Three types of evaluation were built into the initiative: Implementation of the curriculum, the embedded study of student learning by the teachers, and the formal study of student learning through formal instruments administered by a team of external assessors.

The study of implementation was accomplished through a combination of self-report logs and observations conducted by consultants and central office personnel.

Embedded studies of student learning, from the learning of the alphabet in the kindergarten classes to the study of the acquisition of sight vocabulary, were conduced on a regular (generally monthly) basis by each of the teachers.

A team of external assessors was trained to administer the Gunning Procedure in the Kindergarten, and the Gray Oral Reading Test in grades one to five.

The Gray Oral Test is built around a series of passages that the students read to the assessor. The passages proceed from the simple to the complex.

The assessor studies the students' ability to recognize the words and apply strategies for recognizing the words not recognized by sight. The assessor supplies words that are not recognized after a reasonable period of time. After the reading of each passage, questions are asked to assess comprehension of the content. The Gray Test yields scores on fluency and comprehension that have been normed on a substantial population of students. Thus, the results here can be compared with the normative picture.

The Gunning procedure, developed by Thomas Gunning, presents to the students trade books that have been selected because they represent the following levels.

Gunning Levels

1. Level One. PICTURE LEVEL. The vocabularies are very small - sometimes only a half dozen words, and are closely linked to pictures.
2. Level Two. CAPTION LEVEL. There are a few more words and there is more action - more to comprehend. Each page has a phrase that moves the book along.
3. Level Three. EASY SIGHT LEVEL. Extended text is introduced. The student has to read text beyond what is illustrated.
4. Levels Four to Six. BEGINNING READING LEVELS. The vocabularies increase, the complexity of the stories increases, and the understanding of even lavishly illustrated books depend on the reading of complex text.
5. Level Seven. GRADE 2-A. These are larger, more complex books. The student who can read at this level can read a large number of books on many topics and do so independently.

The books are presented to the students and the cover pages are discussed briefly. Then, the students read the books and the procedures described above with respect to the Gray Oral Test are followed, including questions designed to assess comprehension of the major aspects of the books. To ensure that the students are not familiar with the books, they are selected from titles published in Great Britain that have not yet been distributed in Canada.

In the following pages we will deal, first, with the general effects of an initial implementation of the curriculum in eight kindergarten sections. We then proceed to examine the effects on diverse populations. Following that, we will look at the expansion of the initiative into a school with a demographic that enables us to highlight ethnic differences.

Summative Results for the Initial Kindergarten Population

The embedded studies of alphabet recognition and vocabulary acquisition are important, but, for our purposes here, the first question is how did those kindergarten students fare initially, with the use of the Gunning procedure and, second, over the years, as represented by the fifth grade,

The Kindergarten Year

Table 1 presents the results of the initial kindergarten cohort group at the end of the kindergarten year.

TABLE 1 : Percent of Students Reaching Gunning Levels at End-of-Year Testing

Level	*Percent Reaching Level*
Picture (A few words, closely connected to pictures)	2
Caption (Picture books, with text in captions)	26
Easy sight (Simple text carries meaning)	30
Above Easy Sight (extended Text in complex stories)	42

The students learned to read somewhat better than first grade students usually did in our school district with an important addition — they *all* learned to read at some level. In previous years, about 70 percent of the students in those schools learned to read in the primary grades (not in kindergarten) and about 30 percent would have been at the picture level or below, about the same proportion as in United States primary grades in general as reported in the National Assessment of Educational Progress at grade four (Donahue, 1999; NCES, 1999).

All eight sections apparently succeeded in bringing all the students to some level of print literacy. About 40 percent of the students appeared to be able to read extended text and another 30 percent manifested emergent ability to read extended text. Twenty percent reached the "2A" level, which includes long and complex passages and requires the exercise of complex skills both to decode and infer word meanings. All the students could manage at least the simplest level of books. Very important to us was that there were no students who experienced abject failure. Even the student who enters first grade reading independently at the picture level carries alphabet recognition, a substantial storehouse of sight words, and an array of phonetic and structural concepts to the first grade experience. However, half dozen students needed to be watched closely because, even if they were able to handle books at the caption level, they labored at the task, manifesting difficulty either in recognizing text-graphics relationships or using their phonetic or structural generalizations to attack unfamiliar words.

Year One—Comfort and Satisfaction

During the year parents voiced their opinions regularly, and in May we prepared simple questionnaires for both the parents and the children. We asked the parents a series of questions about the progress of their children and whether they and the children believed they were developing satisfactorily. The children were just asked whether they were learning to read and how they felt about their progress. Primarily, we were trying to ferret out whether there were levels of discomfort that were not being detected. Apparently not. No student or parent manifested discomfort or dissatisfaction related to the curriculum. However, some parents were anxious at the beginning and still worried at the end of the year. Some were concerned that we had not taken a "letter by letter" synthetic phonics approach and worried that future problems might develop as a consequence, but they appeared to believe that their children were progressing well "so far."

The Grade Five Year

The Gray Oral Reading Test (GORT) has been administered annually to the initial kindergarten students who have remained in the school division. Currently the initial group has graduated from grade five and we will examine their progress at that point. Sixty-three (46 percent) are still enrolled in division schools. (This is normal attrition for the district. The school on the airbase has considerable mobility and the oil and other mining industries in the area engender mobility as well. There are no systematic demographic differences between the students who have exited and those who are still in residence. For the province as a whole).

At the end of grade five the national GORT average Grade Level Equivalent score in comprehension is 6.0, which is about the average for over the years for students in those schools in the division. For the sixty-three students, the average is GLE 7.5. Contrary to the doctrine that teaching kindergarten students with a formal literacy curriculum will be damaging later, it appears that these students have not been damaged but, rather, have prospered. Importantly, only two students are below the 6.0 level— at 3.2, and 3.7.

Curriculum development may have bypassed the controversies as far as kindergarten is concerns. Also, the balanced curriculum has generated lasting effects much greater than most reported applications of unidimentional approaches (as synthetic-phonics only).

Diversity and the Initial Kindergarten Population

We are concerned here with gender, socioeconomic status (SES), learning disabilities, and ethnicity.

Gender

Gender did not influence levels of success from kindergarten through grade five. The distributions of scores for boys and girls were almost identical. Gender has been a major influence on reading achievement for years.

Socioeconomic Status [SES]

The distributions of scores for students having or not having subsidies for lunch were also approximately equal. Major initiatives, such as the Title One program in the United States, have been directed at socioeconomic status [SES] with indifferent success, despite providing additional resources to schools with sizeable populations of economically poor students.

Learning Disabilities

Typically, in our division, about 28 Kindergarten students would have been referred from the eight classes, as having special needs and that was the case here. Also, at the end of the fifth grade, typically all 28 students would still be coded as having a learning disability. However, in this case, the number dropped to 10.

Ethnicity

In our population area, a major concern is with the achievement of aboriginal students. In the schools where the initial kindergarten initiative was made, only 10 of the 133 students were identified as aboriginal. During the kindergarten year they progressed along with the other students and, by grade five, their average achievement was about 7.5. Just one was below the average exit score for the grade and that student's GLE was. 4.0 — about the average for exiting from grade three.

In Sum

The study was that curriculum development had bypassed the controversies about whether teaching kindergarten students to read is "developmentally inappropriate" and that a strong reading curriculum would address the needs of a very diverse population. The flow of the curriculum is largely built around the Picture Word Inductive Model.

In the Northern Lights, Alberta, school division #69, the thesis has been tested successfully. In eight sections of kindergarten (133 students) a curriculum, based on the Picture Word Inductive Model, was implemented and the students have been followed through their exit from fourth grade. By the end of the kindergarten year they had learned to read about as well as first grade students do except that the number of struggling readers is much smaller than in the typical first grade classes. By the end of grade three, half of the students were at the level of average students exiting grade four, and only a half dozen were below the average of grade three exiting students, and those students could read extended text. The students have much higher than average scores on the provincial tests on reading achievement. Parents, students, and teachers report that no harm was done, but that much has been gained. Referrals to special education dropped dramatically. Diversity yielded — the subgroups performed much better than average. An expanded program has had similar effects in other schools within the division.

Environmental Education through Mass Communication

Potentialities and Opportunities

Abhijit Bora

"Communication is not only a system of information, but also an integral part of education and development"

—McBride Commission Report (1978).

Mass media enjoys the unique distinction of reaching with ease even the remotest areas anywhere on the earth and deliver the messages. As a carrier of messages it has no 'parallel' in the world. Only thing is to prepare messages in the most effective way so that they can actually influence the target audience in the desired manner. It is also one of the most powerful forces for shaping public opinion.

With its enormous power, mass communication has been proving its worth time and again since the early days of its development. This Fourth Pillar of a democracy can claim numerous achievements to its credit in creating popular public opinion as well as correcting the same whenever needed. It has been playing the role of an opinion leader, pathfinder, and provider of solutions at times of crisis to the society constantly like a sentinel on an eternal vigil. Its powers can even move to mountains if the need arises at any point of time.

Situationally every development in this world has positive and negative aspects. It is interesting that when these developments in themselves are neutral, it is the human beings who mould or shape them or decide in which aspect they would be used. For example – nuclear power which can be used for both destructive and constructive uses.

In exactly the same way, mass media in itself is also 'neutral' with all its potential power. And it is up to us how to utilize its powers to reach the unreached or create awareness about anything even among those having ready access to it.

Environmental Education—An Express Need for Intervention

With the development of civilizations across the globe, complicacies in various walks of like are growing at an unprecedented rate. Environmental degradation is one prime problem- area that requires ready attention in a constant manner. So obviously, the world over considerable public movements and awareness drives are being taken up with a well-coordinated effort of a majority of the parties concerned with it.

In our country also, the same development has been taking place more or less in the 'right direction'. Even the Supreme Court as well as the University Grants Commission (UGC) are taking serious note of the issue and have made necessary arrangements for introducing environmental awareness as a subject of study at all levels of education, from primary to postgraduate level.

It needs to be re-emphasized here again that education is the basis of development of an individual and thereby that of the society. And, an efficient and positive communication system is a catalyst for true education so that the educational-messages can be delivered or put across effectively to the larger audiences.

Role of Mass Media

It is worthnoting that mass media is termed as the 'magic-multiplier' and the most persuasive of communications. This is because if a person expresses or communicates something through mass media it is replicated innumerable times and anyone interested in listening to it can do so without much of a difficulty. And if something is repeated again and again for numerous times, it definitely creates a very deep influence and impact upon the listeners or readers.

Right at this point, let us cite the findings of a study done by a communication expert from the USA about exploitation of mass media tools by big time terrorist organizations throughout the world. It concluded that those organizations were quite actively exploiting mass media as tools for reaching out to the masses. This is a novel means of a 'psychological warfare' indulged in by interested parties for getting their messages across to the masses.

A similar 'psychological fight' can also be waged to popularize the concept of environmental awareness and activism. This activism can be either at group or community level or at an individual level.

If mass media can rise up to the extent of transforming even half the target population and if every member of this population lives up to the expectations and does his or her bit effectively then almost half the battle is won.

This will have to take the shape of a development communication mode of activity, which is deliberate, goal-oriented, calculated and aimed at achieving a certain purpose.

In addition to other activities and functions, mass media also performs the role of setting agenda in the society. That is – to decide for the people which issues and aspects - out of so many of them competing for attention - would be focused more than others. Media plays the pivotal role of a 'whip' and leader at times of crisis. In today's world, the environmental problem is also nothing short of a crisis for the humankind. We must exploit this trait or function for deciding the agenda of environmental awareness for the people so that an exhaustive coverage can make them converts to the cause. And if possible, also make them activists.

India, the largest functioning democracy in the world possesses about 18,000 colleges, more than 375 universities including those with 'deemed' status, private ones, institutes of national importance etc. All of them are frantically trying to cater a target population of about 80 crores of youths (8.14 per cent of the country's total population of 105 crores). About 10 million students are pursuing various types of courses in them on any given day.

This number of institutions of higher education may seem to be an enormous one in itself. But don't feel surprised to know that together they are being able to serve just a tiny portion of the total number of youths waiting eagerly to acquire higher education at a given point of time.

As against this let us look at a few other conditions in this connection.

First of all—as the cost of private higher educational institutions are rather on the steep side and situated mostly in urban areas, those from the interiors can hardly afford them.

Secondly, with the present status of infrastructure available in the existing institutions, it will be quite a tall order to expect them to accommodate more than the present population in the near future. Even if the classes are carried out in shifts, it will hardly address the core of the problem.

A few similar issues have made sure that the overall percentage of students' enrollment in higher educational institutions is just a little more than eight per cent. It goes up to 25 per cent of the eligible population attending higher education in some of the western developed nations. While financial constraints and percentage of marks at the qualifying examinations are two important deterrents in this regard, availability of classrooms is another major factor taking its toll.

Also, it is ironical that even after six decades of Independence and quite a few ambitious plans since 1947, the literacy level both for the adults and the children still remain at a not so ideal point. Rather it is discouragingly a poor percentage of about 50.

At this juncture, the question that arises is - what is the scope of roping in the services of the mass communication and media to tackle this major challenge fight towards creating an adequate awareness among the masses about the need for protecting our environment by minimizing the damages already caused. And inculcate new innovative ideas among the human resources for a better and a new environment-friendly world.

In this write up, attempt has been made to look at the possibilities of utilizing mass communication and media exactly for this purpose.

First of all, let us glance at a few of the important aspects related to this entire issue. This includes questions like the levels of formal or informal education to be targeted, use of media—whether traditional mass media, most modern media, folk or traditional media, distribution/circulation of the programme software and most important of all—the job of actually creating an adequate and steady supply of software for feeding all the media on a sustainable basis.

First and foremost, it is to be believed that the motto should be like that of a famous multinational company engaged in apparels and garments which advertise its products as '012' which means from 'age zero to 12'. Similarly, it is strongly felt by the author that it would be doing a better job if we could cultivate the cause of environmental awareness right from the tender age of kindergarten schools up to postgraduate level.

Of course, this does not mean that the development comes to a stop at the postgraduate level itself. There is no end to learning anything in our lifetime and in this direction also the awareness creation has to be carried out in a continuous basis throughout one's lifetime on and on. Only the modes and levels will differ.

The author, being a man from the discipline of Mass Communication, would definitely like to push forward the benefits of this subject of study and practice for extension of the cause of environmental awareness, which is a red corner priority today.

Education through mass media, more so for Television enjoys a much better advantage as it can support, classify and enhance teaching efforts and presents a constant reference to larger masses by an effective presentation.

Formal and Informal Modes of Study

Here there can be two aspects. One is the formal study of mass communication as a course in an institution and then utilizing the skills and knowledge, one acquires for advancing the environmental cause.

The other is the deliberate and effective exposure of the students or people from all other disciplines to this cause. This is necessary because people from other disciplines who might be highly interested in doing something in this regard may feel somewhat handicapped in carrying out the actual task of reaching out to the target audience.

In this connection, steps may be considered seriously for equipping people from other disciplines in the very basic mass media skills to help them put across their views and findings whatever it might be, to the larger audiences in the big broad world. Of course, this might be left simply to the trained professionals in mass communication. But in case of non-availability of this breed of people as well as if the creator of the solution or knowledge would like to address the audiences himself or herself there is no harm in allowing them the opportunity.

Then again, it is not that every one of us would be dedicated to the cause of environmental awareness.

There are two aspects of the matter again – formal and informal education. By 'former' we mean the 'education' imparted through textbooks and may be other related means with specific and fixed curricula in schools, colleges or universities, or in other words 'formal educational institutions'. Following the Supreme Court verdict of 1991, elaborate efforts has been made for introducing the subject from school level to postgraduate levels as it has already mentioned. But, when it is 'institutionalized', there is always a tendency for it to tilt towards a formal entity, which is devoid of any effort at innovation, barring a few good institutions. Ultimately it becomes just a 'subject of study', needed to be studied and score good marks for completion of one's formal degree or diploma whatever it is. Of course, this is not the area of specialization of the author and so he has actually no moral right to advice in this regard. Yet, this has been the observation, so far his professional career in the field as well as in teaching for the last about a decade is concerned.

Our mantra in this regard should be 'catch them young'. The minds of children are always plain and receptive to new ideas and this is the age to bend their minds towards something good and better for themselves as well as the society. So it will be a good idea to start right from primary schooling and continuing it up to postgraduate level, touching secondary and higher levels in between on a continuous basis.

We have also mentioned that the parents of children and students need to be made aware at first so that generation after generation of our children can learn their first lessons on environmental awareness right at their homes even prior to attending a school.

Then there is the mode of 'informal' education. This takes place in a variety of ways not confined to the classroom or formal textbooks. For example – having a club for the purpose and carrying out awareness-campaigns among its members, people in the vicinity of the area where it is located, producing documentaries, street plays for the cause or maybe organizing anything related to the issue and the like.

This mode is advantageous in the aspect that it need not necessarily be confined to the limitations or the classroom textbooks or curricula itself and one can take his or her freedom on the creative side and the phrase is 'sky is the limit'.

In this connection, there is enough scope for exploring the possibilities of integrating all forms of media – mass media (both traditional and modern), folk media, traditional media, informal media and any new media format, which might emerge in the days to come in future.

We can very well say that it can be converted into a very interesting 'multimedia' campaign. This is because here we have the scope for utilizing TV, Radio, films and documentaries, traditional culture in the form of community songs and dramas, internet, mobile telephony – the list if endless and full of potential.

It is observed that during the last few decades or so, many universities have started departments and courses in mass-communication in general as well as its different specializations and disciplines across the country.

This, in addition to the institutes of film and television and radio productions which have also come up in the last about a decade. To contribute to this great cause of creating environmental awareness among the masses, it will be a good idea to include at least one compulsory paper or a full specialization with several papers in this subject in these courses. This will help the coming youngsters and enthusiastic future mass communicators to develop an expertise in this field so that this can be translated into practice later on in their professional life.

Further, as in the last few years, specialized communication courses like sports, agriculture, business, extension education etc. have been introduced by many institutions of the country, where there is high scope and potential for specialized courses in 'Environmental Communication'. The conventional institutions can take this up and universities, already having courses in mass communication or other specialized institutions may be set up mainly for this purpose.

On the other hand the National Council for Science Technology Communication (NCSTC) has been going ahead with a highly ambitious plan for gradually popularizing science communication in the country. And accordingly, an autonomous society has been formed which is looking after this project. It provides active assistance in the form of finance and human resources to interested universities and reputed educational institutions for offering courses in science communication.

As this is just the beginning of a widening network of communication training scheme with far-reaching potential, it would be a good idea to attaché the cause of creating environmental awareness with this scheme.

Further, in all universities and educational institutions, a scheme can be introduced by launching a general interdisciplinary course in communication skills – both written and through the electronic media – for the benefit of the students doing courses other than mass communication. Because even if they like to indulge in this work, lack of communication skills would not be an impediment to it.

Meantime, over the years, the governments – both the central and states as well are progressively making it almost compulsory for intending 'would be teachers' in schools to have possessed the B. Ed or M. Ed degree as a prerequisite for such a job. We need to seriously persuade the policy makers in this scheme for making environmental awareness a major component in this degree so that the youths and children right from formal schooling can take advantage of this development.

In fact, we personally believe that a well-thought out pre-service training system in the form of a course like M.Ed or B.Ed should be introduced for those people interested in a teaching job in colleges and universities. This course also should have such components as mentioned above for the benefit of the students of higher education.

Mass Media Options: An Insight

In view of above, what can be our alternatives to carry forward the messages of environmental awareness to the target audience in this vast country of continental proportions?

Let us consider the options one by one.

In case of the ***print media***, more than 62,000 journals and newspapers of varied kinds are in circulation in the country today with a combined circulation figure of 18 crores copies at present (mid 2007). And the very encouraging fact is that this figure is growing annually at an impressive 18 per cent.

Apart, over the years, there has been a steady and remarkable growth of the vernacular newspapers across the nation. This phenomenon is led by Hindi newspapers with almost 50 per cent of the total circulation figures followed by those in several prominent Indian languages, which means that an ever more number of people of the country spreaded in the remotest parts are being able to read the newspapers in their own language or dialect. From a mass communicator's point of view this is highly important point as every person feels much quite at home in one's own language.

TABLE 1 : Size of Indian Media in Numbers at a Glance (2005)

Media	*Numbers (Rounded)*	*Circulation/Viewers/Readers (in Millions)*
Newspapers	6,000	200 m
Dailies	600	80 m copies daily / 176 m readers
Magazines	22,000	60 m copies
Television	110 million sets	250 – 300 + viewers
Channels available	More than 200	110 m viewer homes / 190 m viewers every week
Colour TV sets	56 m	—
Satellite/Cable connected TV Sets	61 m	—
24 hour news channels	25	—
Radio	135 million sets	Apprx 300 million
No of sets available	135 m	Apprx 300 m listeners
AIR stations	Regional 115, Local 77, Vividh Bharati 39,	60 m listeners a day, 183 m over three months
No of languages in which programmes broadcast	24 languages + 146 dialects,	
FM Channels	37 private and 139 of AIR,	96 m listeners
Cinema		
Cinema theatres	13,000	3.3 billion viewers a year
Multiplexes	130	Account for 1/3rd of collections
Features films made yearly	1,200	—
Telecom		
Landlines	54 m	26 / 1000 people
Mobiles	45 m	7 / 1000 people
Internet		13 m users

Source: Centre for Media Studies (CMS), Delhi Media Lab Compilation, published in the April – June, 2007 issue of the Public Relations Voice (Vol 10, No 3, page 3),

As evident from the Table 1, the number of television viewers is estimated to be around 250 to 300 million – that is 25 to 30 crores on an average. But television and also cable television is basically an urban phenomenon, restricted mostly to the cities and towns across the country.

On the other hand, Radio stations' listenership is supposed to be around 60 million on any given day – that too in 24 languages and 146 dialects cutting across the length and breadth of the nation.

By another estimate right from the AIR Audience Research Unit statistics, this figure is put at a mind-boggling 32 crores on any given day. Further, there are 37 private and 139 AIR FM Radio channels, which boast of a listenership base of 96 million taken together.

One very highly important fact regarding radio coverage of the country is that AIR broadcasting network covers almost 100 per cent of the nation's geographical areas. If utilized properly, this is a landmark and dream-development for any massmedia organization and anyone who may desire to send across their messages to the larger masses.

Next comes the *feature film*. It is estimated that about 1,200 feature films are made in the country in all centers led by Mumbai film world with about 13,000 functioning cinema theatres. This translates into 3.3 billion viewers per year, which is not a number to be easily written off.

The internet is also expanding its base at a faster rate with 13 million users till date. In this direction, there has been a lot of talk about the broadband revolution that is growing at a speedy rate in the country. But in reality, in the remote towns and rural areas of India this revolution is going to take quite a long while to penetrate and become adequately functional. At least in the immediate future it is hardly going to yield much of the desired results.

So we can safely say that if utilized properly, these media can achieve the goals we desire in this connection for development of creating awareness about environmental concerns.

Let us also consider a few other media, which are rightful candidates to this job.

First of all there is the community radio, which has been showing tremendous potential in achieving our goal.

> *"Radio is a combination of the schoolhouse, the church, the public rostrum, the newspaper, the theatre, the concert hall – in fact, all media devoted to the education, enlightenment, and education of the people. Also, it claims a more intimate relationship with the public than any other media or tool of*

information at any given time."

—Anning S Paul, the first Chief Commissioner of the federal Communications Commission of the USA in 1936.

A Community Radio (CR) is a Radio center managed and maintained by the local community in which the center is located through its representatives. The community representatives take care of everything – right from identifying what sort of programmes to be aired, selected, prepared, edited, how to manage funds etc. from A to Z. The best advantage in them is that immediate local problems and issues can be tackled in a minimum loss of time whenever the need is felt.

The community feels empowered as the center airs important and relevant information about local issues and doubles up as a free discussion forum for all local causes and concerns. This is why if selected persons of the local community can be trained in mass media skills – both hard and soft skills, they would go a long way further making the local people informed of the latest developments in different walks of life and a better living style.

Of course, one may argue that the range of these Community Radios is very limited, hardly spanning about 10 to 15 or at the most 25 to 30 kilometers at a stretch. But, there is an interesting and finer way of circumventing this limitation and making the benefits of each of these centers available to the broadest ever-possible target audiences.

This can be done by creating an effective and adequately coordinated network of such CRs across the nation so that the good programmes can be shared in a circuit to allow people from all over the country to enjoy the benefits of it.

In fact, if we look at the history and growth of Community Radio all over the world, we will find that in most of the cases it started out as a means for keeping the community informed as well as making them empowered. Thus why can't we also utilize this wonderful medium for our advantage?

In the process this wonderful medium has accorded a new meaning to the world of 'empowerment of the people at grassroots level'. Imagine a situation - if every block level area of the entire country can have a properly functioning Community Radio, people in those areas would be benefited immensely. The community can identify their own problems, discuss what to air and what not etc., which is a very right candidate for our specific goals. If all these Community Radios become connected through the net or any other means, this will be a never-before development and benefit the people tremendously in the long run.

If it can be made interactive with a phone-in programme or so, that will add a much better flavour to the entire activity.

However, till date the MIB does not allow news, news-based and current affairs programmes to be broadcast by the Community Radios. Because, without the freedom for airing news and news-based current affairs programmes there will hardly any real term benefit for the people. We are optimistic that in the near future this aspect will be taken care of by the MIB for a better service to the people.

Apart, there is the concept of Campus FM Radio centers already launched by several reputed institutions and universities including Anna University (Chennai), Jamia Millia Islamia (Delhi), Vanasthali Vidyapeeth (Rajasthan), IIT, Roorkee etc. And they are rendering yeoman's service to the local community.

This concept of Campus FM Radio serves a very important additional purpose other than the purpose of creating empowerment for the immediate community. That is – the students' community of the institution – more so for those from the departments under which these centers are set up, gets a first hand experience and exposure to the craft of everything related to programme production and airing it in the end. And also carrying out feedback assessment for the programmes and whenever needed assess the feed forward for future usage.

At this point it may be of interest to everyone to know that the Ministry of Information & Broadcasting (MIB) of the Government of India is actually actively encouraging this medium for peoples' development at the grassroots level covering all aspects of our lives. So, obviously environmental awareness can be very well integrated into this scheme of things.

It is to be noted here that when Radio as a medium of entertainment spread widely in the 1920s in the USA, in a short span of time may hundreds of colleges and universities had launched their campus Radio centers. Of course mainly with the purpose of entertainment and providing the students of journalism and mass media with the skills of programme production.

But, it is a sad story that in our case, the MIB has been encouraging it only in the last few years. That too – the obstacles in launching such a center is still daunting due to the need for taking clearances from so many different departments. This needs to be taken care of in an emergent manner.

One other advantage with Community Radio system is that the cost of launching one has been steadily coming down with a short range Community Radio station needing just about Rs 8 lakhs for the whole activity. For a community this is not a very unaffordable amount.

Another fact also needs mention here that in the last part of 2006 the MIB has taken up a landmark decision in case of Community Radio licensing. That is – the Ministry has adopted a decision that any NGO with a good track record of at least three years or more would be allowed to apply for and get a license for launching as well as running a Community Radio station on a priority basis.

I believe this is going to open up a floodgate of good-minded NGOs intent on running Community Radios for the benefit of local communities. And we have already spoken about the potential benefits of programmes aired by these Community Radios through a coordinated network of such centers in future.

Here again there are two types of NGOs involved. First, those dedicated only to the cause of environmental issues while the rest are general purpose NGOs who might take up the environmental cause also. Whatever it is, an all out effort must be adopted for encouraging and empowering both these types of NGOs to further our goals in addition to the others.

At the same time, we must also provide adequate emphasis upon our traditional media like puppetry, folk dances, songs and the like for carrying forward the messages of environmental awareness. As these media or forms of communication are audience-friendly and of a participatory nature they have much potential for achieving very good and effective results in the end. Only problem is that their audience base is limited at one time compared to mass communication and mass media. But they make up for this loss in their being participatory and closely integrated with the masses.

This will be an ideal tool for educating target audiences in both the formal educational sector – at school level – and also in the informal sector.

This aspect has two important sides to it. First of all – we all know that charity begins at home and also that one's home is the first and best university for a child. This is so because the parents and guardians are supposed to be best educators initially when a boy or a girl starts growing in their formative years and whatever is seen or experienced or taught about do have a deep impact upon.

Besides, we also know that today's children are tomorrow's citizens of this nation on whose shoulders there rests a very big responsibility. So, if we can manage to properly educate and influence the parents and guardians of these children and school-going kids, this will have a far reaching and more effective impact upon our future citizens.

This will be in addition to the efforts taken up for the purpose through formal textbooks and study materials used in schools, colleges or universities for popularizing the concept of environmental awareness.

In this connection let us cite the famous examples of the *Kheda project* and the SITE experiment in the mid 1970s which have been considered important milestones in the mass media experimentation in India at a time when nation-building was the prime concern of the leaders of the country.

The Kheda (a backward district of Gujarat) project was implemented by setting up a small-caliber low range television station with an initiative of the Indian Space Research Organization (ISRO), Ahmedabad under its Development Education and Communication Unit (DECU). The television station was utilized primarily for broadcasting programmes for the local people on all facets of their lifestyle. This was a pioneering activity in the field of development communication by which all programmes selected and prepared addressing issues with a positive outlook so that the people of this the then backward area could reap advantages of modern developments delivered to them through mass media.

Each and every programme was previewed by a committee of local elders, selected by the communities before broadcasting. So that nothing offensive or defamatory would go to air. The programme became so successful among the people of the region that when after one year of functioning it was to have been dismantled, there were widespread protests and the programme had to be continued in the face wider popular demand. However, initially it was actually established only for a year on an experimental basis.

On the other hand the Satellite Instructional Television

Experiment (SITE) implemented in 1975 for a year was another major project implemented as an experiment in development communication. The project covered 2400 villages in four states including Delhi and Rajasthan.

It was implemented by placing several hundreds of television receiver sets at different villages and programmes relating a better living style like hygiene, safe child -birth and rearing and other issues were broadcasted for about a couple of hours on a daily basis. Television sets were placed in community centers and common places so that people did not need to face any problem in watching the programmes. More so for the womenfolk as they were especially encouraged to watch the programmes.

This (SITE) experiment was mainly meant for villagers and school-going children. One important objective of the experiment was to study the role of television as a new medium and the changes it might bring about in the existing rural communication networks. Programmes included development educational issues in agriculture and allied subjects, health, family planning and social education. Part of the programme was prepared to study the impact of educational programmes specially produced for the rural primary school children.

Later on, when a proper stock of the achievements were taken up it was found that it also became quite a success.

Worthnoting in this context is that we can still take lessons from these two landmark experiments in the mass media history of the country. Their relevance is still as good as a new one even after a gap of more than three decades till date. In fact, there is sufficient ground to strongly believe that their relevance and necessity have actually grown bigger in today's time – when about 70% of the populations still live in rural areas in an underprivileged manner. We strongly believe that environmental degradation is one important cause of this backwardness. And their backwardness can be attributed to a big extent on the failure of the mass media in India and other so called developing countries in getting across developmental messages effectively to those underprivileged people continuously for several decades on end.

So, in our efforts towards popularizing environmental awareness there is enough scope for initiating similar projects on an urgent basis.

Role of Educational Institutions

Right at this point the institutions of education from primary to higher levels – can also become adequate and the right media of creating awareness on environmental issues in the local areas surroundings those institutions.

In this regard, we can refer to the UGC's provisions and insistence that the colleges and universities affiliated to it supposed to take-up local community development programmes on a priority basis. Even the Bangalore-based National Assessment and Accreditation Council (NAAC) insists on this provision and has made it a major condition for granting accreditation to colleges under UGC.

So this obligation and provision can be very well utilized for creating awareness about environmental issues effectively, especially in those localities where they are situated. Even if there is no such obligation, this is a moral responsibility of such institutions to devote at least some of their resources for development of the local areas.

Distribution Channels for Educational Material

On the other hand having an effective and adequate network of distribution channels is also quite an important aspect. This is because however much one produces good and far-reaching programmes, if they are not able to reach the masses—the target audiences—as desired, there will be hardly any benefit from those programmes.

TABLE 2 : Reach of Mass Media– 2005

(Percentage of adult population)
Overall, one third or more not reached by any or all

Mass Media	*All India*	*Urban*	*Rural*
TV Viewers	45	75	33
Press – Readership	35	58	24
Radio – Listenership	20	21	19
Cinema goers	19	29	15

Source: Readership surveys, (averages rounded up) published in the April-June, 2007 issue of the *Public Relations Voice* (Vol 10, No 3, page 4),

Of course, the broadband is coming up faster though it will take considerable time before it becomes appropriately functional in the near future. In this regard, the major mass media agencies like TV, Radio, cinema, theatres, internet can also doubled up as very effective distribution channels for the programme softwares, prepared by the resources persons.

Meantime, the Ministry of Information Technology (MIT) of the Government of India has adopted an ambitious plan for floating about 1,00,000 Community Service Centers (CSCs) across India for facilitating delivery of services for all possible sorts of requirement – from central and state government departments, private non-governmental agencies etc. The MIT envisions a countrywide network of such delivery centers, which can be quite effortlessly be utilized for the purposes.

So far as we know, in an ideal condition the Ministry plans to set up such canters in every Development Block of the country. Thus we can say that this system would prove to be an ideal delivery channel for software or programmes of creating environmental awareness along with other goals.

Those Beyond the Reach of Formal Institutions

Apart, there are two other very important aspects to be addressed. These are

First of all, we have so far talked about study materials and programme software on the theme of our discussion. We have confined it mainly to the formal mode of education. But who will take care of the needs and interests of those who are already out of the fold of the formal educational institutions. Not only this, there is another equally important aspect to be considered seriously at this juncture. Here, in addition to the target audience, we have been talking about here already, we need to take care of three additional and huge target audiences in the country. These are

1. Those underprivileged people including young children to the adult and matured people who did not enjoy the opportunity of being benefited by formal education due to many factors including financial crisis. In this target audience the children are mostly from such families who can't afford to send them to school and later on when they become matured and adults, they become too old to enroll in a formal institution of study.
2. There are those people who have enjoyed the privilege of getting properly educated in formal schools and

educational institutions and are engaged in various professions for earning their livelihood. And it is not necessary that all of them are aware about the environmental issues.

3. Ours being an agriculture-based economy, even today around 70 % of the people of the country are residents of rural and semi-urban places with hardly any access to adequate and effective mass media outlet.

Now, the million-dollar question is how to take care of this vast majority of people using our resources and distribution channels. This is where the instruments of modern mass media come in handy to reach this 'unreached' people even in the remotest nook and corner of the country. In this regard we can bank upon Radio, more so Community Radio for achieving our goals.

We can carry out this function in the forms of 'continuing education' and 'extension education'. The first one is usually associated with the medical profession where doctors can continue to keep learning all developments in their respective fields of specialization from time to time. The other one is mainly used in relation to agriculture. In fact, agriculture universities invariably do have provisions for such a discipline in their courses curricula at postgraduate level. So, we can provide for continuing education for those persons interested in this direction, irrespective of any professional background and studies. Further, extension education must be exploited for connecting with the masses at the remote corners and rural areas for keeping them updated and informed about the need for being adequately aware about environmental concerns.

Public Service Broadcasting (PSB) in the Service of Environmental Education

'Broadcasting is power', Mahatma Gandhi said in 1948, as this great personality well understood the immense potential of radio as a mass medium even more than six long decades ago. It is ironical that we have actually failed to utilize this medium to our optimum advantage in the intervening period till date.

In the informal sector, radio can take up the responsibility quite easily. AIR being a good example of a Public Service Broadcasting (PSB) needs to gear up its 'public education' component for this purpose. We are pushing the cause of radio more than the others because being an audio-medium, it offers far more scope for utilizing itself for the purpose. Also, it is a cheap and portable medium, which can deliver anywhere anytime.

Then there is encouraging news for those interested in this direction. That is – the MIB is currently implementing an ambitious policy of setting up 336 FM radio stations all over the country in the near future. The process has already been started. As a part of the plan, Radio stations would be set up under AIR, private parties and educational institutions engaged in distance education programmes like IGNOU and a few others. In fact, quite a few stations under the *Gyan Vani* policy of IGNOU have been set up, for extending the benefits of education through mass media to the masses at the grassroots level. This can be very easily utilized also for advancing the cause of environmental education. IGNOU has already been implementing a plan for setting up of 100 such *Gyan Vani* stations in a matter of a few years for taking care of the target audience all over the country.

We strongly believe that herein lays the biggest challenge for the academic community to win with a coordinated effort from all stakeholders concerned about the issues. This is because 'environment' is such a discipline that encompasses almost each and every walk of our lives and even beyond. This is a multidisciplinary subject of study, also involving lots of technical aspects in the process of understanding it in its entirety.

Preparation of Study Materials—The Crucial Question

Another vital question in this direction is preparation of software and programmes. This is quite a difficult and tricky aspect because it is not so easy to prepare programmes, which can be satisfactory and stimulating in all related issues, more so at the primary and high schools rather than graduate and postgraduate levels.

Definitely, there have been efforts by various bodies led by the UGC for preparing teachers in colleges and universities for this task by way of special training courses as well as 'interdisciplinary Refresher Courses' (RCs) conducted through Academic Staff Colleges attached to different universities. These interdisciplinary courses are open for college and university teachers, irrespective of discipline or subject of study.

However, one important lacuna in this approach is that the target audiences generally go through them as mere stepping-stones or requirements for further promotion in their jobs. Besides, there is hardly any component of programme preparation or textbook creation in them. This being a highly technical subject, one requires a good amount of orientation and initiation into its various aspects prior to setting about the task.

The Ahmedabad-based autonomous organization - Center for Environmental Education (CEE) has been at the task for quite some time now though it is believe they are yet to make a major headway in this regard. Besides, writing or preparing study materials for school and college / university levels is quite another thing.

For the formal education sector, already there must be quite a few textbooks and reference books available. But, for the informal sector, there is a sheer lack of study materials, which is posing a big challenge to the academicians, and everyone involved.

Preparation of Study Materials—E-Learning Option

Over the years, with the rapid development of communication technology media including internet, widening bandwidth facility, the recent phenomenon of expansion of Radio are opening up challenging opportunities in this field. These developments have brought in potential opportunities like the 'e-learning' concept to the fore. This is nothing but the creation of learning contents or knowledge contents in such a form which is deliverable through the internet or CD / DVDs. Also they should be replicable unlimited number of times by whoever would like to do so. At present there are several institutions and organizations worldwide offering such study materials, most of which can be downloaded free of cost from the Net while a few of them have to be bought at a certain price for use.

The University Grants Commission (UGC) first conceived an idea in these lines around two decades back. And keeping up with the situation of those days, lessons were prepared in video format. UGC today possesses a rich repository of 4,000-5,000 hours of such study materials. However, with further development of technology and delivery modes of knowledge and information this system seems to be a highly viable option.

In the E - Education mode what is being sought to be achieved is to present a back up, a support system of study materials prepared in the Audio-Visual style. A few characteristics of this mode are—they are study materials on a variety of subjects, virtually any subject for that matter, they are re-usable any number of times if anyone would like to do so, crisp, to the point, complete with all components so that it can supplement the role of the human teacher to a great extent. These e-learning materials are ideally supposed to play the role of both the textbooks and the teachers combined into one.

There is an express need for creating good quality study materials, which must be at the same time–attractive, comprehensive, easily understandable, innovative, cost-effective, interactive, possess adequate scope for future improvements.

The task is far more challenging because of the necessity that these study materials need to be prepared keeping in view that a majority of the target population may not have any exposure to new concepts in the educational field at all. In other words, one has to prepare them for a group of completely novice persons as the target audiences.

Keeping in view the enormous requirements of the growing times we need to develop the e-learning concept as a strong back up of the main face-to-face interactive teaching system aimed primarily at the underprivileged people as mentioned above.

There can be two major advantages in this context:

Firstly, a set of good and ideal E–Contents prepared by a good teacher will be available worldwide as these can be floated in the internet. This will definitely bring in good repute and accolades to the teacher from virtually anywhere in the world.

Secondly, this will also reduce or even minimize the scope of plagiarism, as the contents will be available there for everyone to see. So if anybody attributes something wrongly either deliberately or unintentionally there is a lot of scope that this will be detected and the original creator or the institution may take due note of it.

Further, there is also scope for improvement in this system as anyone who might be interested in those contents may contribute something more to it or point out to discrepancies if there is any. And we are talking of many thousands and lakhs of hours of such E-Content study materials – not something small to be considered before embarking on the big journey.

On the other hand, the Delhi-based Consortium for Educational Communication (CEC) – a component body of UGC, has already been embarking on the path towards creating a library and resource base of materials produced on the 'e-learning mode'. That is – transforming textbook materials into audio-visual and multimedia learning aids. It has 17 Educational Multimedia Research Centers (EMMRCs) at various places of the country for facilitating production of such materials. It has made at least some headway in this direction. With more than 11,000 capsules and 4,000 hours of video contents produced for broadcast over the years, Consortium for Educational Communication (CEC – an autonomous unit of UGC) is in an advantageous position to give the entire initiative a big push to start with.

As the communication technology sector is fast opening up with new promises, things look quite bright for this initiative to grow towards ever-greater heights in the coming days. The launch of the EduSat has also further boosted the development. UGC's countrywide classrooms (CWC) initiative was a right and timely step in this direction. NCERT, IGNOU, *Gyan Darshan*, the 24-hour channels - *Vyas and Eklavya* (a technology channel) followed suit extending the concept and vision of UGC.

Not only this, quite a few other institutions of higher education have been going ahead with such programmes. Besides, the IITs are at present implementing an e-learning project for generating comprehensive and vast pool of such materials for several of their technical subjects. We believe there should be hardly any problem in creating a similar pool for study materials in environmental education too.

Significantly, in the XIth Five Year Plan period, there is a plan for setting up of 'virtual university' for taking care of this mode of study material production. If this becomes a reality we expect to have a good bank of materials on environmental awareness creation in the future.

The UGC is also embarking on an ambitious special plan of connecting all the institutions of higher learning with high-speed internet connection for a better and smoother flow of data and information. This will open up new vistas in the exchange and transfer of data, which will further facilitate 'resource sharing'. This will also allow us to reap rich benefits by sharing high quality study materials through a speedy and seamless transfer method.

Messages Designed to Empower People

Further, the messages or the programmes and software which are to be aired or published or prepared for creating environmental awareness must of be of such standard and nature which can actually make one – the recipient of the messages – a thinking person. That is because mere receiving the messages will hardly address our need. But it must be able to rekindle our thought process and decide what should be adopted and what not in the passage of life. The messages must also be able to make us think rationally so that we can identify and differentiate what is good for us and what not. Then only the process of 'empowerment' will be completed in actual terms, as it will produce at least some changes in the recipients' lifestyle. Our purpose is to bring in a change of behaviour among the people so that they become conscious of their responsibilities and act accordingly to contribute to the greater interests of the world community in general.

Integrating the Stakeholders

We have already said that this is a discipline that involves each and every walk of our lives and thereby things are quite complex compared to other disciplines. It is interesting that here we are speaking of utilizing the different avenues of mass communication and media for getting the messages of environmental awareness among more than 105 crores of population in the nation.

Ironically, even after six long decades of the country's Independence, only about half the people are declared 'officially literate'. But, we all know that the official definition of literacy is 'someone who can juts sign his or her name, nothing more. Thus, in actual terms we can say that only about 25 to 30 crores of these people are actually properly literate. So, it is obvious that it will be quite difficult to make the so-called literate people along with the illiterates aware about our goals. This is because only proper education opens up and liberates our minds, which should be a prime goal for all our positive communication endeavors. This will result in an urgent need for additional shoring up of our efforts, resources and time.

Apart, mass communication is also a discipline of study that encompasses each and every discipline and subject of study of our lives. So we strongly believe that the combination will be highly mutually beneficial one, which will go the extra mile to get us the results, we desire. Of course, we need to move in a systematic concerted way so that nothing is left to chance.

The stakeholders here are the professional communicators engaged in various mass communication and mass media endeavours, academics at all levels from primary to postgraduate levels, students, research institutions, NGOs, government agencies etc. so that an all-out and well-rounded project can be envisaged and implemented.

At the same time adequate care must be taken for making sure that local issues and components are properly integrated into the overall scheme of things so that the efforts do not become too heavy and too centralized to be realistic on the way.

Besides, there must be enough flexibility in the whole scheme so that whenever any new development comes up, the same can be incorporated into the scheme of things without much of a problem. Further, an effective plan for.measuring the feedback of the whole scheme on an ongoing basis must also be kept ready for future usage. Significantly, out of this huge population, about half of them are literates and roughly 70 % of them, in real terms more than 70 crores of people live in rural and semi-urban areas devoid of modern means of mass communication and media.

Conclusion

The endeavours are definitely going to take time to sink in and become successful. Till date, most of the experiments and developments in this direction have met with more or less mixed success. We can't call all of them as outright success stories. Yet, we must also learn from their mistakes and lacuna so that we can refine our efforts for the greater interests of the society.

It is already high time we have started a serious effort in this direction. Yet, we are at least going to start soon. Only thing is that we will need to move fast if we have to make up for the lost time.

However, if we start today, results will start rolling in a few years' time. Let us cite an example in this regard. In June this year while attending the Radio Asia 2007 conference in Singapore, where the author had the opportunity for participating in a workshop on water conservation and efforts for renewing this invaluable resource wisely, sponsored by the Manila (Philippines)-based Asian Development Bank (ADB).

In that workshop, a US citizen of Chinese origin showed us a video film about how a barren almost desert-like land in a remote province of china was completely transformed into forest-covered area in ten years' time. The film was made by integrating film footages taken every year for successive 10 years.

The first of the shots show the barren land with demonstration of how various reckless activities of the residents of the area transformed it into a desert-like place. Then other shots demonstrate how a relentless and coordinated effort of the local people with adequate guidance from an NGO the entire area was again transformed into a green one. So, if those people can achieve it there why can't we?

Of course, it will be a time-consuming process. But we must not shy away from it, as somewhere along the line we will have to confront the problem and do something for solving it. We must set our goals for the next twenty year or so, nothing less.

Trend of Doctoral Research on Environmental Education in Indian Academia

RAJARSHI ROY AND ANJANA PAIRA

The basic requirements for survival of any species may be termed as propensities. Most of our physical needs demand access to natural resources such as land, water and air, which, with the aid of radiant energy from the sun, generate plants and animals. The so-called non-renewable resource such as minerals and fossil fuels, are also needed for human survival and development. All these resources are present on a thin layer of the earth's surface, which we commonly termed as *environment*. It is the environment within which we live. Therefore it is considerably clear that the link remains among the environment, human beings and, their needs.

The basic purpose of environmental education is to provide the individual and social groups sufficient scope so that they should acquire awareness and knowledge, develop attitudes, skills and abilities, and participate in solving real-life environmental problems. The perspective should be integrated following an interdisciplinary approach, and should be holistic in nature. Purpose of environmental education is therefore not to introduce a new subject as such, but to evolve a new approach to education to integrate the concept of preserving environment with the existing content of a subject-discipline. Therefore it may be assumed that environmental education is an approach, which is expected to provide the necessary methodology to integrate the consciousness about environment (both in applied and basic/ theoretical aspects) with education, engineering, socio-economics, ethics, law and other allied disciplines, so that the knowledge will be holistic.

Environmental Education is characterized by its goal of providing education for the enhancement or protection and preservation of human environment. It is not sufficient to teach about the environment. During the end of last century, the term became a jargon. Even today there are controversies about the meaning of environmental education. Many programmes described as 'environmental education' do not attempt to develop appropriate behaviors, psychoeducational attributes, including attitudes, which is implicit in education for the environment. However since the 'Belgrade Charter' was adopted at an environmental workshop in environmental education long back to 1975, there has been an increasing international consensus to focus on affective aims for environmental education.

Environmental issues have a twofold place in adult education. Firstly, they can present problems that need solutions developed by educated people. Secondly, they can be used as relevant and immediate examples in the teaching of much basic adult education such as literacy, health, welfare and competence, obviously following an andragogic approach.

The demand for solutions can be best fulfilled when environmental education produces the following outcomes:

The task to integrate and accumulate environmental concern, knowledge, and skill into all relevant areas of learning - which is mostly progressed in relation to health and hygiene to any significant context, within the domain of education.

The role of education in achieving the goals of environmental education is quite indispensable. Though the task in countries like ours is mostly performed by the non-formal sector and media (both electronic as well as print), however, time has come to integrate it with all possible levels of formal education. It has been realized by the planners and educationists that the prime task of integrating environmental education is best possible if the mass awareness can be created.

It is worthnoting in this context that media help to give a concrete shape to the behavioral patterns and to acquiring values directly. However, it influences from two opposite poles simultaneously. Media creates awareness about *environmental concernes* as well as *detrimental* practices. Therefore a monitoring system is needed so that the positive activities can be prominent over the adverse campaigns. Sometime it appears that media-effectiveness in relation to environmental education is greatly diminished due to their lack of attention to environmental-skill-training as well as their lack of educational goals against environment.

It is noticed that media may be effective in motivating people to become aware of issues than actual teaching. Surveys of attitudes towards pollution control (which is directly linked with environmental issues) and specific environmental problems show a reasonable correlation between awareness of a given problem. When, however, surveys are followed by any form of testing of factual knowledge about a problem, it is evident that educational role of the media has been rather limited. Their contribution to environmental education has been confined mainly to health and conservation issues. As educators recognize that participation in concrete actions directed towards a defined goal greatly enhances learning, much emphasis in environmental education is to be placed on participation in the planning of environment. With a sound environmental education among the masses, the educational importance of participator is expected to be greater than actual input to the planning process.

Though meager, still in Indian scenario, the factual and sustained educational efforts in the sphere of environment consciousness have been made only through NGOs, serving in various spheres and in various geographical regions of the country, evolving a move for environmentalism. Much to meager the attempt is to explore the research-scenario in the direction.

Scope of Disciplinary Approach

The dictionary meaning of the word *discipline* depicts a branch of instruction, or study or, learning. The basic requisites to form any discipline, as we all know, are – *sufficient number of theories of its own, a stable methodology*, accompanied with a *more or less specific boundary*. Environmental education, for its own sake, to emerge as a discipline, should hinge on all these three components, which is best possible with the help of research. Research in any discipline fulfills the need to evolve theory of the very discipline, followed by trying out of methodology, used for research, which in the formative phase, may be borrowed from allied disciplines (i.e., the disciplines which have already taken a structured shape). Reorganization of existing knowledge is best possible through research in the very discipline. Due to massive proliferation of information, related to environment, the scope remains open to carryout multi-disciplinary research, hinging over the environmental education and thereby to generate theories and methodologies in environmental education, with a view to give it a structured shape. Therefore research in environmental education is very much essential. Unfortunately, no such serious attempt has yet been taken up by Indian scholars. A few studies have been initiated by scholars and researchers of the west, though the need for such attempt of research and development(R&D) is much more essential for the so-called developing countries like ours, who are the ultimate and immediate sufferers of environmental degradation. As per information available at this very moment, scholars in Indian universities have completed only sixteen doctoral studies in Education during last few years, centering round the issues and problems of environmental education. It is to be noted that a very small number of them have dealt with affective domain of the students of higher education or similar other sample group. By nature these studies are mere attitude–survey, having restricted significance towards the content of the discipline. Undoubtedly such attempts can hardly contribute towards development of environmental education as a discipline, however useful they may be to explore the trend of attitude towards environmental education. Another factor, worth mentioning in this context is some of those studies evolved popular slogans for environmental education, which may indirectly help in creating a consciousness towards the very area.

In fact, environmental education is the educational process through which it is imparted to its target groups in both formal and non-formal educational institutions, including homes, factories, farms, laboratories and workshops and overall in the society as well. The environmental sensitivity, awareness, knowledge, understanding, attitudes, skills, commitments and civic-actions needed for understanding protection and improvement of the environment and the prevention of solutions of its allied problems. In other words, the mission of environmental education should be to foster environmental literacy among the entire cross-section of the population, who should make sound judgment and decisions and have ethical responsibilities about the environment and its related issues. In this context, environmental education may serve as a common denominator in renewing educational process at all levels of education — by enhancing interdisciplinary approach among the different subjects and by relating education to the real life of its target groups. Environmental education advocates problem-solving approach as a skill, which could help and guide its target groups in the solution of current and future environment and related problems.

Brief Review of Selected Doctoral Research on Envirnomental Education

Since 1997, a trend has emerged in the area of education, where scholars, at the doctoral level started initiating research incorporation environment as a major factor. Prior to these, studies at the very level were reported only in various branches of science (both natural and pure) and technologies, apart from medicine. Though let however studies initiated in the subject like education has made an effort following which environmental education can find a new vista, obviously hinging over the prior studies, contributed by the scholars from other disciplines. We may have a glance perusal of the studies contributed by the scholars form education, listed as follows:

Gupta (1997) carried out a study on *Adolescent's Environmental awareness in connection with religious and scientific attitude and scholastic achievement* over the environmental awareness as a whole. The study was basically a correlational one, where Ex-post-factor research design was used. Stratified random sampling technique was used to select the sample for the study, which includes 500 adolescent students from the district of Hadoti. Inventories for environmental awareness and religious attitude, test for scientific attitude, and poforma for recoding scholastic achievement, constructed by the investigator, were used as tools to collect data for the study. ANOVA, 't' test, and product movement coefficient of correlation were used for analyzing collected data. The study observed that while religious and scientific attitudes, gender, habitation and scholastic achievement of adolescents possesses significant effect over the environmental awareness, religious attitude and managerial background does not possess any significant impact over such awareness.

Gogoi (1998) attempted to explore the major *environmental problems of Assam* in his study, apart from identifying the need for environmental education. While assessing the environmental problems of the very region, special emphasis was given on ecological and pollution problems caused by different industrial activities, initiated mostly in Dibrugarh and Tinsukia district in recent past. 400 high school children from higher secondary (i.e. +2) level were chosen as the human sample for the study. Besides, official records, publications and other print media were also explored as the source to collect information, hinging over the specified objectives. A self-developed 'environmental awareness scale' was used as the basic tools to pull data. Data was further analyzed through basic statistics as well as 't' & chi-squire tests. A normative survey method was followed to carry on the study, apart from a district based juxtaposition approach, to depict the findings of the study, which reveals a lack of awareness towards environment among the sample group with a considerable variation among the respondents. The researcher, on the basis of the study suggests inclusion of environmental education as a subject at high-school level-curriculum.

Apart from suggesting to incorporate environmental science at higher secondary level, studies where also initiated by the scholars to explore and thereby to improve the 'quality of instruction' in environmental science at primary level school children. ***Tomor (1998)***'s study was directed towards this very direction with an objective to prepare intervention programme on seven units in the subject of environmental science for primary school children and thereby to implement the intervention programme to judge the effectiveness of IVth grade students in terms of their academic achievement. In this study, teachers' opinion was also sought about the intervention programme, implemented by the investigator apart from the opinion of the students. The sample of the study incorporates all the students from IVth grade who are offered with environmental science, as well as their teachers. Activity based invention programme, written, oral and activity-based tests and semi-structured interview-schedules were used as tools and techniques to collect data for the study, which where further analyzed through basic statistics and 't' test. The study observed that such programmes are quite helpful to enhance the positive attitude of the student towards environment if those are joyful; it was further observed that such programmes require proper training for the teachers to make those programmes attractive to the students

Singh (1998) initiated a study of scientific temper in relation to personality and environment. His basic objective was to develop and standardize a tool for scientific temperament, along with exploring the inter-relationship of various psychosocial factors including environmental dimensions. Sample for the study incorporates higher secondary students from Haryana with science background. A self-made scientific-temperament-scale, school environment inventory, home environment inventory and Eysenck's Personality questionnaire (Indian adaptation) were the tools used by the researcher to collect data. The study observed that while extraversion is positively related with scientific temperament, neurotic-personality express a negative correlation. The study further observed that home environment and its allied dimensions show a significant positive correlation with scientific temperament. The investigator claims the study as a significant one for counseling the students at under- graduate level.

Rathore (1999)'s study in this direction attempted to examine the scholastic achievement of primary school children towards environmental science with special reference to vernacular, and thereby, development of remedial teaching strategies for those who are attending formal schools as well as non formal education centers. Scholastic achievement test, reading materials and questionnaires were administered over 100 school children and 200 teachers with equal proportion from formal and non formal educational institutions apart from 10 supervisors of non formal education centers from the city and adjoining areas of Khandwa district. The findings of the study are very usual in nature, which depict a comparatively better scenario (in terms of academic achievement of students, methods of teaching used, academic monitoring, duration of study hours etc.) in formal schools compared to non-formal education centers.

Deb (1999) studied the cognitive development in relation to social deprivation and school climate. Initiated with a causal-comparative descriptive method of research, the study aimed to explore whether children exposed to different level of social deprivation, and perceiving different levels of various divisions of classroom climate are differing in their cognitive development or not; apart from examining various dimensions of classroom climate, contributing to prediction of cognitive development among children exposed to different types of social deprivation.

A stratified random sampling technique was followed where sample group incorporates 200 boys and girls with equal ratio from Allahabad city of Uttar Pradesh. Test of conservation ability, concept- formation, and classroom climate inventory where adopted (with modification) to collect data. The study observed heterogeneous differences in terms of class-grade so far their conserverism is concerned. Other factors are also analyzed which revealed that reward, rejection and cognitive-thrust are the best predictors of conservation of volume among highly socially deprived children. Among highly socially deprived children, the study observed that hierarchical classification is negatively related to favoritism, but positively related to rejection. The study ultimately implies that socially deprived students lag behind their non-deprived counterparts in the development of cognitive objectives; various dimensions of classroom climate can promote the cognitive-development of the children.

In her study, ***Indubala (1999)*** explored the scope of video-instructional package as a unique medium of instruction for better comprehension, attention, appeal and fulfillment of instructional objectives among the students in the formal classroom situation. The study followed a two phased design, where in the initial phase, a video-instructional package on 'Environmental Pollution and Education' was developed; which was followed by an experimental tryout of the developed package. A group of 240 students of IXth grade at secondary schools of Gujarat constitute the sample for the study which where further sub- divided into six experimental groups. Video-instructional- package consisted of video-film and Learners' handbook, developed by the investigator was used to conduct the experiment. Criterion tests, attention measures, experts' judgment and opinionnaire (for the students) happened to be the basic tools to collect data, which were further analyzed through 't' test 'f' ratio and analysis of covariance. The study observes that video instructional films on environmental issues are proved to be effective in motivating students and sustaining the attention on the part of the programme.

Mostly to improve the teaching methods in geography following an environmental approach, ***Kidwai (1999)*** initiated her study where she aimed to identify and thereby to critically analyze the instructional objectives of geography curriculum at secondary stage at Delhi based schools, following a descriptive survey method. Paper-pencil test, questionnaire, informal discussion, and interview technique was used to pull data from the sample group of teachers and students. The study observed that importance of natural environment is neglected in formulating the instructional objectives of teaching social science. Related classifications of concepts are required for both teachers and students. Activities in this regard as mentioned in the textbooks published by Government agencies need specific directions. It was also observed that to make the teachers and students aware about environment, public schools are better than the government schools. The study observed the need to strengthen the method of teaching geography through environmental exposure and filed trips, in order to develop the required attitude towards environment.

Sen (1999) studied the learning strategy, it's relationship with environmental factors, course perception, and academic performance of the Xth grade students from Jalpaiguri district of West Bengal. His study basically focused on the learning styles of students in relation to gender, habitation, subject, and other psychosocial factors of a sample group 600 students from five types of schools. A random sampling technique was used for the study. As many as twelve types of tools were administered over the sample group including various scales, inventories and questionnaires. Apart from basic statistics, ANOVA and 'factor analysis' was employed to analyze the collected data. The study observed the role of ecological environment of family and classroom, teaching style, quality of instruction, method of providing feedback, all possess significant impact over the process of developing suitable learning strategy.

In view of developing supplementary curricular programmes on environmental education for high primary schools, ***Sunnetha (2000)*** took up a study to examine the status of basic understanding in environmental education and attitude towards environmental issues among the upper primary school students from Mysore. In all 174 students from four schools constituted the sample for the study. A post-test parallel-group-design was followed in the experimental study in which Basic understanding test in environmental education, and a scale of attitude towards environment were developed and used to pull the data in five basic components of environment viz. biosphere, air, water, soil and energy. ANOVA, Duncan's Multiple Range Test and step wise multiple regression were followed to analyze the pulled data. The study observed that experimental treatments, using specially designed supplementary curricular programme is, significantly much effective in developing favorable attitude towards environment among the school children. Apart from that the study demonstrates its effectiveness in terms of multidisciplinary approach, substantiating the infusion technique for teaching of environmental education.

Hanumanthaiah (2000) studied the effectiveness of curricular creativity inputs in Physics at the secondary school level with a basic aim of preparing lesson plan in physics at Xth grade and to study the effectiveness of such lessons on students, in relation to mental and psychological attributes. A purposive sampling technique was adopted for the study where Baqer Mehdi (1975)'s test of creativity, RSSB test of mental ability, and Socio Economic Status (SES) scale by Kuppaswamy, as well as two reaction questionnaires for experts and students were used as tools to pull the data, which where further analyzed by 't' test. The study observed that such planned Lessons are having their importance in entertaining the attributes among the students, under study.

Nag (2000) studies the ecological perspective of science education among deprived society in West Bengal. The study was mostly correlational, where attempt was made to find out their inter and intra-correlation among various psychosocial factors (in relation to ecological perspectives towards science, scientific aptitude, and knowledge). For the sake of study, a factorial approach was adopted by the researcher, such as level of deprivation, knowledge base of general science along with scientific attitude, verbal entrance, attitude towards science, perception, expectation, aspiration related to science and science education of students, their fathers and teachers. The study followed a factorial research design including students and their fathers and teacher from rural and urban background. Modified version of prolonged deprivation scale, scientific knowledge and aptitude test (Chatterjee & Mukherjee), NCERT- test of general ability, attitude scale towards science, and a questionnaire where used as tools for collecting data; Collected data where analyzed through ANOVA and 'F' ratio. The study reveals that mere improving the 'method of teaching' or 'infrastructurtal facilities' may hardly contribute for realizing the objectives of science education; rather ecology of 'scientific spirit' is much more essential.

Anita (2000) studied the development of hypothetical reasoning in relation to divergent thinking, intelligence and school climate. The sample for the study includes 498 students from Jhind district of Haryana, studying in ten different types of schools. Cattle's intelligence test, Medhi's test of creativity, Mishra's School environment inventory and Piaget's paper-pencil test wear the tools used by the researcher to collect data for the study. Apart from the concrete findings like positive correlation among creativity and its components, the study observed high correlation between intelligence and hypothetical reasoning. It was also observed that habitation of students act as a significant factor so far their hypothetical reasoning capacity is concerned.

Bishnoi (2001) aimed to study the effect of team-game-tournaments on Hindi grammar on students achievement, their inter group relationship, and self-concept under cooperative learning. A group 70 students from IXth grade was taken as sample who where bifurcated in experimental and controlled group. Cattle's Intelligence test, Kulshretha's SES scale, a self developed achievement test and Saraswat's self concept test was used by the researcher to collect required data. The study arrived at a finding that the 'team-game-tournament' approach of teaching Hindi grammar is much more effective, compared to traditional method of teaching grammar. Cooperative learning is also proved to be better; apart from learning grammar, it enhances the sociability among the children. The study advocates that academic achievement can be changed through cooperative learning methods as its interventions are explicitly socially and motivationally guided.

Das (2002) studied the development of environmental awareness through the study of Life science in the secondary schools of West Bengal, with the help of three sets of questionnaires (especially meant for students, teachers and parents). Apart from Survey, Curriculum analysis was also made. The study finds heterogeneity among the groups in terms of their perception of environmental awareness; it was also observed that several approaches related to life science helps in enhancing environmental awareness among the students.

Vandana (2002) studied the managerial skills of educational administrators in relation to organizational climate and certain personality factors. The major aim of the study was to explore the comprehensive profile of educational administrators, apart from their various administrative skills, their interrelationship and to suggest workable guideline for strengthening such skills, related to manage the system of education. A convenient sampling technique was followed for the study, following which a group of 100 college administrators were chosen for the study. A questionnaire was administered over them to fetch the required data on seven dimensions of managerial skills. Apart from exploring the status of the respondent group, the study explored their personality factors and interaction patterns in consonance with their managerial skills.

Srivastava (2003) initiated a comparative study of the life style and value pattern of the students studying in schools with different medium of instruction, where she studied the students from intermediate class grades (i.e. +2 stage) from Hindi and English medium schools. Sample for the study was picked up following a 'Lottery', i.e., random method from 4 Hindi and 4 English medium colleges from Lucknow city. Tools used by the researcher include value scale (by Srivastava & Ram), Life style questionnaire, and socio economic status scale (Urban; by Datta). 't' test was used for analyzing data collected by the researcher. The study observes that the respondents from two different mediums differ in terms of their cognitive, esthetic and health related values, where students from English medium schools found superior. However in terms of economic, patriotic, social, ability and religious values. They are inferior to their counter respondent group from Hindi medium. Gender, as the study observes, does not appear as an intervening factor in this context, The study further reveals a zero difference among the two lingua- groups, so far their scores on 'Modern Indian life style' is concerned.

Rekha (2004) attempted to study the effect of school environment on Creativity and academic achievement of scheduled and non-scheduled caste students at Agra. The study followed a juxtaposition approach over a sample of 400 students, including proportionate ratio of gender and caste affiliation. Tools used for the study includes School Environment Inventory (1986, by Mishra), and Medhi's Verbal Test of creative thinking (1985).

Intermediate Board Examination marks were used as criterion for academic achievement. She observed in her study that institutional environment acts as an important factor, which influence the level of creativity of scheduled caste students; however, in case of the creativity of non-scheduled caste students, it does not possess any impact. The study challenges the prevailing concept of positive correlation between the two factors viz school environment and academic achievement. This may be due to the positive impact of reservation policy which might helped the oppressed sections of the society to express their excellence in favorable atmosphere. So far the level of creativity is concerned, it was found that there exist no significant difference among the scheduled and non-scheduled caste boys and girls.

An Analysis

As it appears from the glimpse of the studies carried out and completed so far since 1997 in the discipline 'Education', major share of these studies are related to school-education. Though they differs in terms of level and direction of objectives. While *Tomor (1998), Rathore (1999), and Sunnetha (2000)*'s studies are focused over the primary school education, studies carried out *by Gupta (1997), Indubala (1999), Kidwai (1999), Sen (1999), Hanumanthaiah (2000), Nag (2000), Anita (2000), Bishnoi (2001), Das (2002)* and *Rekha (2004)'* are dealing with the secondary level of school education. On the other hand, studies carried out by *Gogoi (1998), Singh (1998), Vandana (2002)* and *Srivastava (2003)* are related either with tertiary level of school education or with higher education. The scenario reveals that major share of the studies carried out in the dimension of environmental education are directed towards secondary level, which is followed by higher education, and primary level, respectively. This trend indicates that even today, secondary level of school education draw the attention of the majority of the researchers in the field of environmental education. Apart from the level, (in which the studies are carried out), the studies are directed towards five specific directions, which includes *awareness-study, development of teaching methodology and learning styles, supplementation towards curriculum, school-climate, and interrelationship of environmental education with other psycho-social factors.* Studies carried out by *Gupta (1997)* and *Gogoi (1998)* are *awareness study,* whereas the study carried out by *Das (2002)* is also, to some extent related to the awareness aspect. Studies conducted by *Indubala (1999), Kidwai (1999), Sen (1999), Bishnoi (2001)* and *Das (2002)* are devoted to development of *teaching method of environmental education*, either as an independent subject or in tune with other subjects. *Tomor (1998), Sunnetha (2000)* and *Hanumanthaiah (2000)'s* studies are relating the *curricular aspects in relation to environmental education. School climate* appears as a major concern in the studies carried out by *Rathore (1999), Deb (1999)* and *Vandana (2002).* Psychosocial aspects of environmental education have been explored by *Singh (1988), Nag (2000)* and *Srivastava (2003).* A careful look towards the studies reveals that though they are classified under five categories, however some of those studies may claim a *transitional status.* Studies carried out by *Anita (2000), Rekha (2004)* and *Vandana (2002)* may be the examples of the kind. In their studies, they incorporate variables from both- *psychosocial aspects* as well as *school climate.*

It is interesting to note that all these studies are by nature survey –type, having restricted scope of developing theory. However their importance can't be minimized if one considers the process of validation of methodologies, following which those are completed. Moreover emergence of the subject 'environmental education' may fetch much more contribution from these studies, in terms of dimension, level, area, nature and factors. Ultimately to give environmental education a concrete shape, what we actually need is to explore the more recent trend of research in which studies are in progress in numerous higher learning institutes across the country as well as to initiate studies, capable of contributing theories in the sphere of environmental education.

Taxonomy of Research in Environmental Education

Taxonomy is the systematic classification of a certain activities or phenomenon. While it counts the doctoral research in a decadal period, it involves the type of research in a specific domain or sub-domains, carried out in the very time span. Research in the area of environmental education is just a recent phenomenon. In Indian academia, educational research, encompassing environment as a major factor, was first reported almost a decade back in the year 1997. Even before a couple of decades back since then, environmental education evolved as a move, however in Indian academia, it took almost two decades for the educationists to reflect research-output in the very area. Objectives of Environmental Education, as endorsed in an international Conference, organized jointly by UNESCO and UNEP in the year 1977, held at Tbilisi, the then USSR, [became familiar as Tbilisi Conference in course of time] hinge over developing specific four attributes among the cross section of the population noted as follows:

- **Awareness:** to help social groups and individuals to acquire an awareness of, and sensitivity to the total environment and its allied problems.
- **Knowledge:** to help social groups and individuals to gain a variety of experience in, and acquire a basic understanding of, the environment and its associated problems.
- **Attitudes:** to help social groups and individuals to acquire a set of values and feelings of concern for the environment, and the motivation for actively participating in environmental improvement and protection.
- **Participation:** to provide social groups and individuals with an opportunity to be actively involved at all levels, to work toward resolutions of environmental problems.

In changed scenario, environmental education evolved as a systematic strategy to develop these attributes among the students.

Environmental Education vis-a-vis Ethical and Social Responsibility: What Actually is Needed?

In the sector of higher education during the mid eighties, especially in India, a trend evolved to incorporate the concerns of social responsibility and ethical awareness with a view to protect our environment. It was realized that until and unless we are become conscious about their ethical responsibility, it would be difficult for us to survive on this planet.

To be more specific, ethics refers to the rules or standards of right conduct or practices, especially the standard of a profession, or a field. Environmental ethics emphasized to all those who are the part of the environment and its beneficiaries, to act in such a way so that the deterioration of the environment be prevented. Environment can meet human needs, but not human greed. Therefore the question of ethics and social responsibility towards environment appears as a key issue of environmental education.

It is worth mentioning in this context that the aim of environmental education will go in vain if environmental ethics are not properly taken into consideration. For the sake of survival of the humanity, environment should be used judiciously; simultaneously some minimum ethical acts are necessary so that the environment can be protected for the use of future generations. If this is not followed, environment will take serious revenge on the humankind in specific, and on the biomass in general.

Unfortunately much curriculum development about education for the environment is based on the belief that providing knowledge about an environmental issue will produce correct behavioral exposures. Various teaching schemes have not assumed a direct link between knowledge and attitudes and have concentrated on attitude while sharing the assumption that appropriate action will follow inculcation of attitude.

Development of Environmental Education

To incorporation of Environmental Education into the process of education, it is essential to establish the needed mandate and responsibility for educational institutions to abide with. Without responsibility environmental education will stay as a peripheral subject or activity and it may never be established as an interwoven part of the core of education and curriculum for students and teachers. Research is a prerequisite for this purpose to suggest theory, methodology and thereby reorganizing existing appropriate and indigenous knowledge and skill, following which, it will be easy-accessible for the cross-section of the people of our country to fulfill the objectives of environmental education.

In this context it is essential to focus over curriculum and teaching styles, following which education is imparted to our students. For renewal of the curriculum, it is again essential to initiate special efforts, basing on research-based data, and involving curriculum experts, experienced teachers, environmental-science experts and community representatives. Their task will be to formulate specific aims and objectives for environmental-education, suited to our oriental situation. They will also be entrusted with the responsibilities to examine the curriculum of the primary, secondary and higher secondary schools, as well as colleges and universities, and thereby to identify the concepts of environmental education, already covered, so that it could serve as one of the bases upon which the environmentalisation of curriculum of formal education could rest-on, apart identifying local environmental problems, additional environmental-education contents required, appropriate activities; time needed for different subjects and topics, instructional methodologies and appropriate instructional techniques. However none of these activities should be based on perception of individuals or groups rather should be based on data generated through research in the arena of educational research.

The amalgamation of the above elements and their organization at grade or age levels would form the environmental education dimension of the curriculum. The nature of identified environmental-education objectives and pertinent environmental contents and problems will give the curriculum its essential local dimension or character to suit the local needs.

However research in environmental education in Indian academia is not given desired weightage. Though since a decade, some studies has been initiated in various Indian universities, and some are in progress centering round 'environmental education' and in course doctoral award has been given to those completed. In the forthcoming section, we can have a glance perusal of the status of research on environmental education at doctoral level.

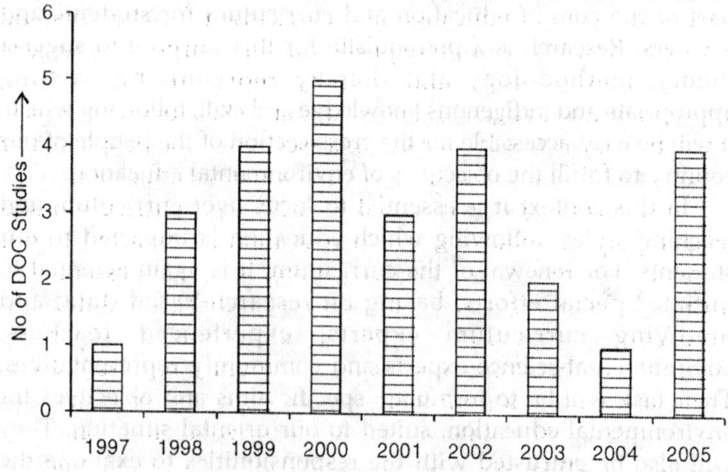

Fig 1 : *Year Wise Number of Ph.D. on Environmental Education Awarded by Indian Universities*

Decadal rate of number of doctoral studies in environmental education reveals that since 1997, up till now, just twenty seven doctoral awards has been made by the Indian universities and similar other higher learning institutes, where the studies are specifically focused on environmental education. A glance perusal over the Figure-1 categorically indicates that during the period, 1997-2001, an increasing trend was prevailed, so far number of studies are concerned. Except the years, 2002 & 2005, just a reverse picture is prominent where the number of studies in environmental education shows a declining trend in terms of number of doctoral awards. However situation in the year 2002 and last year [i.e., 2005] is quite encouraging.

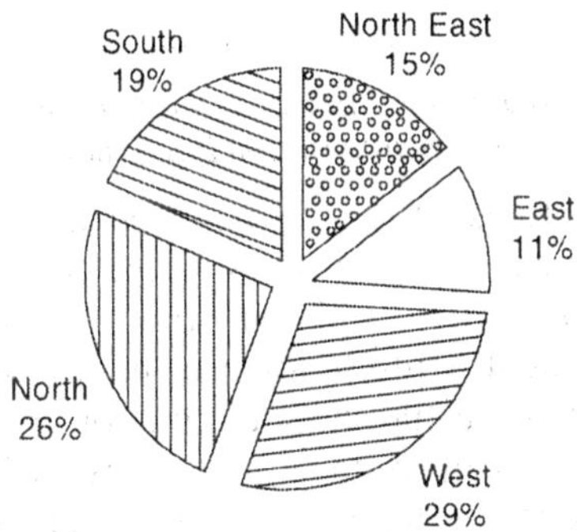

Fig. 2 : *Region-Wise Distribution of Doctoral Studies on Environmental Education*

Figure-2 represents the region wise award made by Indian universities. It is interesting to note that while almost one-third of the bulk of research on environmental education carried out in the university-education departments, situated in the western region of the country, for the universities situated in the northern India, it is little more than a quarter of the total studies in the very direction., which is further followed by southern and northeastern region. Situation in the eastern region reveals that only eleven percent of the studies are hosted and doctoral degrees are awarded by the universities, situated in the very region.

Among the bulk of doctoral research-studies, carried out and degrees awarded by the Indian universities, in the area of environmental education, it was observed that these studies dealt with a sequels of factors and variables. As such an attempt was

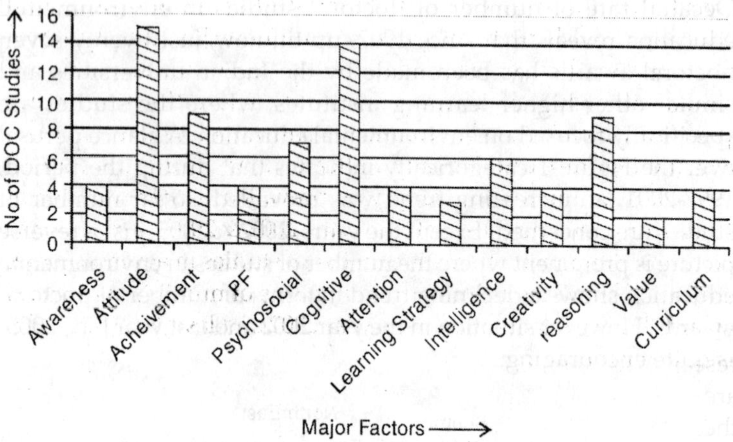

Fig. 3 : *Major Factors Considered in the Studies on Environmental Education*

made to classify those studies, basing on the major factors, on which these studies are based on. Keeping this in view, as many as thirteen major factors are identified. These are awareness towards environment, attitude towards environment and related dimensions, academic achievement, numerous personality factors, various psycho social attributes cognitive styles, level of attention, numerous learning strategies, level of intelligence, creativity, reasoning value-pattern and curriculum. It is to be noted here that none of these studies hinge over a single set of factor. Factor –based distributions, as depicted in the Figure-3 reveals that while factors like attitude, cognitive styles of the learners, reasoning ability of the learners and academic achievement of the learners drew the attention of a sizable number of scholars, who carried out these studies, studies involving value-pattern and curriculum as factors are quite less in number. In other words, it may be said that while some factors are much emphasized in these studies, some other factors are scarcely emphasized. The figure further helps in exploring the direction, towards which these studies are actually directed. As almost all these studies are falling within the broader spectrum of discipline 'education', so, by nature these are educational research in the gamut of environmental education. As such it is quite natural that educational orientation is the basis of these studies and those usually followed methodology of educational research.

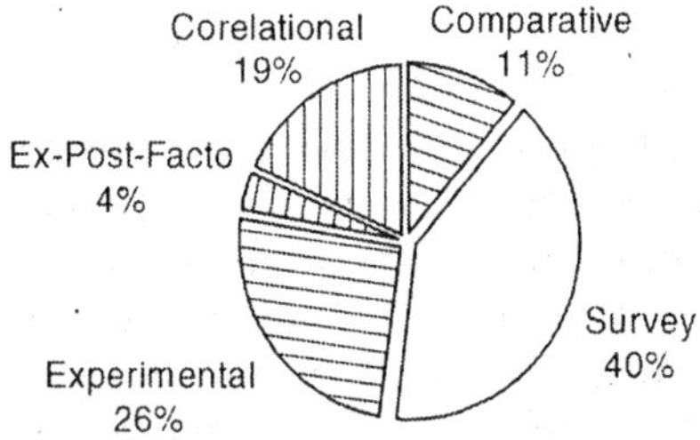

Fig. 4 : *Types of Research on Environmental Education in Terms of Methodology Followed*

Most of these studies followed the conventional types of educational research, so far as the methodology following which these studies are conducted. Figure- 4 depicts the methodological distribution of these doctoral studies.

It is interesting to note that as much as 40% of these doctoral studies followed the survey method to explore the numerous factors of their sample groups. To the extreme contrast, just 4% of these studies followed an Ex-post-facto research design. The researchers in their studies have done juxtapositional-comparison and as such, 11% of these studies are by nature, comparative-studies, where comparison has been made among different factors, variables and sample groups. Experimental and co-relational approach has been followed in 26% and 19% of the studies, respectively. Here the affinity of the researchers towards survey method appears as a trend.

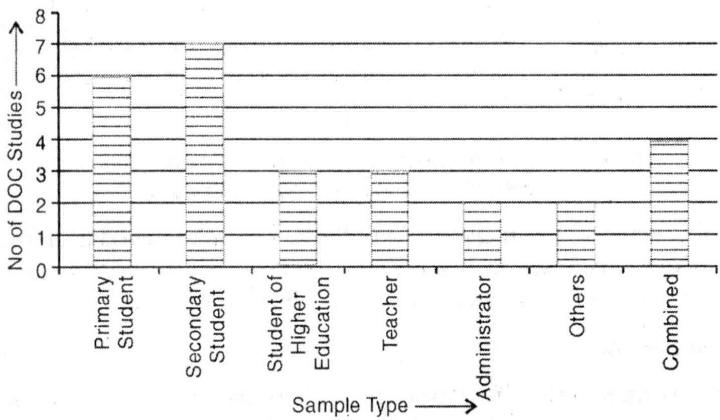

Fig. 5 : *Types of Research on Environmental Education in Terms of Methodology Followed*

So far the nature of human samples, considered in these studies, are concerned, those are classified in seven categories, such as students, belonging to primary, secondary and higher education, teachers, institutional-administrators and management groups, combination of the previously-spelt groups and others.

Table-5 reveals that while major share of these studies accords students from secondary level as their human samplė, followed by students belonging to primary and higher education, just eleven percent of the studies considered only teachers as the human sample. Sizable percentage of the studies (around 15%) used a combination of teachers, students and other human components, directly involved in education, as their sample group. Educational administrators are also considered as human sample in some studies.

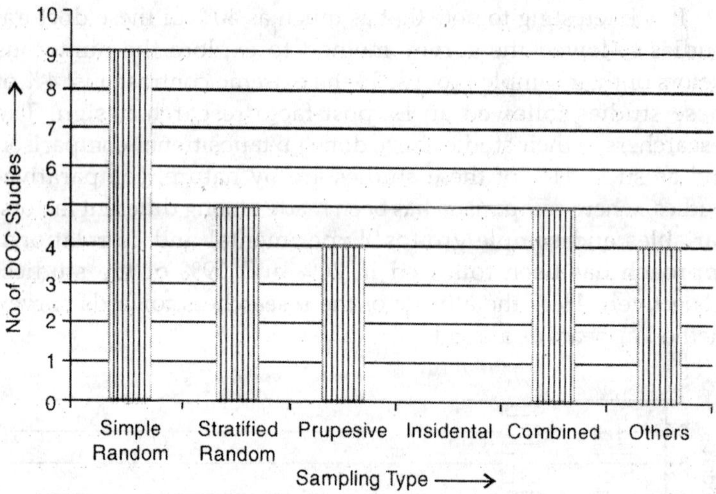

Fig. 6 : *Types of Research on Environmental Education in Terms of Sampling Technique Followed*

In consonance, major share of these studies followed a simple random sampling technique, followed by stratified random, combined and purposive sampling techniques.

Post Script

Environmental education in its broadest sense is about 'empowerment' and developing a sense of 'ownership', improving the capacity of people to address environment and development issues in their own communities. It is about touching people's beliefs and attitudes so that they want to live sustainably, providing sufficient information and knowledge to support these beliefs and to translate attitudes and values into action. Of course this process includes serious research and also encompasses another whole dimension — that which has been placed at the 'core' of the teaching and learning model — the dimension of 'informal' education sources.

A survey of the research in environmental education reveals that most of the studies are macro-survey in nature, where the researches incorporate comparatively more number of factors and variables. As a consequence, most of the researches in the very area are surface level studies. A change in this trend is also required so that in-depth studies can be emphasized. Due to earlier orientation towards education, humanities or allied disciplines, most of the researches in the area use to avoid experimental studies (i.e., the studies, which are carried out following an experimental design). They are more comfortable and biased towards survey type of research. Various organizations and institutions have already reported number of surveys. Keeping in view the findings of such earlier studies, educational researchers in future are to be encouraged to take-up studies, which should be in-depth studies about environmental education and its concerns. Use of experimental design should also be encouraged to explore the effect of various factors and variables, which influence environmental and developmental actions. Comparative studies of different environmental setup, and of the similar environmental setup in different time span, should also be encouraged. Such studies are supposed to follow a juxtaposition approach. Unfortunately educational researchers have overall neglected this very area of research.

Bibliography and References

A Framework for Environmental Learning and Sustainability in Canada (2002), Government of Canada: Ottawa.

A Leokum (1990), *Tell me why*? The Octopus Publishing Co. Limited, London.

Abe, O. and Bishnu Bhandari (1999), *An overview of environmental education in the Asia and Pacific region*. Proceedings of the International Conference on Environmental Education in the Asia-Pacific Region, Yokohama, Japan, 27-28 February 1999.

Agenda 21 (1992), United Nations Conference on Environment and Development. *The Earth Summit*

Albuquerque/Bernalillo County Planning Department (1991), Albuquerque/Bernalillo County Comprehensive Plan. Albuquerque Planning Dept. Office.

Allaby, M. (1994), *Concise Dictionary of Ecology*. Great Britain: Oxford University Press.

Arora, G.L. (1995), *Child centred education for learning without burden*. Gurgaon, Haryana, Krishna Publishing Company.

Arora, G.L. and Ray Shefali (1993), *Towards an enlightened human resource in education*. New Delhi, State Council of Educational Research and Training.

Arora, G.L.; Yadav, S.K (1998), *Self-learning materials for teacher educators*. Vol. 1. New Delhi, NCERT.

Baldes,D.; Cahill,C. and Moretto, F. (2000), *Motivating Students To Learn through Multiple Intelligences, Cooperative Learning, and Positive Discipline*. Masters Action Research Project, Saint Xavier University.

Banister S, Vannatta R. (2006), Beginning with a baseline: insuring productive technology integration in teacher education, *Journal of Technology and Teacher Education*.Norfolk: Vol. 14, Iss. 1; p. 209, p. 27.

Bapat, K.N., *Innovations in household appliances*, Un-published.

Bapat, M.N. (2003), Investigatory Projects and organization of Activities in Secondary School Science, Regional Institute of Science, Mysore.

———, (2005), Insight, *The Journal of Education*, University of Kashmir, p. 94.

———, (2006), Orienting KRP's of Navodaya and that of Andhra Pradesh to encourage children to carry out research based projects in science at secondary level, Regional Institute of Education, Mysore.

Barr, R.B. & Tagg, J. (1995), From Teaching to Learning - A New Paradigm for Undergraduate Education, *Change Magazine*, 27 (6); New York: *pp 13-25*.

Bateson, Gregory (1988), *Mind and Nature: A Necessary Unity*. New York: Bantam.

Bonds, Cox, & Gantt-Bonds (1993), Curriculum Wholeness Through Synergetic Teaching. *The Clearing House*, 4, 66, 252-254.

Bonwell, C.C. & Eison, J.A. (1991), *"Active Learning: Creating Excitement in the Classroom"*, *New* Jercy.

Bowler, P. J. (1992), *"The Fontana History of the Environmental Sciences"*, Fontana, London.

Breault, R. A. (2003), Dewey, Freire, and pedagogy for the oppressed, in *Multicultural Education*: 10, 3, 2-6.

Brooks, D. (2005), Mind over Muscle. *The New York Times*, 16 October, 2005, p. A-12.

Brundtland Commission, 1987 Retrieved from http://www.areadmin.ch/are/en/nachhaltig/international_uno/unterseite02330

Byrne, B.M. (1994), Burnout testing for the validity, replication, and invariance of causal structure across the elementary, intermediate, and secondary teachers, in *American Educational Research Journal*, 31 (3), 645-673.

Caduto, Michael and Bruchac, Joseph (1988), *Keepers of the Earth: Native American and Environmental Activities for Children*. Golden, CO: Fulcrum, Inc.

Calhoun, E. (1997), *Literacy for All*. Saint Simons Island, GA: The Phoenix Alliance.

———, (1999), *Teaching Reading and Writing through the Picture Word Inductive Model*. Alexandria, Virginia: The Association for Superviion and Curriculum Development.

Campbell, B. (1991), Multiple Intelligences in the Classroom, in *Context*, Issue 27, Winter, Langley, WA, USA, Context Institute.

Capra, F. (2002), *The Hidden Connectedness: Integrating the Biological, Cognitive, and Social Dimensions of Life into a Science of Sustainability*. NY: Doubleday.

CEE (1987), *Introducing Environmental Education, Book 2, Schools: Educating for Life, Reading*. Council for Environmental Education.

Chakrabarty, M. K. (1967), *Indian Journal of Industrial Medicine*, 13, 121.

Cooper, D.E. & Palmer, J. A. (eds.) (1992), *The Environment in Question*. Routledge, London.

Cooperative Learning, WWW Page, Accessed on 14th May, 2007. http://edtech.kennesaw.edu/intech/cooperativelearning. htm#elements

Council on Environmental Quality (1976), *The Growth Shapes.* Washington: Government Printing Office.

Curriculum Board for Secondary Education. *Scheme of comprehensive school-based evaluation.* New Delhi, Government of India, n.d.

Cutter, S. L. (1991), et. al.; *Exploitation, Conservation, Preservation: A Geographical Perspective on Natural Resource Use,* Wiley Chichester.

Daniels, H. & Edwards, A. (Eds.) (2004), *The Reader in Psychology of Education,* RoutledgeFalmer, London.

Deshler, D. & Schumaker, J. (2006), *Teaching Adolescents with Disabilities.* Thousand Oaks, California: Corwin.

Dewey, J. (1963), *Experience and Education.* New York: Collier Books.

Donahue, P. (1999), *1998 NAEP Reading Report Card for the Nation and the States.* Washington, D.C.: U.S. Department of Education.

Dorman, P. (2000), *Economics of Occupational Safety and Health, Safe Work,* ILO, Geneva, April, 2000.

Durka, G. (2003), *The Teacher's Calling. A Spirituality for Who Teach.* New York: Paulist Press.

Durkin, D. (1966), *Children Who Read Early.* New York: Teachers College Press.

Dyer, C. (1996), *Moving from Rhetoric to Reality,* RMIT University, Melbourne.

Earthworks Group (1990), 50 Simple Things Kids Can Do to Save the Earth. Andrews and McMeel.

Eblen, William and Ruth (1977), *Experiencing the Total Environment.* New York: Scholastic Book Services.

Ehrlich, P. and R. Ornstein (1989), *New World: New Mind.* New York, Doubleday.

Elkind, D. (2001), Much Too Early. Palo Alto: The Hoover Institute, Stanford University.

Elkind, David. (1987), *Miseducation: Preschoolers at Risk.* New York: Knopf.

Elsom, D. (1987), *Atmospheric Pollution: Causes, Effects And Control Policies,* Blackwell, Oxford.

Elsom, D. (1987), *Atmospheric Pollution: Causes, Effects And Control Policies:* Blackwell, Oxford.

Engeström. Y. (1999), Situated learning at the threshold of the new millennium. In J. Bliss, R. Säljö, & P. Light (Eds.), *Learning sites: Social and technological aspects.* Oxford: Pergamon/Elsevier: pp. 249-257

Feynman, R. P.; Leyton R.B. and Sands, M, *Feynman lectures on Physics,* Narosa Publishing House, New Delhi (1998)

Fink, D., & Stoll, L. (2005), Educational change: Easier said than dome. In Hargreaes, A. (Ed.), *Extended Educational Change,* The Neatherlands: Springer, 17-42.

Finson, S. (1987), Feminist spirituality within the framework of feminist consciousness. *Studies in Religion,* 16(1), 65-77.

Fogarty, R. (1991), *The Mindful School: How to Integrate the Curricula.* Palatine: Skylight Publishing Inc.

Foster, Leila Merrell (1990), *The Story of Rachel Carson and the Environmental Movement*. Children's Press.

Fox, W. (1995), *Towards Transpersonal Ecology*. Boston: Shambhala.

Freire, P. (1970), *Pedagogy of the Oppressed.* New York: Seabury Press.

Gao, Helen (2005), Kindergarten or 'Kindergrind'? School getting tougher for kids. *San Diego Union-Tribune*. April 11, 2005

Gardner, H. (1983), *Frames of Mind: The Theory of Multiple Intelligences.* New York: Basic Books.

———, (1993a), Choice Points as Multiple Intelligences Enter the School. *Intelligence Connections*, III, 1, 3, Fall, 7-8.

———, (1993b), *Multiple Intelligences: The Theory in Practice.* New York: Basic Books.

———, (1993c), *Frames of Mind: The Theory of Multiple Intelligences*, 10th Anniversary Edition. New York: Basic Books.

———, (1995), Reflections on Multiple Intelligences. *Phi Delta Kappan*, 77(3), 200-208.

———, (1996), Probing More Deeply into the Theory of Multiple Intelligences. *Bulletin*, November, 1-7.

———, (1998), Are there Additional Intelligences? The Case for Naturalist, Spiritual, and Existential Intelligences, in J. Kane (Ed.), *Education, Information, and Transformation*. Upper Saddle River, NJ: Merrill-Prentice Hall, pp. 111-131

———, (1999), *Intelligence Reframed: Multiple Intelligences for the 21st Century*. New York: Basic Books.

Gebara, I. (1999), *Longing for running water: Ecofeminism and liberation*. Minneapolis, MN: Fortress Press.

Geimer, M.; Getz, J.; Pochert,T.; Pullam, K. (2000), Improving Student Achievement in Language Arts through Implementation of Multiple Intelligences Strategies. Master of Arts Action Research Project, Saint Xavier University and SkyLight Professional Development.

George, M.; Mitofsky,J.; Peter, M. (2001), Improving Student Interest in Social Studies through the Use of Multiple Intelligences. Master of Arts Action Research Project, Saint Xavier University and SkyLight Professional Development Field-Based Master's Program.

Goudic, A. S. (1984), *The Nature of the Environment*: Blackwell, Oxford.

Government of India (1999), *Operationalization of the suggestions for teacher fundamental duties to the citizens of the country. Interim report*. New Delhi.

Grabovska, R. (2006), Sustainability as a pedagogical category and its perspective in teacher education, in A. Pipere (ed.) (2006). *Education and Sustainable Development*. Daugavpils: Saule, 211-223.

Gunning, T. (1998), Best Books for Beginning Readers. Boston, Allyn Bacon.

Hanson, R. & Farrell, D. (1995), The long-term effects on high school seniors of learning to read in kindergarten. *Reading Research Quarterly*, 30 (4). 908-933.

Harrow, A.J. (1992), *A Taxonomy of the Psychomotor Domain*, New York: David McKay Co., Inc.

Harten, W. (1991), *"Science Concept and Skills"*, Cit in *International Encyclopaedia of Curriculum*, Pergamon Press, Oxford.

Hawkins, David (1974), *The Informed Vision*. New York: Agathon Press.

Haysom, J.J. and C.R. Sutton (Edited) (1974), *Innovation in Teacher Education*, Mc Graw Hills, London.

Heilweil, I. (2002), *Teachers and technology: from training to implementation*, PHD dissertation, University of Leicester.

Hopkins, Susan and Winters, Jeffery (1990), *Discover the World: Empowering Children to Value Themselves, Others and the Earth*. Santa Cruz, CA New Society Publishers.

Hutchison, D. (1998), *Growing up Green. Educating for Ecological Renewal*. New York Teachers College Press.

ICMR. (2001), Report of the working group on "Environmental and occupational Health" for 10th five year plan, prepared by Indian Council of Medical Research, New Delhi, pp. 1-117.

ICR, (1996), Preparedness and response to chemical emergencies, India Country Report (for World Health Organization), June 1996.

Iliško, Dz. (2004), Developing sensitivities towards 'the other' in an ecologically sustainable global community, in *International Journal of Comparative Religious Education and Values*, 16, 33-43.

Iliško, Dz. (2005), Pedagogical challenges for implementing holistic curriculum in Latvia, in *Journal of Teacher Education and Training*. Daugavpils: Saule, 5, 28-40.

———, (2006), Ecofeminism – a healing perspective for reshaping religious education, in M de Souza, (ed.) *International Handbook of the Religious, Moral and Spiritual Dimensions in Education*. The Netherlands: Springer, 127-141.

———, (2006), The challenges of pedagogy: Reclaiming one's voice to construct a just world, in S. Smita & A. Gupta (ed.) (2006). *At Risk population*. Sociolinguistic Educational Issues. New Delhi: Dominate Publishers and Distributors.

———, (2007), Teachers as Agents of Societal Change. In A. Pipere (Eds). *Journal of Teacher Education for Sustainability*. 11, 1, 14-27

International Reading Association and The National Association for the Education of Young Children. (1998). Position Statement on Learning to Read and Write: Developmentally Appropriate Practices for Young Children. Newark, Delaware: International Reading Association.

International Reading Association. (1998), Position Statement on Phonemic Awareness and the Teaching of Reading. Newark, Deleware: International Reading Association

Jacobs, Jane (1961), *Death and Life of Great American Cities*. (A Vintage Book) New York: Random House.

James, Charity (1974), *Beyond Customs*. New York; Agathan Press.

Janes, L.M.; Koutsopanagos, C.L.; Mason, D.S.; Villaranda, I. (2000), Improving Student Motivation through the Use of Engaged Learning, Cooperative Learning and Multiple Intelligences. Master's Action Research Project, Saint Xavier University and SkyLight Field-Based Master's Program.

Jonassen, D. H. (2000), *Computers as mindtools for schools: Engaging critical thinking* (2nd ed.). Upper Saddle River, NJ: Prentice-Hall.

Jonassen, D. H., & Rohrer-Murphy, L. (1999), Activity theory as a framework for designing constructivist learning environments. *Educational Technology: Research & Development*, 47 (1), 61-72. Available on line: http://tiger.coe.missouri.edu/~jonassen/courses/CLE/documents/activity.pdf.

Jones, A. J. (2003), ICT and future teachers: Are we preparing for e-learning? http://crpit.com/confpapers/CRPITV23Jones.pdf.

Joyce, B., Calhoun, E., & Hrycauk, M. (2001), A second chance for struggling readers. *Educational Leadership*. 58, 6, 42-47.

———, (2003), Learning to read in kindergarten. *Phi Delta Kappan*, 85, 2, 126-132.

Joyce, B.R. & Weil, M. (1980), *Models of Teaching*. Englewood Cliffs, N.J., Prentice Hall Inc.

Kahn, Herman and Wiener, Anthony J. (1967), *The Year 2000*. New York: MacMillan.

Kaul, L. (2003), *"Methodology of Educational Research"*, Vikas Publishing, New Delhi.

Kemp. D. D. (1994), *"Global Environmental Issues: A Climatological Approach"*, Routeledge, London.

Lakatos, G. & Meszaros, I. (2004), Actual issues of education of sustainable development in Eastern and Central European countries, in the Proceedings of 3rd International JTET Conference in Tallin 'Sustainable Development. Culture. Education.' *Latvia Human Development Report* (LHDR) (2001) Riga: UNESCO.

Lappe, Francis M. (1975), *Diet for a Small Planet*. New York: Ballantine Press.

Lele, S. M. (1991), Sustainable development: A Critical Review, in *World Development*, 19 (6), 607-621.

Leopold, Aldo (1949), *Sand County Almanac*. New York: Oxford University Press.

Leopold, Aldo (1977), *Sand County Almanac Illustrated* (new edition). Madison, WI: Tamarack Press.

Mannion, A. M. & Bowlby, S. R. (1992), (Eds.): *Environmental issues in the 1990s*; Wiley: Chichester.

Mannion, A. M. (1991), "*Global Environmental change: A Natural and Cultural Environmental History*", Longman, Harlow.

McFague, S. (1993), *The Body of God: An Ecological theology*. Minneapolis, MN: Fortress Press.

McFague, S. (1995), An earthly theological agenda, in M.H. MacKinnon & M.MacIntyre (Eds). *Readings in Ecology and Feminist Theology*. Kansas City, MO: Sheed & Ward, 327-334.

McHarg, Ian. (1969), *Design with Nature*. Garden City, NJ: Natural History Press.

McInnis, Noel (1972), *You Are An Environment*. Evanston, IL: Center for Curriculum Design.

McInnis, Noel and Albrecht, Don (1975), *What Makes Education Environmental*? Washington and Louisville, KY: Environmental Educators, Inc., and Data Courier.

Meadows, Donna H., (1972), et al. *The Limits to Growth*. New York: Universe Books.

Mezirow, J. (1991), *Transformative Dimensions of Adult Learning*. San Francisco: Jossey-Bass.

Miller, J.P. (1996), *The Holistic Curriculum*. Toronto: Ontario Institute for Studies in Education Press.

Ministry of Human Resource Development (1986). *National policy on education*. New Delhi, Government of India.

Ministry of Human Resource Development (1991), Department of Education. *Minimum levels of learning at the primary stage*. New Delhi, Government of India.

Moore, E. M. (1998), *Ministering with the Earth*. St.Louis, MO: Chalice Press.

Mor, N. (2001), Changes in conceptions of learning as a function of experiencing novel learning environments. Dissertation, Faculty of Education, University of Haifa.

Natale, J. (2001), Early learners: Are full day academic kindergartens too much, too soon. *American School Board Journal*. 188, 3, 22-25.

National Advisory Committee (1993), Ministry of Human Resource Development. *Learning without burden*. New Delhi, Government of India, National Council of Educational Research and Training.

National Center for Educational Statistics (1998), *Long term trends in reading performance*. NAEP Facts. Washington, D.C.: Office of Educational Research and Improvement, U.S. Department of Education.

National Council of Educational Research and Training (2005), *National Curriculum Framework, 2005. NCERT, New Delhi.*

National Council of Educational Research and Training (NA), WWW Page, Accessed on 29th April, 2007 from http://ncert.nic.in/sites/publication/envstudies/perspective_EES.htm.

National curriculum for elementary and secondary education (1988). *A framework*. New Delhi, Government of India.

National Institute of Child Health and Human Development (2000), *Report of the National Reading Panel: Teaching children to read: An evidence-based assessment of the scientific research literature on reading and its implications for reading instruction*. Rockville, MD: National Institute of Child Health and Human Development. Washington, D.C.: U.S. Government Printing Office.

National Recreation and Park Association. Energy. Arlington, VA: Energy Conservation Project.

National Wildlife Federation (1991), *Conservation Directory*. National Wildlife Federation, 1400 16th Street, NW Washington, D.C. 20036-2266.

Natural Resources Defense Council. *NRDC Newsletter*. New York.

New Mexico State University Cooperative Extension Service (1965), *Range Management: Then and Now*. University Park, NM.

Novak, J. D. (1990), Concept maps and Vee diagrams: Two metacognitive tools for science and mathematics education. *Instructional Science*, 19, 29-52.

Novak, J.D. (1991), Clarify with concept maps: A tool for students and teachers alike. *The Science Teacher*, 58 (7), 45-49.

O'Sullivan, E. (2001), *Transformative Learning. Educational Vision for the 21st century*. London: Zed Books.

Ohanian, H C (1994), *Principles of Physics*, W W Norton & Co. New York.

Orr, D.W. (1992), *Ecological Literacy. Education and the Transition to a Postmodern World*. New York: State University of New York Press.

Palmer, J. & Neal, P. (1996), *The Handbook of Environmental Education*. Routledge, London.

Parikh, D. J. and Kashyap, S. K. (1995), Industrialization and its impact on Occupational Hygiene, *Indian Journal of Industrial Medicine*, 41(4), 167-170.

Phoon, W. O. (1985), Occupational Health in developing countries in Asia, South-East Asia Medical Information Centre, Tokyo.

Pickering, K. T. & Owen, L. A. (1994), *"An Introduction to Global Environmental Issues"*, Routeledge, London.

Pipere, A. (2006), Philosophy of education for sustainable development: Perspectives of doctoral students in education, in A. Pipere. (Ed). *Education & Sustainable Development. First Steps Towards Changes*. Daugavpils: Saule, 43-58.

Plitz, Albert (1960), *How Your Body Uses Food*. Chicago: National Dairy Council.

Proceedings, (1986), International Conference and workshop on "Training and Education in Occupational Hygiene", *Luxembourg*, 19-20 June, 1986.

Putnam-Northern Westchester Board of Cooperative Educational Services. *Environment: A Humanistic Approach*. Heights, NY: ECOS Training Institute.

Queitzsch, M. (1997), The Northwest regional profile: Integration of technology in preservice teacher education programs. http://www.netc.org/preservice/challenge.html.

Raj, S. (2004), *Teaching of Environmental Education*. IVY Publishing House, New Delhi.

Rajgopal, T. (2002), Occupational Health Status in India–An Overview Published by *National Safety Council*, in 10th National Conference on HSE Challengers in the Era of Globalizations, 1-11th April, 2002, Vigyan Bhavan, New Delhi, pp. 1-7.

Ranade, M.D. (2006), Computer-based Instruction on "Multiple Intelligences Approach to Teaching": Research Studies in Teacher Education, Hong Kong, APERA Conference Proceedings.

Rao, M. N. and Lundgren, N. P. V. (1955), A review of Occupational Health Research in India, ICMR, New Delhi.

Redinger, C. (1997), BS 8800 : 1996–A British Occupational Health and Safety Management System, *The Synergist*, 8, 32.

Roberts, N. (Ed.) (1994), *"The Changing Global Environment"*, Blackwell, Oxford.

Roosevelt, Theodore (1976), "Opening Address at Conference of Governors, 1901," Nash, Roderci, et al,. The American Environment, Readings in the History of Conservation. Reading, Mass: Addison-Wesley.

Roy, R, Chakraborty, S.K., & Mondal, N.K. (September, 2004), Technology and Education for Human Resource Development in Asia and Pacific, Cit. in the post-seminar proceedings of International Conference on New challenges in Technology Education for HRD in Asia and Pacific Region [*HRDAP*, 2004], pp. 114 - 125, Kolkata.

Roy, R. (2002), "Information Based Instruction and Future", *Journal of North East India Education Society*, February, Shillong: pp 150-158.

Salîte, I. (2002), Teacher's views on the aim of education for sustainable development. *Journal of Teacher Education and Training*. Daugavpils: Saule, 1, 68-80.

———, (2006), Aim of education in the context of present and future educational issues: Perspectives of teachers, in A. Pipere (ed.). (2006). *Education & Sustainable Development. First Steps Towards Changes.* Daugavpils: Saule, 390 - 408.

Savery, J. R., & Duffy, T. M. (1995), Problem based learning: An instructional model and its constructivist framework. *Educational Technology*, 35(5), 31-38.

Schaffer, S., P. & Richardson, J. V. (2004), Supporting technology integration within a teacher education system. *Journal of Educational Computing Research*, 31(4), 423-435

Schlitz Audubon Center (1990), *Living Lightly on the Planet*. Milwaukee, WI 53217.

Schmoker, Mike (2001), The "crayola curriculum." *Education Week*, October 24.

Schreiner, P., Baney, E., & Oxley, S. (2006), *Holistic Education. Resource Book*. Munchen: Clopenburg.

Scott, W. (2002), *Sustainability and Learning: What role for the Curriculum?* UK: Council for Environmental Education in association with the Centre for Research in Education and the Environment, University of Bath.

Sharp, Bill, and the Environmental Careers Organization (1993). The New Complete Guide to Environmental Careers. *Island Press*, Washington, D.C.

Sherry, L., & Gibson, D. (2002), The path to teacher leadership in educational technology. *Contemporary Issues in Technology and Teacher Education* [Online serial], 2(2). http://www.citejournal.org/vol2/iss2/general/article2.cfm.

Siembieda, William and Lupsha, Peter (1978), "The Poverty of Public Services in the Sunbelt" in Perry and Watkins, eds., *The Rise of Sunbelt Cities*. Beverly Hills, CA: Sage Publications.

Sierra Club. *The Green Guide*. Sierra Club, Dept. SA, P.O. Box 7959, San Francisco, CA 94120.

Simmons, I. G. (1956), *Changing The Face of the Earth*: Blackwell, Oxford, 1996.

Snow, C., Burns, M., & Griffin, P. (1998), *Preventing Reading Difficulties in Young Children*. Washington, D.C.: National Academy Press.

Soelle, D. (1984), *To work and to love: A theology of creation*. Philadelphia: Fortress Press.

Stapp, William and Cox, Dorothy A. *Environmental Education Activities Manual*. Dexter, MI: Thomson-Shore, Inc.

Stauffer, R. (1970), *The Lauguage-Experience Approach to the Teaching of Reading*. New York: Harper and Row.

Sterling, S. (1992), Mapping Environmental Education, in W.D.S. Leal Filho & J.A. Palmer (eds.), *Key Issues in Environmental Education*, University of Bradford / UNESCO, Paris.

Straus, S. (1980), "*U-Shaped Behavioural Growth*", Academic Press, London.

Students about Sustainability (2007), [Studenti par Ilgtspçjîbu] Daugavpils: Saule.

Successful models of environmental education in urban schools with a special focus on sustainability project proposal by centre for environmental research and education (CERE).

Taylor, Anne and George Vlastos (1983), *School Zones: Learning Environments for Children*. Corrales, NM: School Zones, Inc.

Taylor, E.W. (1998), The theory and practice of transformative learning: A critical review, in Information *Series*, 374. Columbus: Center on

Education and Training for Employment, College of Education, The Ohio State University.

The Brubach Corporation. Environmental Career Opportunities. 1776 Eye St. NW #710, Washington D.C. 20006.

The Earth Chapter (2000), in www.zb-zeme.lv/Zemes_harta.htm.

The Student Conservation Association (1994), *Earth Work: Resource Guide to Nationwide Green Jobs*. Harper Collins West. New York.

Thomas, W. L. (Ed.) (1956), *"Man's Role in Changing The Face of the Earth"*, University of Chicago.

Titscher, S., Meyer, M., Wodak, R., & Vetter, E. (2000), *Methods of text and discourse analysis*. London: Sage.

UNESCO (1977), Final Report, First Intergovernmental Conference on Environmental Education. *Tbilisi*, UNESCO, Paris.

UNESCO (1987), Environmental Education in the Light of the Tbilisi Conference. *Education on the Move*, UNESCO, Paris.

UNESCO (2002), *Education for Sustainability. From Rio to Johannesburg: Lessons learned from a decade of commitment*. Paris, UNESCO

United Nations Environmental Program/Worldwide Fund for Nature/ World Conservation Union, *Caring for the Earth*.

United Nations World Summit on Sustainable Development. *Johannesburg, South Africa*, August 26 – September 4, 2002.

Vrasidas, C. & G. V. Glass (2004), (Ed.) *Current perspectives on applied information technologies: Online professional development of teachers.* Greenwich, CT: Information Age Publishing.

Vrasidas, C., & McIsaac, M. (2001), Integrating technology in teaching and teacher education: Implications for policy and curriculum reform. *Educational Media International*, 38 (2/3), 127-132. http://www.cait.org/vrasidas/Integrate.pdf.

Warner, David (1992), *Environmental Careers: A Practical Guide to Opportunities in the 90s*. Lewis Publishers, Boca Raton, FL.

Wedman, J & Diggs, L. (2001), Identifying barriers to technology-enhanced learning environments in teacher education. *Computers in Human Behavior*, 17: 421-430.

Wiederholt, J.L & Bryant, B. (2001), *Gray Oral Reading Tests* (Austin, Texas: Pro-Ed.

Wilson, B. G. (2001a), Sense of community as a valued outcome for electronic courses, cohorts, and programs. Paper written for *Vision Quest PT3 Conference* held in Denver, July. http://www.pt3.org/technology/html/wilson.html.

Wilson, B. G. (2001b), Constructivist Learning on the web. In L. Burge (Ed.), *Learning Technologies: Reflective and Strategic Thinking*. San Francisco: Jossey-Bass.

Wilson, B. G., & Ryder, M. (1998), *Dynamic learning communities: An alternative to designed instructional systems*. http://carbon.cudenver.edu/~mryder/dlc.html.

Wilson, S., Wineburg S. & Samuel S. (1988) Peering at history through different lenses: The role of disciplinary perspectives in teaching history. *Teacher College Record*, 89 (4), 525-539.

Wolfensohn, J. D.; *Entering the 21st Century: World Development Report: 1999/2000.* Oxford University Press: Inc., New York.

Wood, K. & Tinajero, J. (2002), Using Pictures to Teach Content to Second Language Learners. *Middle School Journal*. May, 47-51.

World Commission on Environment and Development (WCED), (1987), *Our Common Future.* Oxford, UK: Oxford University Press

World Health Organization Collaborating Center in Occupational Health, (1995), *News Letter,* Vol. 6, Page 1, may, 1995.

World Wildlife Fund (1987), *How to Plan a Conservation Education Program.* World Wildlife Fund, P.O. Box 4866, Hampden Post Office, Baltimore, MD 21211.

Young, H D & Freedman, R A, (1996), *University Physics*, Addison Wesley.

Zellermayer, M., Mor, N., Heilweil, I., (2004), Preparing teachers for e-teaching via e-learning, in Charalambos V. & Gene V.G. (Eds) *Current Perspectives in Applied Information Technologies* , Cyprus

Zhu, Z. T., & Yan, H. (2001), *ICT and pre-service teacher education: Towards an integrated approach.* Paper presented at the 7th Annual UNESCO-ACEID International Conference on Education. Available in: http://www.unescobkk.org/education/aceid/conference/conf7/doc/zhou.pdf.

Contributors

Bapat, Mukund N., Ph.D., is the member of faculty in Regional Institute of Education [RIE], Bhopal, under NCERT, India. His areas of special interest include Experimental Physics, Electronic transport, Innovative methods & Constructivism.

Bora, Abhijit is a member of faculty and presently Head of the Dept of Mass-Communication & Journalism in Gauhati University, Assam, India.

Calhoun, Emily, Ph.D., is a specialist in action research, the teaching of literacy, and staff development. Presently she is associated with Them Phoenix Alliance at Saint Simons Island, Georgia, USA.

Ghosh, Sanat K. Ph.D., is Professor of Education. Presently he is Director of Adult Education Center as well as Dean of faculty of Humanities & Education in Rabindra Bharati University, Kolkata, India.

Heilweil, Ida, Ph.D,. is Associate Professor of Levinsky College of Education at Israel.

Hrycauk, Marilyn, Ph.D,. served as Director of Curriculum and Instruction in USA. Presently she is Consultant for Northern Lights School Division. She was also the recipient of prestigious Alberta Premier's Award for School Board Innovation and Excellence in 2002.

Hrycauk, Walter, Ph.D,. is associated with The Northern Lights School Division #69, Bonnyville, Alberta, Canada. Presently he is Chair of the Northern Lights School Division Board of Trustees in USA.

Iliško, Dzintra, Ph.D, is Professor of Educational Studies in Institute of Sustainable Education at Daugavpils University, Latvia.

Joyce, Bruce, Ph.D., specializes in instruction and one of the early propounder of teaching Models. Presently he is associated with Booksend Laboratories, Saint Simons Island, Georgia, USA. His book, *Models of Teaching,* is in its eighth edition, first published in 1972. In addition he has conducted extensive research on staff development and institution improvement

Kar, Sandeep, M.Sc., is a research scholar in the Department of Environmental Science, University of Kalyani, West Bengal, India

Molia, Maganlal S, Ph.D., is Assistant Professor in the Department of Education, Saurashtra University, Gujarat, India.

Mor, Nili, Ph.D. is Associate Professor of Levinsky College of Education at Israel.

Paira, Anjana, M.A, M.Ed. is Research Scholar in faculty of Education, Visva-Bharati, Santiniketan, India.

Ranade, Mridula, Ph.D. is a senior member of faculty in the Department of Education, SNDT Women's University, Pune, India.

Roy, Rajarshi, Ph.D. is Assistant Professor of Education and Curriculum Development Center at National Institute of Technical Teachers' Training and Research (NITTTR), Kolkata, India.

Samal, Aloke Chandra, Ph.D,. is Programme Officer and Post-Doctoral fellow in the Department of Environmental Science, University of Kalyani, India.

Santra, Subhash Chandra, Ph.D. is Professor in the Department of Environmental Science, University of Kalyani and Coordinator of Ministry of Environment and Forest (MoEF), Government of India supported ENVIS Centre on Environmental Biotechnology at University of Kalyani. He is also a PRS Fellow from University of Calcutta, India.

Siddiqui, Tauseef Zia is a post-graduate in Technology and associated with Indian School of Mines, Dhanbad, India.

Siddiqui, Faisal Zia is member of faculty in the Department of Civil & Environmental Engineering, University Poly, Faculty of Engineering and Technology, Aligarh Muslim University, Aligarh, India.

Singh, R.P., Ph. D,. is a Fulbright Fellow, holds his master's and doctoral degrees from the University of London. He was the former Joint Secretary of Ministry of Human Resource Development, Government of India. He retired from the NCERT, where he was Dean of Research, Chairman of Educational Research and Innovation Committee (ERIC) and Head, Department of Teacher Education. He has written numerous books and won several awards. He is currently President, All India Association of Teacher Educators, New Delhi.